Praise for *The Doctrine o*

MW01283715

"Brad East writes about the Bible with joy, verve, and insight. His presentation is highly readable, opening the subject up to all those who want to explore a theological perspective on Scripture. His strategy of working from church practice back to the nature and qualities of the text gives us all much to ponder."

—DARREN SARISKY, Institute for Religion and Critical Inquiry, Australian Catholic University

"What an exciting book! East's basic moves are recognizable: he carries forward and integrates elements of the doctrines of Scripture of Webster, Boersma, and Jenson. This would be accomplishment enough for a normal book, but East is even bolder ecumenically than the masters upon whom he builds. Without ceasing to value the Reformers, he challenges *sola scriptura* and the perspicacity of Scripture, and he offers a deeply Catholic account of dogma and apostolicity. This book is a rare gift—a richly comprehensive theology of Scripture that lays the foundation for real ecumenical breakthroughs."

—MATTHEW LEVERING, Mundelein Seminary

"It would be hard to imagine a more winsome and helpful introduction to the Christian doctrine of Scripture than this. In an area that has been a minefield of controversy, Brad East writes with clarity yet without polemic, with ecumenical sympathy yet without failing to take a clear position on all the important and contested issues. Whatever your convictions about the Bible and how it should be read, you will benefit from this book."

—BRUCE D. MARSHALL, Perkins School of Theology, Southern Methodist University

"A magnificent achievement! Brad East has taken his years of theological reflection upon the Bible and crafted a compelling and synoptic discussion of Scripture's divinely granted being and place within the Christian church's life and vision of reality. In the end, East's volume provides a modernized version of a generally classical view of Scripture's form and function, respectfully taking up traditional claims with a critical eye, and weaving old and new perspectives into a lucidly ordered whole that is fundamentally grounded in a living and humble faith. Sprightly written, substantively resourced, carefully argued, and pastorally adept, East's *Doctrine of Scripture* should be required reading for theological students and scholars alike."

—EPHRAIM RADNER, Wycliffe College, University of Toronto

"Brad East's *The Doctrine of Scripture* raises all the key issues for theologians and biblical scholars to think about with regard to the nature and place of Scripture in a Christian theological framework. In a lucid and highly accessible style, he makes a compelling case for why these issues matter for theology and Scriptural interpretation."

—STEPHEN FOWL, Loyola University Maryland

The Doctrine of Scripture

The Doctrine of Scripture

BRAD EAST

Foreword by Katherine Sonderegger

![logo] CASCADE *Books* · Eugene, Oregon

THE DOCTRINE OF SCRIPTURE

Cascade Books
An Imprint of Wipf and Stock Publishers
199 W. 8th Ave., Suite 3
Eugene, OR 97401

www.wipfandstock.com

PAPERBACK ISBN: 978-1-5326-6498-4
HARDCOVER ISBN: 978-1-5326-6499-1
EBOOK ISBN: 978-1-5326-6500-4

Cataloguing-in-Publication data:

Names: East, Brad, author. | Sonderegger, Katherine, foreword writer

Title: The doctrine of scripture / Brad East.

Description: Eugene, OR: Cascade Books, 2021 | Includes bibliographical references and index.

Identifiers: ISBN 978-1-5326-6498-4 (paperback) | ISBN 978-1-5326-6499-1 (hardcover) | ISBN 978-1-5326-6500-4 (ebook)

Subjects: LCSH: Bible—Criticism, interpretation, etc. | Bible—Evidences, authority, etc. | The Bible—Inspiration | Authority—Religious aspects

Classification: BS480 E17 2021 (paperback) | BS480 (ebook)

08/25/21

For Spencer Bogle:
minister and mentor,
missionary and theologian,
and now friend

The Bunch of Grapes

By George Herbert

Joy, I did lock thee up: but some bad man
               Hath let thee out again:
And now, me thinks, I am where I began
                  Sev'n yeares ago: one vogue and vein,
                  One aire of thoughts usurps my brain
I did towards Canaan draw; but now I am
Brought back to the Red sea, the sea of shame.

For as the Jews of old by Gods command
               Travell'd, and saw no town;
So now each Christian hath his journeys spann'd:
                  Their storie pennes and sets us down.
                  A single deed is small renown.
Gods works are wide, and let in future times;
His ancient justice overflows our crimes.

Then have we too our guardian fires and clouds;
               Our Scripture-dew drops fast:
We have our sands and serpents, tents and shrowds;
                  Alas! our murmurings come not last.
                  But where's the cluster? where's the taste
Of mine inheritance? Lord, if I must borrow,
Let me as well take up their joy, as sorrow.

But can he want the grape, who hath the wine?
               I have their fruit and more.
Blessed be God, who prosper'd *Noahs* vine,
                  And made it bring forth grapes good store.
                  But much more him I must adore,
Who of the Laws sowre juice sweet wine did make,
Ev'n God himself being pressed for my sake.

Contents

Foreword

In a celebrated collect, Archbishop Thomas Cranmer prayed that a Christian would "hear the holy Scriptures, read, mark, learn, and inwardly digest them." *The Doctrine of Scripture* is a book Cranmer would recognize and welcome. In this eloquent book, Brad East shows us just what it looks like to encounter the Bible as Cranmer proposed. This is a far more difficult task than simply *saying* these honorifics about the Holy Scriptures, for East actually *enacts* them. Since the Reformation, treatises about Holy Scripture have poured forth from Protestant and Catholic scholars. In our day, these have taken the forms of histories of interpretation, theories of hermeneutics, accounts of canonicity and genre within the texts, and post-colonial readings of central narratives within Israel's Scriptures. This book, while apparently taking its place quietly among these many neighbors, in truth is not such a book at all. *The Doctrine of Scripture* lays out and, more, demonstrates what it is like to "stand under the Word of God," as the Reformers put this. Brad East places us within the textual world of the medieval and patristic church where, most daringly, the Song of Solomon strikes the keynote. Drawing a page from von Balthasar, East speaks of the nuptial and conjugal love of Christ for his people, declaimed in the pages of Scripture. Taking the reader patiently through the nature, purpose, perfection, and authority of Scripture, East demonstrates how a modern Christian might "take up and read" in the company of the pre-modern church.

In all these ways, *The Doctrine of Scripture* turns aside from much modernist, critical reading of the Bible. But I should be quick to say that this is decidedly not an antiquarian book. It *is* devotional, but a devotion of the intellect, bringing the insights, the intellectual challenges, and the preoccupations of a modern reader to the well of rich exegesis of the ancient church. The Bible, East underscores as a *basso continuo*, belongs in the church, not in the lecture hall, on the shelf of ancient texts, nor principally in individual readers' hands. Some of the sternest language of the book is reserved for the modernist turn to higher criticism. It simply has no place in the proper reading of this unique text. Certainly, Scripture is a historical text; it is a creaturely work in service of the Commanding God. But the Bible turns to ash when no longer treated as holy, when snatched out of the church's nave to be read in Jowett's fateful phrase, "as any other book." Holy Scripture, East teaches, is to be proclaimed in liturgy, held up, processed, kissed, and signed. It is a book, above all, to be *loved*.

In the midst of this hieratic language, East does not shy away from argument or from daring conclusions. He knows that any full exposition of Scripture must acknowledge its two-fold form, a witness issuing forth from Israel and the nascent apostolic community. East recognizes the complex terrain of supersessionism, and he firmly endorses the plenary stature of the Old Testament in the Christian Bible. But he stoutly defends the Christological reading of the whole, and repudiates the worried Christian claim that the Old Testament has been appropriated or worse, stolen, from the people Israel and from Judaism. The sections devoted to the Old Testament as *magistra* are some of the most incisive and instructive of the entire volume.

East knows too that he cannot avoid the polarizing elements of Protestant doctrines of Scripture, especially in the modern era. He takes up the problems of inerrancy, of plenary inspiration, and of originary autographs with a sure hand. Not surprisingly, East places these neuralgic topics in a larger, calmer room: the pre-modern church. There we see a Bible that is simply assumed to be guide, teacher, authority, and the history and figures it relates reliable and accurate. This is the *tenor* East hopes to evoke when treating these topics. But he parts with St. Augustine and St. Thomas on matters of accuracy. Following Luther here, East can draw distinctions between the high places of Scripture and the out-lying districts. The Bible is the work of human authors, and it may contain errors of historical detail and sequence—it will bear the mark of its frail, human scribes. But Scripture is not merely human! It is commanded by the Holy God, and he dwells in it as in a temple. In this, East follows some recent proposals that Scripture be understood not so much on the pattern of Chalcedonian two-nature Christology as on the Sacrament of the Holy Eucharist. Even as bread and wine are the artifice of human creatures—the grapes and wheat *made* into the staff of life—so Holy Scripture is the work of scribes and tradents and redactors, and contain, as do bread and wine, the anomalies of human craft; but they are put in service of, set apart for, the Indwelling God. This proposal is not far from the "two tables of Scripture and the Altar" of *Dei Verbum*, the Constitution on Scripture promulgated at Vatican II.

East does not shy away from controversy. In his discussion on Biblical authority—which he wisely leaves to the final chapter—East carefully follows Michael Rae's lead in distinguishing regulative from sacramental or devotional use, and he demarcates areas of authority, restricting Scripture's teaching office to domains of its own competence. (No scriptural ruling on proper restaurants, ways to keep score at ball games, or preferences for Petrarchan and Shakespearian sonnets.) The authority of the Bible is complex, properly delimited, but in its domain, sovereign. Still, East does hold that Scripture requires interpretive guidance: this is the magisterium of the church. His quiet insistence on Scripture as the *church's* book now gathers steam. He places the Scriptures firmly in the "matrix of the church," echoing some of the path-breaking language of *Dei Verbum* in its joining of Scripture and Tradition as from a single source. He considers this embedding of the Scriptures within the teaching office of the church to demand a rejection of the Reformation *sola Scriptura*. The notions of perspicuity, self-authentication, and interior inspiration by the Holy Spirit are not, in his judgement, sufficient to allay worries about proper interpretation, reading, and application of the Bible's authority. Whether this touches too the venerable Reformation doctrine of the sufficiency of Scripture (sufficient for what?, East might say) is another question East's far-reaching proposal will raise. This is the clearest indication of East's catholic commitments, and he is willing to follow wherever they lead, even to distant or unfamiliar lands.

The Doctrine of Scripture is a wonderfully ecumenical text. Here we find St. Francis de Sales next to Calvin and Turretin; they in turn next to St. Thomas, St. John of Damascus, St. Cyril, and St. Augustine. Not surprisingly, the list of authors is decidedly pre-modern. East has, it seems, followed C. S. Lewis's dictum *ad litteram:* Read old books! The book sings. The text displays a clear, poetic style, and wisely reserves the disputation with authors ancient and modern, across several communions, to footnotes. The whole work dedicates itself to showing how Holy Scripture, in its unique yet creaturely status, must be interpreted as the *Viva Vox Dei*, the living voice of the Living God. *The Doctrine of Scripture* is an ambitious, learned, and deeply moving work of *Ressourcement* theology, and I am grateful to have learned from this fine teacher.

KATHERINE SONDEREGGER
William Meade Chair in Systematic Theology
Virginia Theological Seminary

Acknowledgments

As I say in the introduction, the doctrine of Scripture is an occasion for joy. But that does not mean writing a doctrine of Scripture is necessarily a joyful activity. In this case, however, it was, from start to finish. It has been nothing but a pleasure to work on this book, from the initial idea to the first draft to the multiple revisions that followed. In the process I have accrued many debts, which I am happy to register here as a token of my gratitude.

First of all, to Robin Parry, who not only accepted my initial proposal but also approved, rather late in the game, a shift from publishing the book in the Cascade Companions series to publishing it as a stand-alone work. I am thankful for his flexibility and kindness throughout the course of the book's creation.

I am similarly thankful to all those friends and colleagues who read the manuscript and offered comments on it, especially Ken Cukrowski, Jamie Dunn, Garrett East, Mitch East, Justin Hawkins, Ross McCullough, Bradley Steele, and Myles Werntz. That they did so during a global pandemic speaks to the depth of their generosity, manifest also in their feedback, since most of them maintain strong disagreements with me in this area. A special thanks to Ken for his extraordinarily detailed notes on the whole manuscript; it is uncommon to work for a dean as kind and supportive as Ken is, and I am grateful that I do.

Nearly as uncommon is to inhabit a department as friendly and collegial as the Department of Bible, Missions, and Ministry in the College of Biblical Studies at Abilene Christian University. The conception, birth, and growth of this book have occurred entirely during my time here, and it could not have found a more nurturing environment. My thanks to all my colleagues, especially Rodney Ashlock and Chris Hutson (for making my life easy); Amanda Pittman and John Boyles (for all the texts and hallway chats); and Steve Hare, Vic McCracken, David Kneip, Cliff Barbarick, and

Jerry Taylor (for conversations relevant to the matter of this book). Thanks also to Carlene Harrison and (across the way) Fred Aquino.

The preparation of this or any other manuscript would be impossible without my intrepid graduate assistant Luke Roberts, who along with Débora Viana prepared the bibliography. My thanks to both of them for their tireless work.

Though I neither conceived nor began writing this book during my graduate studies at Emory and Yale, once I had the idea, it came out quickly, more or less fully formed. That is a testament to my teachers, especially those who helped shape my understanding of biblical interpretation, the doctrine of Scripture, and the church's theological tradition. I cannot speak to their approval of the result of my labors, but it nevertheless would have been impossible without them. My thanks in particular to Ian McFarland, Luke Timothy Johnson, Carol Newsom, Felix Asiedu, Steffen Lösel, Kathryn Tanner, Christopher Beeley, John Hare, Denys Turner, David Kelsey, Miroslav Volf, Linn Tonstad, and Dale Martin, as well as (from afar) Steve Fowl and Stanley Hauerwas.

I have been arguing about the doctrine and interpretation of Scripture with Mark Lackowski, Liv Stuart Lester, Mark Lester, and Laura Carlson Hasler for a decade. I am grateful for our countless conversations and for their friendship, as also for that of Wes Hill, if only through the dread Zoom; for the priestly rapport of Zac Koons and Kester Smith; for the pastoral and intellectual hospitality of Richard Beck; and for the supererogatory mentorship and encouragement of Darren Sarisky.

I am blessed with an extraordinary family. Thanks to my parents, Ray and Georgine, for their unwavering support of my vocation and above all for igniting in me from my earliest years a love for Holy Scripture that, I hope, still burns bright in these pages. To Garrett and Mitch: what a wonderful thing to have best friends for brothers, not to mention theologians in their own right! Thanks for the lifelong conversation, and thanks to Stacy and Allison for tolerating the ferocity of the arguments.

There are no words adequate to the love and gratitude I have for my wife, Katelin, or to her role in my life and the lives of our children, or to her bottomless support for my work. We have traveled the country together, and now we have put down roots in west Texas, the land of beautiful sunsets. There's nowhere I'd rather be, and no one else I'd rather be here with.

Well, besides Sam, Rowan, Paige, and Liv. Even in lockdown, even in Covidtide, our house has continued to brim over with life. I wouldn't have it any other way. Thanks to each of them for following the Spirit's prompting by doing their level-headed best to interrupt my sleep, my reading, my teaching, my writing. Books are straw, but these four souls are imperishable, their value immeasurable. God won't let me forget it, and for that I am grateful.

This book is dedicated to Spencer Bogle. Spence was my youth minister at Round Rock Church of Christ during my teenage years. Humanly speaking, he is the reason I am a theologian. He put books into my hands at a very young age, books written by authors I'd never heard of: Lewis, Chesterton, Bonhoeffer, Kierkegaard. He met with me time and again, fielding my questions and indulging an adolescent's budding intellectual affection for God and all things in God. He then served in east Africa as a missionary while I earned my Bachelor's and Master's degrees in Bible and divinity. But he beat me to a PhD program by a year: he at SMU, I at Yale. We became doctors—of philosophy, technically, but in truth of sacred doctrine—at one and the same time. I still marvel at the wry humor of providence. I would not be who I am or where I am, this book would not exist, were it not for Spence. I will never be able to thank him enough.

BRAD EAST
First week of Advent 2020
Feast of St. John Damascene

Introduction

The doctrine of Holy Scripture is a matter of joy. Before it is an occasion for disputation, disagreement, or division, prior to hassling over terms, definitions, and scholarship, the doctrine of Scripture is a cause for praise. The theologian pauses before the astonishing claim—the fact—that here, in this book, through these words, the living God speaks.

God speaks: this confession is at the heart of what Holy Scripture is, what it is about, and why it matters. Few statements are closer to the center of either Scripture's testimony as such or the faith to which it testifies. If God has not spoken, then of all people Christians are most to be pitied. "In many and various ways," we find written in Hebrews 1:1–2, "God spoke of old to our fathers by the prophets; but in these last days he has spoken to us by a Son," Jesus of Nazareth.[1] God speaks by means of his Son; the identity of Sonship and divine speech in Jesus is so complete that in the prologue to St. John's Gospel he is called, simply, God's Word or *Logos*.[2] Nor is this merely a designation, like Savior or Messiah, that obtains in time. God's Son is God's Word from everlasting to everlasting: God speaks eternally; God *is* the eternal act *of speaking* his own Word. God never tires of this Word. When and where God speaks, this Word is what he speaks. Spoken eternally, he is with God and is God, God from God, Son of the Father.

---

1. Unless otherwise indicated, all quotations from Scripture are taken from the Revised Standard Version.

2. In this book I will designate those persons canonized as saints by the church (East and West both) by the relevant abbreviated title. The reasons why will be clear in the following, but in short, theology should not spurn its status as *churchly* discourse; remembering that Mary and Peter and Paul—and Macrina and Maximus and Thomas—are *saints*, and not merely members of some generic mortal guild, is salutary for the mind approaching the task of thinking, talking, and writing about God. It also works to keep us from forgetting that they are not dead but alive in Christ. Theology mindful of heaven knows that it does its work not only before God but before the whole communion of saints.

Spoken in time, he is Jesus, Mary's son, the Nazarene crucified under Pontius Pilate. Jesus is divine speech perfectly spoken in human flesh and blood, complete from beginning to end, definitively communicating what the one true and ever-living God is and wills, as one of us, visible and perceptible to creaturely ears and eyes.

That God speaks is good news; there is no gospel apart from God's saving word. As the Wisdom of Solomon puts it, "your all-powerful word leaped from heaven, from the royal throne, into the midst of the land that was doomed" (18:15). The Word, that is, "became flesh and dwelt among us" (John 1:14). That is news, to be sure. "And from his fullness have we all received, grace upon grace": that is what makes it good (v. 16). God has spoken, once for all, and the good news of Jesus Christ attests the fact. The Word and Son of God is at once Immanuel, God with us, and Yeshua, divine salvation in a person (see Matt 1:20–23).[3] In speaking, God saves; in saving, God comes near. God's speech is an occasion for joy, wonder, and praise.

Thus we see the twofold character of God's speech: *eternal in nature, incarnate in time*. Plotted as a narrative, the latter moment is the center and climax of God's speech in human affairs. But it is not the only instance of humans' hearing God speak. Starting from Christ, the center, we can move in both directions, backwards and forwards in time. As the passage from Hebrews says, God's speech in Christ was neither the first such occurrence nor did it conclude the series. The God whose Word is manifest in Mary's son is the God of Abraham, just as Mary is Abraham's daughter; and between God's conversations with Abraham and Mary, respectively, God spoke to and through countless individuals in myriad episodes in the history of Abraham's family (and not a few outsiders too). Nor do references to God's word dry up after the saving events of Jesus's life, death, resurrection, and ascension: they continue on in the ministry and teaching of the apostles. Though the advent of Jesus qualifies what it means to say that God speaks, has spoken, or continues to speak, it does not nullify or cancel such claims but rather defines and clarifies their meaning in light of Christ, the final Word.

3. Moreover, inasmuch as the good news that Jesus proclaims is the advent of God's kingdom (Matt 4:17), Origen is right to call Jesus *autobasileia*, that is, the kingdom in person, God's reign embodied in a single human being. See Origen, *Commentary on Matthew* 4.17 (commenting on Matt 18:23). In addition to *autobasileia* Origen also includes *autosophia*, *autodikaiosyne*, and *autoasphaleia*: Jesus is himself *wisdom* as such, *justice* as such, *truth* as such—incarnate in and as a man. To these, given my claim above that he is "salvation in a person," and in light of the reiterated theme in St. Luke's Gospel that to see Jesus is to "see the salvation of God" (3:6; cf. 2:15–20, 25–32; 7:22–23; 8:10; 9:27–36; 10:23–24; 19:1–10; 21:25–28; 23:44–49; 24:13–43), we might finally add *autosoteria*. A short post by Fred Sanders ("The Kingdom in Person") brought my attention to the wider context of this passage in Origen.

God spoke through the prophets, for to be a prophet just is to speak a word given to one by God to speak. All such words were granted by the Word himself, and anticipated his coming in Mary's womb. After the outpouring of Christ's Spirit on all flesh, by faith the baptized are prophets one and all, united to Jesus and enlivened by his own Spirit to speak the saving word of Christ, which is the gospel. Prophecy in either case, then—whether in old Israel by discrete persons or by apostles in the new age or by all God's people after them—has Christ as its source and Christ as its principal *res* or subject matter. Phrased differently, the incarnate Word is he *from whom* prophetic speech comes and he *to whom* such speech bears witness (whether hiddenly or explicitly). Prophecy therefore is Christ-inflected speech concerning the things of God for the people of God, since prophecy is God's Word in human words, and God's Word enfleshed is Christ, the risen Lord.

But prophecy, on this broader understanding, was not and is not exclusively a "live" event. It could be and was recorded. "Written prophecy" is not an oxymoron. Which means "God's word written" is not a self-contradiction in terms. Tanakh—the Torah, the Prophets, and the Psalms and other writings—was received among the Jews as (among other things) the record of God's verbal dealings with Israel; and not only the record, but the means of God's ongoing dealings, precisely verbal, with Israel in the present and into the future. So that a text, written centuries before by a named or anonymous Israelite, could be cited as God's own speech, in the present tense.

This is what it means for the words of David, or Moses, or Isaiah to be the word of the Lord in and for the Lord's people *today*. And that in turn is why the designation "the writings" (*hai graphai*) to describe the histories and testimonies of the patriarchs and prophets and kings of Israel could come to signify what we mean by "the scriptures." Holy Scripture is the Lord's speech fixed in written form, which is to say, composed, edited, transmitted, collected, republished, and used liturgically and otherwise by individuals and communities within the Lord's people across generations and geography. This entity or artifact is what the church continues to mean by "Scripture," because the church inherited both the selfsame sacred writings of Israel and the concept of their prophetic-scriptural character (which is to say, the practice of receiving them as the Lord's mediated word to his people). Had the ascended Lord returned within the lifetime of the longest living apostles, any addenda to Tanakh would have been unnecessary. In the event, the letters, memories, histories, visions, and sermons of the apostles and their deputies were transcribed as a kind of lasting library, a portable sample and deposit of the faith once for all delivered to the saints. In the wake of their passing and in the face of ongoing missionary challenges, it was clear that the writings of Israel (collectively "the prophets") and the writings of the church (collectively "the apostles") ought to be joined together. And so they were, unofficially then officially under two headings: the old covenant and the new covenant. Thus it is that, for nearly two millennia, when a text from either of these collections is read aloud in the assembly of Christ's people, the lector announces: "The word of the Lord." To which the company of the baptized responds in unison: "Thanks be to God."

What does the church mean when it says that, and how can what it says be true? That is what this book is about, because that is what the Christian doctrine of Holy Scripture is about.

This book began as a concise companion to the doctrine of Scripture, but rather quickly swelled beyond its bounds. My approach has remained the same, however, and I continue to think of it as a sort of extended companion or compendium: an ecumenical sketch in service to the universal church.[4] As I outlined above, the doctrine of Scripture is an occasion for joy because Scripture attests the good news of Christ, who is the living Word of God incarnate. The doctrine of Scripture names the theological task of understanding and describing what the Bible is in the economy of God's grace manifested in Christ: its source in the Holy Trinity's being and works, its nature and attributes as a result of the divine action and will, and its role—in terms of authority, interpretation, and ends—in Christ's corporate body, the church. This book is a companion to that doctrine in that it seeks to present an account of the doctrine that is at once representative, constructive, exhibitive, and explanatory. What do I mean by those modifiers?

By *representative*, I mean that the account I offer in what follows is intended to be neither my idiosyncratic opinion nor cutting-edge innovation in the field, but instead sufficiently broad and inclusive so that those new to the doctrine get a sense for its scope, breadth, and depths, while those familiar with the doctrine do not think I cut corners or left their views out. At the same time, the work is *constructive*, by which I mean that though I am wanting to represent the doctrine as a whole, this is not a survey; I am not offering an exhaustive, much less a historical, sampling of the varieties of bibliology on offer in the church's many traditions. This book is not viewpoint neutral. There is a slant. My aim is to be fair, but not to be all things to all people.

---

4. The epitome of what I have in mind may be found in Davison, *Why Sacraments?* Within the doctrine of Scripture, and not the sister doctrine of sacramentology, see the theologically rich but accessibly written works by Bryan, *And God Spoke*; Bryan, *Listening to the Bible.*

Though I will represent particular positions that require support, I will by and large not be offering that support: that is to say, the following chapters will be *exhibitive* more than argumentative. There will be assertions aplenty that lack the necessary reasons to justify those assertions. In other words, I will be showing more than telling, offering variations on themes the Christian tradition in general and I in particular find beautiful and compelling. My goal is to introduce you to those themes, and to render them in their most appealing forms, not to persuade you (at least not by direct argumentation) that they are true. That would require a larger and quite different book than this one.

Having said that, though this book is not an argument, at least in the way we ordinarily use that term, it is *explanatory*. By that I mean that I want you to understand the terms, concepts, claims, and explanations that constitute the Christian doctrine of Scripture. Even if you close the book unconvinced, or half-convinced, or eager for larger, more systematic treatments, I will have succeeded if you are not confused, and I will have failed if you do not have a basic sense of the overall vision as well as the grammar of the doctrine. In other words, most of the time, sections of chapters will not take the form, "Here is why X claim is true and thus why you should believe it." Rather, they will usually take the form, "Here is what X claim means, how it connects to other theological loci, and why Christians of many stripes have thought it crucial to a full account of the Bible."

In this way the tone of the book is meant to avoid polemic as far as possible. Even where I voice disagreement with certain common positions in the doctrine of Scripture (say, Reformed accounts of perspicuity), my aim is not to draw the battle lines or denigrate long-standing doctrinal commitments. The madness of the theologians is evident in every doctrine, but beginning in the sixteenth century the doctrine of Scripture has been a magnet and a magnifier for a very special kind of madness. Not here, at least if I can help it. Nor will I stoop to spying fundamentalism behind every bush and beneath every rock on the theological map. Spend time in a mainline seminary or even with a random group of biblical scholars, and you will quickly discover that the "fundies" are the ever-present bogeymen. "Oceania was at war with Eurasia: therefore Oceania had always been at war with Eurasia": *mutatis mutandis* for historical critics and Protestant evangelicals.[5] This book, however, will not assume that inerrancy or infallibility or plenary verbal inspiration or the like are bygone terms of an unenlightened era, lingering on in unavoidable but pitiable half-lives. When and where I discuss

5. Orwell, *1984*, 32.

or disagree with these or other ideas, I will say so, but I will not do so smugly or glibly—at least that is my hope.

No theology gets off the ground without assumptions, and the assumptions of this work are catholic. The canon of Scripture,[6] the Rule of Faith found in variable early forms and creeds, the first seven ecumenical councils:[7] I take all these for granted. Indeed, one curiosity of the account that follows is that I will have one foot planted in two different time periods. On the one hand, Lutheran and Reformed scholastic and later theological reflection on Scripture contains insights it would be foolish for any thinker on these matters to ignore. It is a veritable storehouse of riches. On the other hand, most of what I have to say, perhaps all of it, is presented in such a way that it would have made sense to a Christian living before the Reformation—St. Anselm of Canterbury, say, living in the eleventh century (and born before the Great Schism with the East), or St. John Damascene, living in the eighth. Let me explain why. Although the church's wisdom and knowledge regarding Holy Scripture have expanded in the last millennium, and especially in the centuries since Luther and Calvin, the essence of Scripture—what it is, what it is for, its authority, its reception—has not changed, nor could it have once the canon was codified in the middle patristic period. This will emerge as a theme in the book: the right interpretation or use of Scripture is not the sort of thing one can "discover" late in the game, that is, fifteen or nineteen centuries after Pentecost. At least not on a properly Christian understanding of history and divine providence. Church doctrine develops across time, and development involves pruning. But the church catholic does not, because it cannot, come to realize that for centuries it was absolutely wrong about central matters; that, in this case, it was unable to understand even the basics of the faith until person X or idea Y or method Z came along. Historians, theorists, and critics may make such moves. Theologians may not.

In short, this is a deeply un-Protestant work, albeit written by an ambivalent sort of Protestant.[8] I do not take either the arguments of the

6. Whose canon? See below, esp. chapters 1 and 2.

7. Division still lingers over the Council of Chalcedon in 451, but I do not mean to exclude the Oriental Orthodox or the Church of the East. As ecumenical dialogues between Chalcedonian and non-Chalcedonian communions have shown, the anathemas of that Council need no longer obtain; the substance of what is affirmed about Christ is common to the separated traditions; differing formulations are semantic and thus need not be church-dividing.

8. In this I find a model in what we might call the catholic ecumenism of Robert Jenson, who remained a confessional Lutheran all his life yet exemplified, across his work, a compelling vision of theological catholicity in express resistance to the church's currently divided state. "Theology is the church's enterprise of thought, and the only

reformers or the traditions descended from them as the point of departure for the doctrine of Scripture, and in certain areas—far from all—I think they are profoundly mistaken. A full theological account of the Christian Bible, to repeat myself, is one that would be at home in centuries prior to the sixteenth, and familiar to the martyrs, saints, and doctors who populated that great span of time. Prior commitments in christology, ecclesiology, and pneumatology require this, it seems to me, as well as a simple fact: when one reads patristic and medieval theology, the exegesis on display, the evident deference to Scripture's authority, the subtle interactions glimpsed between text and tradition and natural reason and missionary challenge—these are not an obstacle to overcome or a detour to correct, but exemplary. They embody the doctrine of Scripture in rich, manifold practice. We should all want to understand, read, and relate to Holy Scripture as St. Irenaeus, St. Augustine, St. Maximus, St. Gregory of Narek, and St. Bernard of Clairvaux do. They are our forebears, trailblazers, and guides, our beatified Virgil and Beatrice in the spiritual ascent of Scripture.[9] If what I offer in what follows approximates even a fraction of their vision of the sacred page, I will have succeeded far beyond what I dared to expect.

A final word, this time on style. I am persuaded by Paul Griffiths that Anglophone theologians write bad prose, and that this is a problem.[10] Theologians in our context are usually academics, and academic training is often a formation in the worst possible writing habits: jumbled syntax, dense constructions, lack of conceptual clarity, volume over depth, phraseology too clever by half, jargon in droves, endlessly unnecessary quotations interrupting the flow of thought, and so on. Moreover, the principal subject matter of theology is God, and the mother tongue for God-talk is prayer. Yet academic theology rarely reads as prayer, even though some of the greatest theological

---

church conceivably in question is the unique and unitary church of the creeds. . . . To live as the church in the situation of a divided church—if this can happen at all—must at least mean that we confess we live in radical self-contradiction and that by every churchly act we contradict that contradiction. Also theology must make this double contradiction at and by every step of its way" (*Triune God*, vii). See also, from the other side of the divide, the extraordinary comments of Joseph Ratzinger in his 1986 letter to the *Theologische Quartalschrift*, "On the Progress of Ecumenism," now gathered in *Church, Ecumenism, and Politics*, 132–38.

9. If one prefers a Christian to Virgil (however imaginatively beatified), then perhaps substitute George MacDonald, as C. S. Lewis does in *The Great Divorce*.

10. Griffiths, *Christian Flesh*, xi–xiii.

works are themselves written as prayer.[11] Often it is not clear whether the theologian writing prays herself, or has as one of the goals of her writing the life of the Christian soul found in prayer. It is true that theology, as a work of the intellect and a second-order reflection on the grammar and claims of the faith, is a genre distinct from prayer or proclamation. Theology is not liturgy. But it is not disconnected from liturgy, nor need theology always be non-liturgical. For—again, lest we forget, though it is odd that we do—theology concerns God. And to speak of God, even in academic books, even while considering highly technical or abstract matters that require rigor and concentration, is to speak not of a hypothesis or an inert object but of the transcendent Living One, the Holy Trinity, who was and is and is to come. And our words ought to be fitting to that *res*, that subject matter, even when they are at the extreme end of second- or third-order philosophical abstraction.[12]

In this book, therefore, I have borne in mind that charge. I have sought to speak with fittingness about, above all, the God to whom Holy Scripture bears witness, and in light of that resplendent reality, the sacred texts that mediate his speech and communicate his saving love. Where I have done so poorly, I ask for patience and charity, from the Lord and yourself, the reader. Where I have done so faithfully, it is because of the patience and charity I have already received, from the Lord and others, graces I first learned as a child listening to stories about Jesus in the Bible. This is a book about that book, the book of Christ.

11. E.g., St. Augustine, *Confessions*; St. Anselm, *Proslogion*.

12. See Charry, *Renewing of Your Minds*, which not only is a splendid book about this topic—what she calls the pastoral function or salutary character of Christian doctrine—but embodies the point, both in her style and in the attentive generosity she extends to patristic and medieval texts.

I

Source

> *First of all you must understand this, that no prophecy of scripture*
> *is a matter of one's own interpretation, because no prophecy ever*
> *came by the impulse of man, but men moved by the Holy Spirit*
> *spoke from God.*
> —2 Peter 1:20–21

The Bible comes from God: this is the first thing to say in the doctrine of Scripture. But the Bible is, on its face, a human product; that the Bible is a collection of texts written, collected, and transmitted by women and men across centuries and cultures is disputed by no one. So the claim that the Bible is, in some unspecified sense, "from God" requires clarification, expansion, and argument. What does it mean for human artifacts to have their source in God in a manner distinct from the way in which all things have their source in God? Both the nature of the claim—that is, how a canon of writings can come simultaneously from God and from human beings—and the process or mechanism by which it comes about are together in view.

If Scripture is "from God," moreover, then *who* is the God in question? There are many claimants to that designation. The texts of the Christian canon are not ascribed, or indeed ascribable, to deity in general, or to a pantheon of plausible candidates. These texts have a particular God as their source, or so the synagogue and church confess. That God is the God of Israel, who is one and the same as the Holy Trinity of Christian confession.[1]

---

1. Or in the words of Robert Jenson, "God is whoever raised Jesus from the dead, having before raised Israel from Egypt" (*The Triune God*, 63). For wider discussion, see 63–89.

Having revealed himself in, through, among, and to his covenant people, this God, the one God—the Lord—is unique, holy, transcendent, and jealous. He communicates knowledge of himself as he is in himself, manifesting who he is on behalf of his beloved, the seed of Abraham, which is the object of his saving affections. This relationship includes knowledge not just of who he is but also of his character. For the Lord is not interchangeable with Moloch or Asherah or Baal or Zeus or Mars or Mammon; and to know him means to know that, too.

Scripture is instrumental (in more than one way) in the communication of this knowledge. To know God entails attending to this book, for it comes from him; one attends to this book in order to know God and/or because one already knows God. If we seek adequate theological description of Scripture as a uniquely God-sourced collection of texts, then, we ought to expect, first, that the collection in question will be correspondingly unique; second, that its uniqueness will be a function of God's uniqueness; third, that knowledge of the identity and character of the One from whom these texts come will be central to our understanding them; and, fourth, that the role and purposes for which Scripture exists will have their basis in the divine will and action. In sum, Scripture comes from the sovereign Lord, who is both its source and its subject matter.

But before turning to the God of Scripture, I will address how it is that we begin the doctrine of Scripture with beliefs that are themselves derived from Scripture. How, in other words, to avoid a vicious circularity? Then, following a discussion of the character of the God attested by Scripture, who is himself the wellspring of the living water that flows through Scripture's words, I will turn to the economy of grace, that is, the great drama narrated by the Bible. The third section will explore the twofold authorship of Scripture and the theological terms best suited to describe God's activity in Scripture's composition and codification. Last, the fourth section will conclude the chapter by considering Scripture as a human artifact, one produced and preserved within and for God's covenant people, and the implications that follow for text criticism and translation.

1. The Faith of Scripture

The lone individual taking up and reading the Bible and making sense of it all on her own is a common cultural trope. Think of the proverbial man on a desert island alone with a Bible, or the hotel guest who opens her drawer to find a book left for her by the Gideons: *Could such a person be converted by the text itself, devoid of context or the ministrations of priest and church and creed and the rest?* The answer, if we must offer one, is yes, because God is God, and because such things have in fact happened. But hard cases make bad law, and exceptions prove the rule. Very few people come to Scripture "cold," as it were, a blank slate upon which the text may write faith in the gospel.[2] Moreover, even the island reader or hotel guest is not alone, strictly speaking; the situation masks the mediated character of such an encounter with the Bible. For we are not posing that God miraculously brought the book into existence apart from secondary causes (though, again, God is free to do as God pleases). The Gideons placed the Bible in the drawer—itself a misleadingly simple statement, given the complex coordination of actions that led to the Bible's being placed there—and the Bible that washed up on the shore in a water-proof box likewise has a history. Someone, or rather someones, made it. A chain of human activity led from the original manuscripts to their being copied by scribes or monks to their being passed down through the centuries to their being vetted and compared by scholars for antiquity and accuracy to their being translated by a team of linguists and historians in service to a larger project—that of producing Christian Holy Scripture in the same language in a single bound volume between two covers—and *then* actually mass-producing and distributing said volumes across (in this case) the English-speaking world. Not only does "the" Bible have a history, but each and every version of the Bible, in whatever form, has its own small history within that greater history. It follows that even in the most extreme of lonely encounters between the church's Holy Scripture and a curious pagan ignorant of the faith, the reading that results is not unmediated. It is anything but. Better therefore to imagine that island shore or hotel room as populated by an invisible but all-too-present cloud of witnesses, the providential assembly line delivering God's word to this person, at this moment, through innumerable human hands across continents, cultures, and centuries. We are all Ethiopian eunuchs, whether we know it or not, in need of someone to help us understand the scriptures (see Acts 8:26–40). And whether we see them or not, we all have our St. Philips, too.

Having said that, most of us, most of the time, come to the text with some measure of knowledge and expectations. Not only is the artifact of the text mediated to us, but what it is, what it means in the world, what it means to us, the role it plays in our lives and the lives of those around us: this is all given in advance, charged with significance, brimming over with

---

2. I do not mean very few people in raw numbers; millions of people around the globe have not encountered Scripture, and each generation does so anew. I mean that, once one *has* encountered Scripture, one cannot do so again for the first time. If that initial engagement spawns a lifetime of engagement, then the latter, by definition, is not a species of the former, which is unique, standing as it does at the head of a series.

hopes and fears. And the theological point to note here, at the outset, is that this is as it should be. The extraordinary thing is to approach Scripture for the first time, without anticipation or prior acquaintance. The ordinary thing is to approach it for the ten-thousandth time, knowing—or thinking one knows—exactly what it is and what it says. That is what happens in the liturgy, and the church's liturgy is the native habitat, the first home, of Holy Scripture. For Scripture is a document of devotion, the means of God's gathered people hearkening to his voice and responding with thanks and praise. Through Scripture, God the Father "uninterruptedly converses with the bride of His beloved Son."[3] Scripture is the language of love, which is just another way of saying it is the language and medium of prayer. The opening petition of the beloved in the Song of Songs—"O that he would kiss me with the kisses of his mouth!" (1:2)—is a supremely fitting figure for the church at worship: we beg with longing to hear the bridegroom speak. The *responsum* to the lector's parting words signifies at least temporary satisfaction.[4]

Apart from ecclesial context, then, Scripture is not well understood. The reason is simple: Scripture has no *existence* apart from ecclesial context. Scripture is what it is within and in light of the church's tradition. So in the doctrine of Scripture we do not begin from the ground up, analyzing each discrete text of the canon, reenacting or play-acting the arguments and processes that generated either the canon or the dogmas and assumptions that accompanied its transmission across time. The doctrine of Scripture begins with what we have, with the long-standing practices of using and relating to Scripture that have built up in the church's life. Just as Tanakh was a given for the apostolic church, so the two-testament Bible is a given for the church after the apostles and church fathers. We rightly approach it in the faith of the church, under the teaching of the church, within the worship of the church, with the whole company of the church—that is to say, the communion of saints, past, present, and future. We open its pages with the words of the Shema and the Nicene Creed on our lips and in our hearts. Doing so will lead us into its depths, not obstruct our path.

The same goes for theological reflection on Scripture, with one caveat. The Bible does not, as it were, "know" of its own existence. How could it, after all? Parts of the canon certainly know other parts. But the texts of canonical Scripture, considered individually and as a whole, are unaware

---

3. *Dei Verbum* 2.8.

4. Rachel Held Evans writes of the Eucharist, "Jesus slips in, through my parted lips" (*Searching for Sunday*, 143). The evocative phrasing would be right at home in a medieval commentary on the Song of Songs, and is equally appropriate for the hearing of Scripture in the liturgy, where, like Mary, we receive the Word—"Jesus slips in"— through the ears.

of canonical Scripture as such. For the latter, logically and historically, is subsequent to the former. Even if the aged beloved disciple penned the final text of the New Testament, hoping or trusting that it would complete the apostolic deposit of faith in written form, he would still not have been in a position to know, conceive, or relate to what eventually became the two-testament canonical scriptures of the Christian church. Which means, necessarily, that in their original historical settings, the texts of the Bible have nothing to say directly about the literary document we colloquially refer to today as "the Bible" or "the Christian canon" or "Holy Scripture."[5]

Of what help, then, is the Bible for a theological account *of* the Bible? Can Scripture be used in the doctrine of Scripture?

The answer is yes, in at least three ways. First, inasmuch as the biblical texts speak of "the word of God," and the church confesses in faith that Holy Scripture is—bears, attests, mediates—God's word, what Scripture says about the one may be taken to be true of the other. This process requires making the necessary changes, so that not every statement about the word of the Lord in Scripture may or need be lifted out of context and applied without modification to Scripture. But done well, the procedure is both reasonable and fruitful. Second, because parts of Scripture do talk about other parts, particularly the New Testament about the Old, we have a sizable sample within Scripture of explicit commentary on and usage of canonical texts *as* Scripture. Indeed, much of the model for a Christian doctrine of Scripture *in toto* is taken whole cloth from what is effectively an informal apostolic doctrine of Tanakh-as-Scripture contained within the New Testament. Third, Christians believe that the texts of canonical Scripture are sanctified media of divine speech because, in plain terms, the church tells them so. Rare is the individual Christian who investigates such claims to the fullest and, departing here and there from the church's tradition, proceeds to create her own canon, with her own understanding of the meaning of Scripture, and so on. Not only do few persons have the interest or capacity to undertake such an investigation; it would render the church's mission impossible. Most of us simply take the church at its word that *these* texts, in *this* book, are God's word to us. We have reasons, antecedent or consequent to encountering that teaching, that supplement or justify our consent. But our consent is finally a matter of trust.[6] Trust, to be sure, in the Holy Spirit's work in history and the people of God. But also trust in the church that is

5. Here and throughout the book, I use these terms more or less interchangeably, unless the wider context suggests a more specific meaning (e.g., "the Bible" implying a pandect volume or "the canon" an officially authoritative list of sacred writings).

6. For rich reflection on these matters, see Aquino, *Communities of Informed Judgment.*

the temple of the Spirit: guided by the Spirit into the fullness of truth and empowered by the Spirit to teach that truth to successive generations of believers (cf. John 16:12–15; 2 Tim 1:13–14).[7]

So canonical texts either are or are not Holy Scripture, the medium of divine speech to the church. If they are not, then all this is moot anyway. If they are, then—and this picks up the third way in which the Bible can teach us about itself—they have the eternal God as their source; and since God is eternal, his word to us is not bound by the strictures of time or the limits of the human authors whom he inspired. It follows both that Scripture can say more than what its human authors could have meant to say and that Scripture (considered theologically) can speak about "itself," even though the texts of Scripture (considered historically) lack awareness of "itself" qua canonical Scripture. In other words, in the doctrine of Scripture we are permitted to read Scripture anachronistically. And so the church has, and so we will in what follows, with abandon. Which is not to say we will read irresponsibly; there are hermeneutical criteria for the sort of anachronistic reading I am proposing here. But the mere avoidance of historical anachronism is not among them.[8]

We have discovered the particular hermeneutical circle that encompasses (1) the texts of Scripture, (2) the community in which Scripture has its home, and (3) the readers in that community who seek to understand it. On the one hand, all reading participates in just such a circle. On the other hand, the foregoing description just is the justification that this specific circle is not vicious: there is nothing else to be said, save for one detail. The added benefit of reading Holy Scripture within the church is that, at every level—the text, the community, and the reading activity—the one true God is active and present, indwelling, enabling, and securing our fellowship in a hermeneutical process that may stumble and, in this life, will always be imperfect, but will never finally fail.[9] And if that is not true, then there is no good reason to be reading the Bible in the church in the first place.

2. The God of Scripture

When the church confesses in faith that the words found in canonical Scripture are "the word of the Lord," the second term of the phrase—that is, the

7. More on this below, in section 4.

8. For further discussion, see chapter 6. See also East, "Reading the Trinity"; "Standards of Excellence."

9. Here, as elsewhere, Christ's promise that the gates of hell shall not prevail against his church (Matt 16:18) applies with particular force.

Lord whose word is heard in the text—is also a confession of faith. The identity of this Lord is not unknown. The Lord in question is the one God of Israel, whom believers know to be the God and Father of our Lord Jesus Christ. The Father of Jesus is the God of Abraham; God's Son is the crucified and risen Messiah of Israel. The Spirit of the Father, moreover, is one and the same as the Spirit of Jesus. Together, these identities or persons—Father, Son, and Holy Spirit—are not three gods or three personas the one God assumes in time but, eternally, the one Lord confessed in the Shema. So that the Holy One of Israel, YHWH, is from everlasting to everlasting the Holy Trinity of Christian confession.

It is *this* God whom we find in Scripture, his voice we hear in its words. This, as I have said, is not ordinarily an inference drawn from a first-time read-through of the Bible. It is the proper presupposition of Christian exegesis. But beyond identifying the God attested in and by the Bible, what more ought we to specify as this bears on the doctrine of Scripture? For there is much more to be said about God *in se*, that is, God considered from the perspective of God's own life apart from his relationship to creation. It is true enough to name God as Trinity, but that does not tell us much about what the triune God is *like*. Not that we can have any sense what it is like for God to be God "from the inside," as it were.[10] Rather, on the basis of Scripture and tradition, what do we know of the character of this God, his being and works and attributes?

First, the life of God is a perfectly realized and utterly complete movement of mutual presence, inexhaustible communication, and self-giving love. God is the fullness of life and being itself. He lacks for nothing, and nothing could be added to him or taken from him. He exists without limit in the unbroken circle of beatitude comprising the Father's begetting of the Son in the Spirit and breathing of the Spirit upon the Son. The Father gives all that he is and has to the Son, who receives all that he is and has from the Father without loss or remainder. The Spirit who proceeds from the Father alights upon the Son—a gift so comprehensive as to constitute, from all eternity, the bond of unity between them. The unreserved transparency of each to the others is total: "each in each, and each in all, and all in each, and all in all, and all are one."[11] The Father is not the Son, nor the Son the Father, nor the Spirit either the Father or the Son; but each is God, and all are one God. This is the one blessed and undivided Trinity to whom the prophets and apostles bear witness.

10. See here Kilby, *God, Evil, and the Limits of Theology*.
11. St. Augustine, *De Trinitate* 6.12.

Second, God is not "enclosed" within the triune life: the subsistent re-lations of Father, Son, and Spirit do not form a sort of tripartite cage beyond which aught else matters, the cosmos reduced to a void of darkness and un-being sealed off from a shackled divinity. The generosity and love beheld in the everlasting relationship between Father and Son, a relationship in which the Son perfectly images the Father even as he is spoken forth as his eternal Word, overflows "externally" to that which is not God. Which is not a way of saying that the triune love rivers outward to what already exists, for the rivering outward is itself the act of bringing into existence what was not and need not be at all. God creates from nothing: he speaks, only now the word of his power is not solely the drumbeat repetition of his own resplendent being; it brings into being that which has no existence in and of itself. The Spirit hovers, the Father speaks, the Word figures forth—and there was light (Gen 1:3). What was not, is; what is—all that is—comes from God through the Word: "all things were made through him, and without him was not anything made that was made" (John 1:3). The Trinity alone is the Creator, and the resulting creation is good (Gen 1:31). Its goodness is a reflection of its Creator, from whom all things and only good things come (Jas 1:17), but it does not share in the fullness of God's life or perfections. It is finite (limited), contingent (not necessary), gratuitous (sheer gift), and dependent at every moment, in every way, upon God, who as Creator upholds it in be-ing from start to finish. To be a creature is to exist "eccentrically," having the ultimate ground of one's being outside of oneself.[12] To flourish as a creature is to accept this fact with gratitude and joy, to relate to God as a beneficent and gracious giver, who withholds nothing from us, but provides for our needs and empowers us for life in accordance with our several natures.[13]

If we were to stop there, having only scratched the surface of God's "in-ner" identity as Trinity and "outer" work as Creator, we would already have a rich catalogue of God's personal character. He is eternal, infinite, perfect; living, present, happy; loving, giving, glorious; powerful, wise, sovereign. This is who God is, in his own life and in his actions. This is the God at work in creation, the God who calls Abraham and Mary, the God revealed in Jesus, the God who speaks in Scripture. We are right, as we open Scripture, to expect to find these and other attributes narrated and elaborated in beau-tiful, clarifying, and surprising ways.

What else ought we to say? We not only know something of God's identity and character as we approach the sacred page.[14] We also read the

12. See Kelsey, *Eccentric Existence*.

13. See McFarland, *From Nothing*, esp. 57–107.

14. Known, that is, not apart from Scripture, but because of the church's confession

text in the light of faith in God's saving works, as that finds concise shape in what is called the Rule of Faith. The Rule of Faith is a précis of the economy of grace. One ancient and widely received form of the Rule is the Apostles' Creed; what the church calls the Nicene Creed is its definitive ecumenical expansion.[15] We have already, in effect, begun commentary on the Creed, a process we cannot continue in detail without swamping the other purposes of this book. But as far back as we go in the early church, its teachers and leaders took for granted that Scripture could not and should not be read "alone." The scriptures are complex, diverse in genre, difficult to understand in places—a vast territory in which well-intending pilgrims are liable to get lost. The Rule of Faith is the map for Scripture's geography. It says, *You are here*. It paints with broad brush strokes the lay of the land. Initially this took the form of a flexible shorthand based on baptismal confessions: "Do you believe in . . . ?" Answer: "I do: I believe in . . . ." Remove the questions, and you have a rule of thumb both for guiding and for measuring interpretation of the canon. The Rule "rules" by saying, *Should you read in such a way that God is judged not to be one, or Jesus not to be Lord, or Mary not to be a virgin, or the body not to be raised—read again, for you have erred; you have lost your way and need to find the proper path again*. St. Irenaeus of Lyons acknowledged the extraordinary diversity of Scripture; he likened it to a vast mosaic, each discrete book a separate tile coming together to form an image of the royal Son. But tiles can be rearranged. Heretics—or rather, the heresies they wittingly or unwittingly teach—are rearrangers of tiles: they move Exodus to the periphery, or shift Revelation to the center, or excise St. James entirely. The result is certainly a mosaic, but instead of a handsome prince it images a dog or a fox. The Rule, in this case, is the instruction manual that ensures the puzzle turns out right.[16]

As codified in the early creeds, the Rule of Faith serves not as a summary of Scripture but rather as a condensed, trustworthy statement of the identity of God as revealed in his saving work through Jesus and the Spirit. Later statements of faith (like that of Chalcedon), dogmas (like Mary's acclamation as Theotokos), and conciliar teaching (like the two wills of Christ, or the veneration of icons) serve a similar function as the Creed; together, the total tradition of the church, official and unofficial, is a kind of global or master Rule. Overlaid on Scripture, it offers ever clearer and more detailed aid in navigating the terrain, for over the centuries the church has

---

of faith, itself rooted in Scripture's testimony, and bequeathed to us through liturgy, catechesis, and baptism.

15. For the Rule of Faith in action, see St. Irenaeus, *Against Heresies*. For the history, see Kelly, *Early Christian Creeds*; Ferguson, *Rule of Faith*.

16. St. Irenaeus, *Against Heresies* 1.8.1.

had more time to explore, noting both the beauties of the landscape and the dangers to avoid. Consider the alternative. Imagine each generation having to approach Scripture blind, uninformed about the book's contents and thus forced to relive and rehash every question, every argument, every controversy from the preceding generations of the church. Those traditions today that insist on something like this (what I will call "biblicist" traditions) seek simplicity and unadorned faith in a restoration of the apostolic age. Such a project is quixotic. It will not do for the tasks of Christian mission generally, and it will not do for a doctrine of Scripture.[17]

For the purposes of this book, the fulsome Rule presupposed is that of the two Creeds mentioned above (along with the Athanasian), combined with (at a minimum) the first seven ecumenical councils of the church, and more broadly the faith as taught by the church fathers and common to the one church prior to the Great Schism. With that division and the later Protestant fracturing, things become more complicated, and I cannot attend to the complexities of what that entails for Christians attempting theology across divided communions (beyond lamenting and begging the Spirit for what only he can give: the bond of unity).[18] What I can do, instead, is conclude this section with a restatement of the Rule and its basic claims as they bear on the narrative, teaching, and status of Holy Scripture.

Though creation is good, God's rational creatures (angelic and human) fall from grace, that is, they transgress God's good commands and rupture (from their side) the integrity of the relationship between themselves and God. They sin. But God's grace knows no limits. He longs to be intimate with us, that is to say, he wills for us to know the fullness of his felicity, the nearness of his presence, the very thing we have spurned in our rebellion. In his mercy and patience he purposes the plan of redemption. In love he forms a people for himself, his treasured possession among all the nations. He calls Abraham and promises irrevocably that his seed, his children, will be God's beloved elect to the end of time. This promise is sealed in covenant. Later, the God of Abraham delivers Abraham's family from slavery in Egypt.

---

17. Magisterial Protestant traditions are for the most part not in view here, because for the most part they are not biblicist in character. For a contemporary treatment of these issues, see Gordon, *Divine Scripture*; for a constructive patristic approach, see Behr, *Mystery of Christ*; for post-Reformation Protestant hermeneutics, see Gerhard, *Interpreting Sacred Scripture*; for post-Reformation Catholic polemic on this topic, see St. Francis de Sales, *Catholic Controversy*.

18. See further Radner, *End of the Church*; Ratzinger, *Church, Ecumenism, and Politics*; Jenson, *Unbaptized God*.

He covenants again with them through Moses and the Law, or Torah, which he establishes for their common life, to make them holy—to make them his. He gives them the land he promised on oath to Abraham, and he makes them to flourish. He appoints a king, a royal line that also receives a covenant promise: that David's seed will sit on Israel's throne now and till the end of time. The Lord thus builds David a house, and David's son builds the Lord a house: the temple in Jerusalem. There the Lord's name abides, there his powerful saving presence—once on the move, tabernacling among the people in their sojourn from Egypt to the Land—takes up residence. The Lord can now be found on a map; he has an address: Number 1, Temple Avenue, Jerusalem.[19]

But as in the Garden, as at Sinai, the people rebel. They do not keep their side of the agreement: they break the Law; they commit injustice; they worship other gods. Through the prophets the Lord threatens and woos, alternately, but repentance is lacking and doom arrives: first in the north, then in the south. Invasion, destruction, and exile. Finally, the razing of the temple to its foundations. All seems lost.[20]

But the Lord is true. He provides for his people as he did Adam and Eve, exiled from Eden. And he returns them to the Land, foretelling a fuller, deeper obedience (Deut 30:1–10): a Law written on the heart (Jer 31:33); a Spirit poured out on all flesh (Joel 2:28); a temple restored to heavenly perfection (Ezek 40–48); a servant who suffers for the people's transgressions (Isa 52:1—53:12); a king who brings God's reign to earth (Zech 9:9–17), drawing the gentiles from every corner of the compass to Zion (14:16–21), where they will unlearn the ways of war and idolatry and receive instruction from the mouth of the Lord (Mic 4:1–4).

And so it was that "in those days Jesus came from Nazareth in Galilee and was baptized by John in the Jordan" (Mark 1:9). In all that he does as the One he is, Jesus accomplishes the saving work of the Lord, fulfilling all of God's promises—to Abraham, to Moses, to Israel, to David—in his person and his deeds. He is God's only and eternal Son, drawn near in flesh and blood, like unto us in all ways apart from sin (Heb 2:17; 4:15). He is the very Word of God's breath,[21] the inner intelligible wisdom and power of the

19. See Wyschogrod, "Incarnation." See also his *Body of Faith* and *Abraham's Promise*, esp. 165–78.

20. I am summarizing whole swaths of the Old Testament, but focal passages for this and the previous paragraph include Gen 1–4; 12–22; Exod 1–40; Josh 1–12; 1 Sam 8–31; 2 Sam 1–7; 1 Kgs 1–8; 11–14; 17–22; 2 Kgs 17–25; Amos 1–9; Hos 1–14; Isa 1–13; Jer 1–11; Lam 1–5.

21. See Tanner, *Christ the Key*, 191–98: "The Word does not come out of the Spirit as the Word does from the Father, but is carried away from the Father with the Spirit's

triune life through which all things were made and are sustained in being (1:1–4). He is the human prophet who bears God's word, the glad tidings of the kingdom, to God's people (Luke 4:14–44; 7:11–17). He is the king of Israel, David's son, rightful heir to the throne, and liberator of the captives in bondage not only to Pilate and Herod but to sin, death, and the devil (Matt 1:1—2:12; Mark 10:35—11:11; 12:35–37; 14:1—15:39; Rom 1:1–6; 8:1—11:36). More: He is a true and faithful high priest in the service of God who makes the once-for-all sacrifice for the forgiveness of sins, both here on earth and in the heavenly sanctuary (Heb 4:14—10:18). He is the bearer and giver of the Holy Spirit (John 15:26; 16:7; 20:22), alive and transparent in his humanity to the working of God's own living presence (10:30; 14:9), for "in him the whole fullness of deity dwells bodily" (Col 2:9). He, Jesus, is God incarnate, the Lord of heaven and earth.

Conceived in the womb of Mary, he lives a fully human life. He is tempted (Matt 4:1–11); he travels while teaching, preaching, healing, and casting out demons (Mark 1:21—7:37); he prays (Luke 3:21; 5:16; 6:12; 9:18); he eats and sleeps and gets tired (Matt 8:24; John 4:6-8); he weeps over loved ones lost to death (John 11:32–37) and beloved cities lost to sin (Luke 19:41–44; Matt 23:37–39). He calls the Twelve and forms friendships with them and others, including the women who follow him and provide for his needs (Luke 8:1–3). He befriends the outcast, touches the diseased, blesses the poor, and dwells among the needy, hopeless, lost, and vulnerable. By his authority, prostitutes and tax collectors are pronounced first among all entrants to God's kingdom (Matt 21:31). His solidarity with the meek and lowly is total. He lives in perfect submission to the Father as a child of Abraham obedient to the Law of Moses. And when the time comes, he journeys to Jerusalem knowing what his fate will be there (Mark 10:32–34). After his betrayal and arrest, he suffers the shame of mockery, rejection, and execution fit for a gentile slave, not the King of the Jews (14:53—15:39). Except for a few of the women, his own followers scatter, deserting and disclaiming even the knowledge of his name (14:50–52; 15:40–41). He dies on a cross, by all accounts a failed Messiah and accursed false prophet. He is buried in another man's tomb (15:42–47; John 19:38–42).

"But God raised him up": that is the fearless refrain of the early apostles' teaching (Acts 2:24, 32; 3:15, 26; 4:10; 5:30). Jesus, dead and buried, rises from the dead to new and unconquerable life in the Spirit of the Father (Rom 8:9–11; 1 Tim 3:16). His resurrection is at once his vindication, the inauguration of the Lord's reign on earth, the last days of the old age and the first days

---

support, like a word carried away by a breath of air from someone's mouth. . . . The creative Word of God the Father is . . . always accompanied by the animating breath of the Spirit that surrounds it" (194, 196).

of the new,[22] and the sign of the fate of those who call on him as Messiah and Lord. Upon ascending to heaven to sit at the right hand of the Father, he pours out their Spirit on "all flesh," enlivening the Twelve and those baptized into his name with the power to live as subjects of the kingdom in advance of its full arrival. Together, the baptized establish The Way: a community centered on allegiance to Jesus, come what may. As a community, they are sent by the risen Jesus into the world to bear witness to his Way. And early on they realize the good news about Jesus is not only for Abraham's seed according to the flesh but also for all the nations, who through baptism and the reception of Christ's Spirit within them may become, through God's inestimable grace, Abraham's seed by faith and thus God's children by adoption (Gal 3:1—4:31).[23] And so this community, the church, is the Israel of the End planted, as it were, backwards in time: a foretaste of the day when the nations will stream to Zion, seeking *torah* from the Lord (Isa 2:3) and bowing the knee before his Son and Messiah, Jesus (Phil 2:10–11). A single people of Jews and gentiles constitutes a sign to the world that not only have the powers of evil and darkness been defeated but God's will for all humanity to be united in fellowship with one another and himself is coming to fruition even now (Eph 1:3—3:13), in anticipation of its perfection when, on the last day, God will be all in all (1 Cor 15:28; Col 3:11).

Until then, the church continues in its mission to the nations in the power of the Holy Spirit, whose presence enables the church to judge rightly, teach truthfully, live faithfully, and communicate the blessings of Christ in word and sacrament. The assembly of the baptized worships the Father in Spirit and truth, gathering to hear the words of the prophets and apostles read aloud and the appointed leader to proclaim the good news out of their words. And they share in the sacred meal instituted by Christ, in which the Spirit works hiddenly so to sanctify the ordinary elements of bread and wine that, just as human words become the word of the Lord, so these simple tokens become—are and are called—the body and blood of Christ. Christ thus makes himself present to his people as they make their way toward him. But the Eucharist is bread for the journey, a meal on the run, a sign of twinned presence and absence, not the fullness of union itself. Christ has come, Christ is risen, Christ will come again: "For as often as [we] eat this bread and drink the cup, [we] proclaim the Lord's death until he comes" (1 Cor 11:26). The supper of the Lord partaken of now points forward to the wedding supper of the Lamb (Rev 19:9), the final and unending banquet with and before the Lord who, with the Jerusalem above, will

22. This phrasing comes from Wright, *Paul*, 405.

23. See further Thiessen, *Paul and the Gentile Problem*.

descend to earth from heaven once for all, and make his dwelling among mortals forever.

Such is the conclusion of the story Scripture tells; such is the consummation of the cosmos God created from nothing; such is the telos of human creatures in Christ. Not only will we be restored to what we were, or were intended to be. We will be elevated to what never could have or would have been ours by right: we will be "partakers of the divine nature" (2 Pet 1:4). We will, through the humanity of the incarnate Word and by the Spirit's omnipotent power within us, be "inserted" into that perfect circle of love, glory, and beatitude that is the eternal life of Father, Son, and Holy Spirit. God will dwell with us, and we will indwell him. We will see him as he is—a gift beyond measure. Christ with his saints will reign over the new creation, and together with him we will re-pronounce the words of blessing initially spoken through him at the world's creation: It is good. Indeed, it is *very good*.

3. The Authors of Scripture

In one form or another, the foregoing account is the "given" we bring to Scripture, and rightly so. It is the encompassing context that tradition has provided, principally through the church's liturgy, for the reception of Scripture within the community that is defined by faith in the One to whom Scripture bears witness. Scripture, the church thus argues, makes sense—more sense than the alternative, at least, and possibly the only sense it can properly make—when read and heard in the eucharistic assembly, before and during and after prayer and confession and praise, kneeling and making the sign of the cross, giving glory to the Father and the Son and the Holy Spirit, communicating in the consecrated elements, and being sent into the world to love and serve the Lord.[24] Scripture is the church's book, not in spite of its exalted divine status, but precisely in virtue of its being the Lord's word to the church.

What then of Scripture's composition, its authorship? All things have their source in God, the Bible included. But what makes it different? What

---

24. "To understand the word of God, then, we need to appreciate and experience the essential meaning and value of the liturgical action. *A faith-filled understanding of sacred Scripture must always refer back to the liturgy*, in which the word of God is celebrated as a timely and living word . . . . Word and Eucharist are so deeply bound together that we cannot understand one without the other: the word of God sacramentally takes flesh in the event of the Eucharist. The Eucharist opens us to an understanding of Scripture, just as Scripture for its part illumines and explains the mystery of the Eucharist": Benedict XVI, *Verbum Domini* 2.52, 55.

justifies the claims the church makes for it, the practices that attend it in the liturgy and in private devotion? And whatever the justification, how should Scripture's divine difference be understood in relation to the human authors and other hands that have made it what it is?

It will be helpful at this point to introduce and define a number of important terms in the doctrine of Scripture. I will do so cumulatively, each building on the others, while clarifying my own usage and deployment of them.

Before coming to the all-important term "inspiration," it is crucial to recognize that the church got along quite well for centuries without overmuch reliance on that concept. For the first few centuries, the scriptures of Israel paired with a relatively consistent but not officially formalized collection of apostolic writings served as the norm for church doctrine and practice and as the source for hearing the ascended Christ speak to his people in the Spirit—all without recourse to what we think of as divine inspiration, or at least a systematically elaborated doctrine thereof. Remember that for the first millennium neither individuals nor families nor churches would have had a single pandect volume of "Old Testament" and "New Testament" bound in a book titled "Holy Scripture." What they had were scrolls and parchments and indices and codices and florilegia and any number of other technological modes of inscription and transmission of the written word. The texts of the canon lacked literal binding in a single *biblos*, but they were not therefore "unbound": what held them together was the worship of the church. Or in the words of Alastair Roberts, "the binding of the text was the liturgy."[25]

In this way "scriptures" and "holy" are worth highlighting as terms logically, historically, and perhaps theologically prior to "inspiration." That the writings of the prophets and apostles were "scriptures" meant that they reliably taught God's will to God's people, and ought to be read aloud in corporate worship and, at the individual level, consulted, studied, contemplated, and memorized so far as opportunity and aptitude permitted. That they were holy, or sacred, meant both that they were set apart from all other writings—however useful, true, spiritual, renowned, or ancient the latter might be—and that their status, as a collection of texts, was different not in degree but in kind from all other texts, given the nature and source of their content. In other words, what "made" them holy was not per se the church's decision to set them aside from other writings; rather, the church set them aside from

25. The phrase comes from an interview Roberts did with Gerald McDermott on the *Via Media Podcast*, Episode 21, 26 September 2019.

other writings because they were received and confessed as qualitatively distinct, owing to their mediation of the Lord's speech to the church.[26]

In this way, too, other terms take historical and liturgical priority to inspiration, such as "word" or "speech" as well as "author." These will be explored in greater detail below as well as in the next chapter, but it is important to see how the liturgical and devotional claims—or rather, theological presuppositions revealed in ecclesial practices—precede doctrinal inquiry into the grounds of such claims. It is only when, in countless regional contexts across a dozen generations, the texts of Scripture are read in the liturgy *as* the present-tense speech of the living God that the theological question makes itself known: *How does that work, after all?* It became axiomatic to say, as St. Thomas Aquinas does, that the principal author of Holy Scripture is the triune God;[27] but this never meant a denial of the human authors of the scriptural texts. Thus and only thus does the question come: What

---

26. This issue is not, or should not be, a source of ecumenical tension. No less than St. Francis de Sales, in *Catholic Controversy*, affirms the principle: "the Church cannot give truth or certitude to the Scripture or make a book canonical if it were not so but the Church can make a book known as canonical and make us certain of its certitude and is fully able to declare that a book is canonical which is not held as such by every one and thus to give it credit in Christendom, not changing the substance of the book which of itself was canonical, but changing the persuasion of Christians, making it quite assured where previously it had not been so" (1.6). Now, I think a stronger case can be made than the merely epistemic one offered by de Sales, on analogy to eucharistic consecration, miracles, or the forgiveness of sins. When Jesus deputizes the disciples in the Upper Room ("If you forgive the sins of any, they are forgiven; if you retain the sins of any, they are retained"; John 20:23), he does not thereby make them the *source* of the forgiveness of sins. Rather, he is specifying the medium of *God's* forgiveness of sins: namely, through these human beings; indeed, through their all too human deeds and words. So that, when the church canonizes texts—or, put differently, when the church's ordained leaders formally recognize as canonical a particular collection of texts—though their actions are not the *source* of the authority invested in the texts, their actions are nonetheless the human *medium* of the divine action whereby those texts antecedently inspired by the Spirit are definitively and authoritatively identified and set apart as such by the selfsame Spirit, through his ecclesial servants and ministers. Thus and only thus are they *made* canonical. That "making," moreover, is a crucial part of the divine-human work of confecting the scriptures: divine in origin and primacy, human in authorized instrumentality. We may remain agnostic about whether the divine authority with which Scripture is endowed as a result is owed wholly to the act of inspiration or to the larger sweep of historical processes that I am gathering under the term "confection." Either way, authority is not a matter of human conferral but rather of human activities that mediate—sometimes wittingly, sometimes not—the Holy Spirit's sovereign activity of bestowing sacred texts upon his beloved people: revelatory texts that bear God's own authority.

27. Or any one of the persons, usually appropriated to the Spirit; see, e.g., St. Thomas Aquinas, *Quodlibetal Questions* VII, Q6, A1, resp. For critique and reformulation, see Rahner, SJ, *Inspiration in the Bible*.

SOURCE 25

makes Scripture qualitatively different from all other texts? What accounts for this difference, and how did or does it happen?

So we come to inspiration. Consider St. John Damascene's comment in the early eighth century: "It is one and the same God whom both the Old and the New Testament proclaim, who is praised and glorified in the Trinity: 'I am come,' says the Lord, 'not to destroy the law but to fulfill it.' For he himself worked out our salvation for which all Scripture and all mystery exists." After quoting Jesus in the Gospel of St. John and the opening of Hebrews, he continues: "Through the Holy Spirit, therefore, both the law and the prophets, the evangelists and apostles and pastors and teachers, spoke. All Scripture, then, is given by inspiration of God and is also assuredly profitable."[28] The passage on which he draws here is the master text for all Christian talk of inspiration: "All scripture is inspired by God and profitable for teaching, for reproof, for correction, and for training in righteousness, that the man of God may be complete, equipped for every good work" (2 Tim 3:16–17). The Damascene goes on to outline the purpose of Scripture and how to engage it, but he treats inspiration more as a premise (having as much to do, interestingly, with unity across the testaments as with the canon's divine source) than as a metaphysical claim requiring elaboration. Such elaboration came later in the Middle Ages but above all in and after the Protestant Reformation.[29] In light of that history, then, what does it mean theologically to affirm that Scripture is inspired by God?

At a formal level, it means that, unlike in ordinary speech and writing, the origin of the canonical texts' words as well as their meaning does not terminate in the creaturely volition or intention of the human authors. For the human authors are the proximate but not the ultimate source of the words, including both their sense and their reference. These wholly human words may be predicated of God as God's own. Now, because they are creaturely signs, they continue to bear all the marks of their production and transmission; they are neither exhaustive nor, in the colloquial sense of the term, perfect. The only living, perfect, and eternal Word is the second

28. St. John of Damascus, *Exposition of the Orthodox Faith* 4.17. Cf. Origen, *On First Principles*: "This just and good God, the Father of our Lord Jesus Christ, himself gave the law and the prophets and the Gospels, who is also the God of the apostles and of the Old and New Testaments. . . . That [the] Holy Spirit inspired each one of the saints, both the prophets and the apostles, and that there was not one Spirit in those of old but another in those who were inspired at the coming of Christ, is indeed most clearly taught throughout the churches" (Pr.4); "the Scriptures were written by the Spirit of God" (Pr.8); "[the] Scriptures . . . were inspired by the Holy Spirit, that is, the evangelical and apostolic Scriptures and also, according to the statement of Christ himself, those of the law and the prophets" (1.3.1).

29. See, e.g., Muller, *Holy Scripture*; Robert Preus, *Inspiration of Scripture*.

person of the Trinity, incarnate in the man Jesus. The Bible is not Jesus, nor the Word he incarnates, and ought not to be treated as such.[30] But because of the Holy Spirit's inspiration of just these texts (and no others), their lexical and syntactical features bear, as a medium or mirror, God's speech to God's people in the present tense.

What of the act of inspiration? Answer: God the Spirit so works in, on, and through the canon's authors—using "author" broadly to include amanuenses, redactors, and those who dictate aloud—that the words they naturally will to write are one and the same as those which God wills them to write. God does not take command of their wills: they are not possessed; they are not automatons; they are not mindless secretaries of the Spirit "dictating" in their ears.[31] A proper account of Scripture's inspiration requires an account of divine transcendence, rooted in creation from nothing, that understands divine activity to be compatible with human activity. That is to say, the Creator is not in competition with his creatures. Because God is not a discrete entity in the cosmos—one in a series alongside us—it follows that for God to do something does not exclude our doing it, or vice versa. The paradigm here is the divine-human activity of Christ, every one of whose actions is simultaneously the Creator's and a creature's.[32] But consider also a miraculous healing performed by a human being: Did St. Peter "do" that, or did God? Yes; both.[33] Or consider the Eucharist: Who confects the elements to be Christ's body and blood for the people? Is it God, the minister, or God-through-the-minister? The answer is the same for Scripture's composition. Isaiah and Ezekiel and St. Luke and St. Paul and St. John the Seer: each put human thought and planning and intentionality into their texts, and when they wrote, the words that appeared on the page were the product of their wills and bore the unique stamp of their personalities, their

30. The identity and non-identity of Scripture and God's word will be discussed further in the next chapter.

31. Though one can understand the conceptual confusion created by descriptions like Johann Gerhard's: the canonical authors "neither spoke nor wrote by human or their own will; rather, they were moved, driven, led, impelled by the Holy Spirit and controlled by him. They did not write as men but as 'holy men of God,' that is, they wrote as God's servants and as the unique instruments of the Holy Spirit" (*On the Nature of Holy Scripture* 1.18.2).

32. See Tanner, *God and Creation*; Wittman, *God and Creation*; Williams, *Christ the Heart of Creation*; Sokolowski, *God of Faith and Reason*; McFarland, *Word Made Flesh*.

33. But see Farkasfalvy, O Cist, *Theology of the Christian Bible*, 29–63, 111–20, for a subtle critique and reformulation of Scripture's twofold authorship. Farkasfalvy's account of inspiration, I should add, differs from the one offered here; he understands the term to include God's work beyond the writing of the texts into their transmission and reception, whereas I differentiate those moments with distinct terminology.

histories, their sociocultural contexts, and their communicative purposes. So far so good; the doctrine of Scripture affirms this natural description of the act of composing scriptural texts. But the doctrine goes on to offer a theological description. For coterminous with the whole process of writing, simultaneous with every moment and activity constituting it, the Spirit of God moved the wills of the human authors—from within, infallibly but not coercively[34]—such that their thoughts, plans, and intentions in the act of writing were in accordance with the divine will. With the result that their words, willed humanly, were just the words willed by God to be his own, set apart as the medium of his speech and ordered to particular ends in the economy of salvation and the mission of God's people.

A number of points are worth mentioning here. First, inspiration is a confession of faith: it is not verifiable or falsifiable, any more than is the substantial change of the elements in Communion. Second, inspiration is a second-order claim: it follows upon the first-order liturgical and devotional practice of receiving, with trust and thanksgiving, the words of Scripture as the word of the Lord to us and for our sake. Properly speaking, we do not begin with inspiration and work our way "up" to the Bible. We begin with the Bible, living with it in our midst and attending to its teaching, and only thereupon do we seek the grounds for our according it the authority we do. Third, the implications of inspiration are contested, and indeed are the subject of the rest of this book. For in what way is a narrative or a poem or a song or a legend or a history or a letter or an apocalypse or a theodicy "God's inspired word"? In what way is a ceremonial or dietary command of the Torah "God's inspired word" for a gentile believer today? Given Scripture's inspiration, must every empirical fact or historical reference found in Scripture be "accurate"? These are good questions, but their answers are neither simple nor self-evident; they do not follow as a matter of course. Fourth, one hermeneutical matter is worth addressing at this juncture. Although the biblical texts were composed with fully human authorial intentions, there is no reason to conclude that these intentions are synonymous with God's, exhaust God's, or are affirmed by God. It may be the case, that is, not only that God's authorial intentions go beyond those of the human authors, but also that God's intentions actively qualify, subvert, or repudiate the human author's intentions.[35] At a minimum, this means that to know the original or historical meaning of the text is not, from the perspective of the Christian

34. This language comes from St. Thomas Aquinas; see, e.g., *Summa Theologica* I-II, Q 112, A3, resp.

35. See chapter 5 for further discussion; see also East, "Hermeneutics of Theological Interpretation." For another approach, see Wiarda, "Scripture between the Incarnate Christ and the Illuminating Spirit."

doctrine of Scripture, necessarily thereby to know the text's true meaning in and for the church.

Fifth and finally, inspiration is not the only theological term we have at our disposal to describe Scripture's ultimate source in the divine will and work. Three other terms are useful in this respect: sanctification, confection, and illumination. In reverse order, *illumination* names the work of the Holy Spirit in our reception of Scripture. It marks the other pole in the movement begun with inspiration. The same God at work in authoring the texts that attest God's word is equally present in their being read or heard. The Spirit accompanies the word wherever it goes. In this case, the Spirit's hidden activity prepares the souls of the community of faith and of individual believers to hear God's word, to receive it as such, and with gratitude and teachableness to be converted to the gospel, edified in the mind, ever more conformed to the image of Christ. So St. Paul: "And we also thank God constantly for this, that when you received the word of God which you heard from us, you accepted it not as the word of men but as what it really is, the word of God, which is at work in you believers" (1 Thess 2:13). Divine illumination gives the baptized ears to hear and eyes to see the word of the Lord in the words of the apostles and prophets; and not only to hear, but to obey (Jas 1:22). Nor is illumination optional or extra; it is necessary, for our sinful hearts and stubborn pride need God's help, in this as in all things: "Open my eyes, that I may behold wondrous things out of your law" (Ps 119:18).

Confection is the technical term for what occurs in the eucharistic rite within catholic tradition. *Sanctification* is the biblical term for the act or process of being made holy; in Christian usage it usually refers to God's work, begun in baptism, of making sinners into saints. Recent theologians have appropriated these terms, deploying them analogously as descriptions of God's relationship to the Bible.[36] In the case of confection, the term applies to the entire millennia-long sweep of Scripture's coming-to-be (I suggest the reader take a large breath): from its origins in historical events and human experiences to oral retellings and initial transcription through extensive processes of composition and redaction and, in turn, transmission and usage of the texts thus produced thence to the gathering, reproducing, collecting, certifying, and canonizing of such texts *as* an officially authoritative compilation of different texts, all of which, severally and together, *are* the church's sacred book: Holy Scripture, the word of the Lord Christ in and for Christ's church.[37] Whereas inspiration has more to do with the

36. See Griffiths, *Song of Songs*, xxiii–xlii; Webster, *Holy Scripture* 17–30.

37. Is translation a component of confection? Yes, according to Griffiths. For discussion see the next section.

specific activity of writing (and perhaps revision), confection identifies the vast complex movement as itself requiring theological description indexed to the Spirit's work. And confection recommends itself both as an account of divine-human activity within the church's worship and as an analogy to the Eucharist, given the parallels between them (celebrant : consecration : epiclesis : elements :: author : writing : inspiration : texts) and the inherently sacramental character of Scripture.[38] For the church trusts not only that the original words written in the texts that became Scripture come from God, but also that their preservation, collection, and canonization are all alike and equally a product of the Spirit's superintendence. God is not merely the author of the (original manuscripts—possibly corrupted, possibly lost—of the) discrete texts in the canon. God is the author of Scripture *as a book*, considered as a whole, as a single thing. Confection is a useful term by which to name and ground that fact.[39]

Sanctification takes a final step back, in order to consider the whole in the widest frame possible. It encompasses inspiration, confection, and illumination. It names God's ongoing activity to set Scripture apart as the holy means of the self-communication of the saving presence of his word (the periphrasis is intentional), an activity neither relegated to the past nor concluded in canonization, but in principle having no end until the End. It is the work of the Holy Spirit through multifarious historical, human, and liturgical processes to make the living voice of the ascended Christ heard in history, to the glory of the Father. Sanctification connects inspiration

38 The analogy is inexact, unless one affirms something like consubstantiation. For further discussion of Scripture as sacramental (but not a sacrament), see chapter 2. See also the comments of Henri de Lubac in *Medieval Exegesis*, 241: "The Action of Christ in fulfilling the Scriptures and conferring on them, at the same time, the fullness of their meaning is still compared by Christian tradition to the act of eucharistic consecration. For, in truth, Scripture is bread, but for the Christian this bread does not become the living food that it ought to be until it has been consecrated by Jesus."

39. Incidentally, the upshot of the set of claims made here is that "Jesus wrote the Bible" or "Jesus is the author of Scripture" is a perfectly orthodox statement. For Jesus is the Word incarnate, and thus fully God; all that may be said of God as such may be said of Jesus. So that, if God is the principal author of Scripture, then Jesus is, too. And though "author" and "wrote" are analogical terms—that is, they are not only not literal (in the way that "God is good" is a literal predication) but, as applied to the production of the canonical texts, even their meaning in terms of the texts having God as their ultimate source is not univocal with, e.g., our saying the same of a text dictated to a secretary by a human author—they are nonetheless true predications, of God and therefore of Jesus. "Confection" as a term gets this dynamic just right, since it is true to say that Jesus is the "author" of the change of the elements in the Eucharist, precisely because (not in spite of the fact that) the celebrant is the visible human being performing the rite. For the celebrant acts *in persona Christi*, representing and mediating the activity of the living Jesus in the eucharistic meal.

(Scripture's from-ness) and confection (Scripture's what-ness) to illumination (Scripture's now-ness); it renders the act of hearing the inspired words of the canonical text as above all an event, one that is essentially spiritual, laden with God's presence and action. The Spirit's work is not limited to the production of Scripture ("made" "back then") or to my inward appropriation of an ostensibly inert object ("received" "within me"). It binds them together in the form of an ecclesially mediated, Spirit-enabled encounter, in which the creatures (we humans) and creaturely entities (these texts comprising these signs) are instruments and recipients of divine grace.[40] God *uses* Scripture to *do* things. He does this, without ceasing, in the daily life of the church, and in the manifold relationships the church's members have with Scripture. Accordingly, the church, its members, and Scripture itself are sanctified, "commanded and molded to enter into the divine service."[41] If Scripture is the sword of the Spirit (Eph 6:17), then sanctification names the Spirit's ongoing work, this side of glory, in battle "against the principalities, against the powers, against the world rulers of this present darkness, against the spiritual hosts of wickedness in the heavenly places" (v. 12). It follows that the work of Scripture, too, will remain unfinished until, through its words, we are made holy as the One whose words they are is holy.

4. The Artifact of Scripture

The Bible is an artifact, a product of human making. So far I have emphasized Scripture's ultimate ground in God the Trinity, antecedent to as well as active in and through the creaturely processes of its coming to be. But this emphasis, while crucial to maintain in the doctrine of Scripture, is not meant to overbalance the doubled set of claims regarding Scripture's creation. Though the Lord is the great and incomparable Artificer, he is a Maker of makers whose distant imitation of his creative activity results in, among other things, texts.[42] The texts of Scripture belong in that cultural category without qualification. That is, there is nothing in their literary or phenomenal character that sets them apart from other texts, considered

---

40. See the discussion in Barth, *Church Dogmatics* I/2, 457–537.

41. Webster, *Holy Scripture*, 27.

42. This brings to mind the work of J. R. R. Tolkien and Dorothy Sayers, as well as the poetry of the Catholic convert Franz Wright; from the latter, see esp. "Icon from Childhood" ("all things are shining words, busy silently saying themselves—they don't need me") and "Maker" ("the way, always, being a maker reminds: you were made") in *Walking to Martha's Vineyard*, 37, 68. Cf. Wiman, *He Held Radical Light*; Fujimura, *Art and Faith*.

in terms of their natural properties.[43] They are not the oldest texts, or the most beautiful, or the most philosophically acute, or the most religiously profound. Such judgments are arguable. What sets them apart instead is the good pleasure of God, who deputizes them to communicate his saving word to the church and the world until kingdom come.

There will be time in later chapters to give greater attention to the historicity of the biblical texts, their particular location in sociocultural and linguistic contexts and how that bears on their reception in the church. What I want to do in this section is discuss, not the divine or even the human *from-ness* of Scripture, but rather its *ecclesial* from-ness. And, in turn, address some of the specifically textual issues that arise in the interplay between Scripture's divine and ecclesial artefaction.

First, Holy Scripture is a specifically ecclesial artifact. It is a product of the people of God. To the question, "Which human persons, belonging to which human community, created the Christian Bible?" the only reasonable answer is, "The Christian church." For our purposes, we are using that term expansively, to include the whole company of Christ, before and after his advent: Abraham's seed circumcised in the flesh together with his seed circumcised in the Spirit through baptism (Col 2:11–12; Rom 3:21—5:11; 8:1–17; 11:1–32). The one covenant community of God the Lord, therefore, is the corporate human author and artificer of the texts of the old and new covenants. If, in short, we stipulate that "church" is the name the New Testament gives to eschatological Israel, sent as Jews and gentiles in one body to proclaim the gospel to the nations in between the Messiah's first and second comings, then we are permitted to affirm that the Bible's human author is the church.

This is true at a less theologically precarious level, too. For the scriptures as such are not distinct from the church's tradition as a whole.[44] The scriptures, rather, are an item within that tradition. That is a sociological fact not worth disputing. The relevant question is what role the texts of the prophets and apostles play within the church's larger tradition. And indeed,

43. Those trained in rhetoric in the premodern church were quick to admit this, such as Origen, St. Augustine, even Calvin. But Protestant traditions in the wake of the Reformation can sometimes fall into the trap of elevating the human or literary qualities of the text simply in virtue of its status as inspired canon; see, e.g., the Westminster Confession of Faith: "the heavenliness of the matter, the efficacy of the doctrine, the majesty of the style, the consent of all the parts, . . . the many other incomparable excellencies, and the entire perfection thereof, are arguments whereby [Scripture] doth abundantly evidence itself to be the Word of God" (1.5).

44. Better to say: they are distinct within the tradition, *as* preeminent tradition. See Florovsky, *Bible, Church, Tradition*; Congar, OP, *The Meaning of Tradition*. Barth admits as much in *Church Dogmatics* I/1, 102. Cf. Schneiders, *Revelatory Text*, esp. 27–93.

all are agreed that they play a controlling role: that is what it means to say they bear authority. The devil is in the details. For how is that authority exercised? And how can texts, which must be interpreted in conjunction with other (non-scriptural) texts as well as innumerable unanticipated questions, function as a "control" apart from living human readers and teachers? Furthermore, how is the authority of the latter related to the authority of the former? We will return to these questions in chapter 6. For now, it is enough to accept the irreducibly ecclesial character of Holy Scripture as a product of God's covenant people and therefore as an element of that people's historical tradition of worship and faith.

Second, if "inspiration" is paired with "confection" for an adequate description of the divine activity in bringing Scripture into being, then "authorship" also stands in need of a second term. That term is "canonization."[45] Scripture comes "from" the church not only in the sense that its texts have God's people (prophets and apostles) as its corporate author. Scripture is "from" the church, additionally, in the form of the official canon of texts that the church counts *as* Scripture. And that, too, is an utterly human and historical act. Just as the Bible's texts did not descend from heaven inscribed

---

45. Following Griffiths's lead, I would like to suggest an alternative formal term, one also borrowed from the sacraments, by which to designate the theological and not merely human or ecclesial activity of canonization: *chrismation*. This is the name of the Eastern sacrament of anointing that follows immediately upon baptism (by contrast to the West, which eventually separated confirmation from the initial baptism of infants). Chrismation makes little Christs of the baptized, sealing them with oil that signifies and imparts the gift and graces of the Holy Spirit. As a seal, it confirms and completes the sacrament of baptism while charging the baptizand, now anointed with the Spirit of Christ, with the lifelong tasks of discipleship to Christ himself, the holy Anointed One of God. Applied analogously to the doctrine of Scripture, chrismation names the specific work of the Holy Spirit, in and through the temporally extended actions of the church, to seal, certify, and complete the scriptures as a collection—that is to say, as a canon. No less than in the scriptures' inspiration or reception, the Spirit is at work in their canonization as the church's sovereign Lord. Chrismation presents itself as a fitting term for this particular work given its association with the Spirit, its ecumenical purchase, and the analogous activity of (a) bringing to completion the Spirit's own prior sacramental work in and on fallen creaturely entities and (b) charging those creatures just anointed with a particular mission within the church. The result for theological description of Scripture's creation is something of a mixed sacramental metaphor, but that is part of the appeal, since all the terms in question are analogous in one way or another. In sum: The Holy Spirit's sanctification of Holy Scripture encompasses both confection (the Spirit's comprehensive "making" of the canon from beginning to end) and reception (which the Spirit facilitates through the ongoing illumination of the faithful); while the Spirit's confection of the canon includes both inspiration (the Spirit's work in the people of God to speak aloud in human words, and later to transcribe in fixed form, the word of God) and chrismation (the Spirit's work to transmit, gather, collect, and canonize the inspired texts of the prophets and apostles).

by the divine finger, so the list of texts to be included in the Bible was not re-vealed by miracle (much less appended to the final page of the Apocalypse). The question of which texts ought to be included was left to the church to sort out for itself.

"For itself": under the guidance of the Holy Spirit, that is. But I am of-fering a natural description. And understood as an extended series of occa-sional but increasingly formal decisions spanning centuries and continents, canonization is a fully human process, akin to the composition of the texts themselves, one that terminates, finally, in a (relatively) fixed list of which books are Holy Scripture for the church, and which books are not. Prior to the Reformation, though there was minor disagreement on the margins, the issue of the canon was not a pressing one.[46] With the reformers, their proposal of *sola scriptura*, and their excision of certain long-standing ca-nonical texts (e.g., the Wisdom of Solomon), the canon became a matter not only of theological controversy but of division between communions. For our purposes, though, the point to highlight is that no one disputes the need for an official canon. The more controversial point is that the canon is itself a decision of the church and thus an item of tradition. Though some argue that the canon is in principle perpetually open and therefore subject to revision—as a function of the church's fallibility, standing beneath the di-vine sovereignty—as a matter of practice all treat the canon as closed.[47] The question is who closed it and on the basis of what, or whose, authority. But regardless of the answer, the truth is that ordinary believers receive what-ever canon their particular church presents to them (perhaps quite literally whatever Bible is in the pew before them), and they do so with simple trust. The ultimate object of this trust is God's Spirit. Its proximate object, though, is God's church.

If, then, the canon of texts that constitute Holy Scripture is, humanly speaking, a product of the church in both its composition and its final form (which books, in what order, organized thus, in a single collection), two questions follow. Which manuscripts of the ancient scriptural texts count as the authorized standard for the canon? And what of the status of transla-tions of those manuscripts?

The answer to the first question is relatively straightforward. We do not have the so-called "original autographs" of the biblical texts. That is not a theological problem, as we have seen, because God's work in establishing

46. I mean once the Marcionite challenge was decisively rejected—say, in the mil-lennium or more between the early councils and Luther. On canon formation see, e.g., Metzger, *Canon of the New Testament*; Barton, *Holy Writings, Sacred Text*; McDonald, *Biblical Canon*.

47. See, e.g., the discussion in Barth, *Church Dogmatics* I/1, 99–11; I/2, 473–81.

Scripture for the church did not cease with the composition of the texts. The activity of the Spirit in providentially guiding and preserving the texts means that what we have is sufficient to the Spirit's purposes. (Indeed, the changes produced in their "preservation" are potentially, from this perspective, the work of the Spirit. That is why there need be no anxiety about lacking the "originals.")[48] And so the specifically text-critical questions are best handled by the experts, whose centuries-long labors on this very issue are a peerless example of historical and linguistic scholarship at its best. From the Christian side, the work can be undertaken free of either worry (what if we lack what we need?) or mania (we must discover the *ipsissima verba* of the apostles!), for the Lord has graciously provided all that we require to hear and obey his voice. Here, too, we arrive at trust.

Translation is a trickier question, but it too permits a plain answer. If the doctrine of Scripture is a theological investigation into what must be the case for it to be true, good, and right for the church to acclaim words read from the Bible as "the word of the Lord," then we must clarify whether it is proper for that acclamation to follow exclusively for words read in the original languages—largely Hebrew and Greek—or also for words read from the Bible in translation. And once posed, the question answers itself. The Bible is "the word of the Lord" in translation or it is not the Lord's word at all. For we begin with practice, not theory. And what must be true, given our starting point, is that the Hebrew scriptures translated into Greek, and the apostles' words translated into Latin, and the texts of both translated into English *are*, without qualification, "the word of the Lord" to and for Christ's body, gathered in his name. What alternative is there? We aren't building Christianity from scratch. We are beginning in the middle (there is nowhere else to begin), with faith that Christ is risen and has sent his disciples into the world. That mission is constitutive of the church's identity and work until the Lord's return. Mission means translation, both of culture and of language. The apostles embodied this in the first generation,

---

48. I do not mean to deny the possibility and prevalence of corruption in textual transmission. See chapter 2 for further discussion of the issues raised by translation. For now I will note, first, that passages like John 8:2–11 suggest later interpolations can be received in the church catholic as inspired, canonical Scripture; and, second, that the line drawn between presumptive "original autographs" and later redactional work is arbitrary, given the state of the texts as we have them. What if, e.g., Philippians or 2 Corinthians is in fact a later literary creation by students or delegates of St. Paul, stitched together out of distinct letters or fragments thereof? Or what if, e.g., St. John's Gospel was revised following its primary author's death, as some scholars suppose? What we have is the final form of the text, which may or may not have passed through many hands and many revisions before reaching us, just like canonical texts in the Old Testament. By comparison, emendations in transmission are a difference only of degree, not in kind.

moving from Jewish Palestine through Greek roads and cities to the Roman imperial capital within a few decades. They went telling of a *christos* called *kyrios* and *theou huios* and *soter*, names elaborated through reference to the Septuagint, the Tanakh in Greek. And when St. Paul and others in the New Testament cite the Septuagint, they do not issue the qualification, "As a translation of the word of the Lord says . . ." They treat it as God's word *simpliciter*. To offer only one example, Hebrews introduces a quotation from Psalm 95 in the Greek with the bare words, "As the Holy Spirit says" (*kathos legei to pneuma to hagion*; 3:7).[49]

The church has proceeded on the same basis ever since. What, again, would be the alternative? Either converts from every corner of the globe would need to become fluent in Greek, Aramaic, and Hebrew, or less than 1 percent of the church at any given time would have true and unvarnished access to God's word; whereas the ordinary baptized—all 99 percent of them—would live their lives, not least in the church's public worship, having heard only a simulacrum of the Lord's speech to his people: not the genuine article but merely a representation or best-possible-rendering thereof. But there is no asterisk in the liturgy when the sacred text is read. There are no qualifications made. "Hear the word of the Lord from . . ." is the wholly proper and theologically justified formulation preceding any and all reading from the Bible. What the doctrine of Scripture has to do is make sense of how that can be the case.

I will not make that fulsome case here. At a minimum, I want to flag the issue and clarify what Christian convictions about Scripture entail here. The claims made above about translation do indeed raise questions regarding regnant assumptions about the meaning of texts, the nature of Scripture's authority, "originalism" in text criticism as well as interpretation, and finally the church's own authority in making judgments in this area. It raises further questions regarding the criteria by which decisions might be made (and by whom?) regarding the status of translations, and how to weigh translations against one another (if all are the Lord's word, how could any be "superior" to another?). These are important theoretical and practical considerations. But, like the doctrine of Scripture, they follow from prior givens; they are not the starting point. And the starting point is not a matter of dry abstraction: *Say such-and-such and not otherwise in theological formulations about the Bible*. No, the starting point is part and parcel of the good news: that the One we receive in faith and baptism is not remote from us, not hard to find; he is the One we hear, here and now, in the words of the

49. See, e.g., Law, *When God Spoke Greek*. See also Gerhard, *Nature of Holy Scripture*, ch. 25; Turretin, *Institutes*, Questions 10–15. I will say more on these matters in the next chapter when we consider the nature or ontology of Scripture in translation.

prophets and apostles. For Christ promised that he, Immanuel, would be with us till the end of the age (Matt 1:23; 28:20); that where two or three are gathered in his name, there he will be with them (18:20); that heaven and earth may pass away, but his words will never pass away (24:35; cf. 5:18). He, the risen One, is not far from any of us (Acts 17:27); he has not left us orphans (John 14:18); we are not bereft of his word (17:17; 15:26; 16:13). The flock knows the voice of the shepherd, and this shepherd is good (10:4, 11). His gentle speech will not cease until we find our way home to him.

2

Nature

> *And we also thank God constantly for this, that when you re-*
> *ceived the word of God which you heard from us, you accepted it*
> *not as the word of men but as what it really is, the word of God,*
> *which is at work in you believers.*
> —1 Thessalonians 2:13

Because the Bible comes from God, it is more (though not less) than a human product. To ask "what" the Bible is, then, requires more (though not less) than a natural description. It calls above all for a theological answer. Only an account of the Christian Bible with substantive, irreducible reference to the God revealed in Jesus Christ will prove adequate to the fullness of its nature. But reference to the church is also necessary, and not only because, as shown in the last chapter, the church, broadly speaking, is the human "source" of the canon. Rather, the church is itself a theological entity. The "more (though not less) than human" appellation applies as much to the church as to its sacred text. The same Spirit that inspired the latter fills the former, rendering it a temple for the Lord's presence. Indeed, as St. Augustine says, Holy Scripture is itself a sort of sacred temple from which the mouth of the Lord speaks by the Spirit.[1] Scripture is thus both a product of the church and a defining fact of its ongoing existence. That "fact-ness" tells us something, too, about what Scripture is.

---

1. St. Augustine, *De Doctrina* Pr.6.

"What Scripture is": a curious phrase. For "Scripture" has no self-evident or easily locatable referent. We might expand it to say "the canonical scriptures of the Christian church." But whose church? Which canon? And even if we stick with one canon of one church, there are countless concrete instances of said canon, most of which (call them "versions") contain different words than the others, and each of which is a discrete artifact. We are not asking a question along the lines of, "What is the Kaaba?" That would admit of a fairly straightforward answer, for there is only one object in the world that answers to that name, and the consequent description (also potentially theological!) would prove clear to any who spent more than a few minutes considering it. In this case, however, there is no Ur-canon to which all questions about the nature of Scripture refer; nor will imaginary reference to Ur-texts—the fabled autographs of yore—do the trick, both because we have no access to them and because we are not referring to past-tense historical objects but to a single object in the present tense: the church's Holy Scripture. How then do we make sense of the question, "What is Scripture?"—much less offer an answer?

That will be the burden of this chapter and the next. Chapter 3 will offer an account of the particular attributes (unity, sufficiency, etc.) proper to Scripture in virtue of the triune Lord's action in and upon it. This chapter remains at the more general level of how it is that Scripture *is* a "what," a "this" not "that," and thus *has* a "what-ness," an ontology. The first section addresses that issue specifically. The second section discusses the range of claims and concepts central to a theological description of Scripture's nature, considered as a sacrament of revelation and thus a means of grace, the word of the Lord, and more besides. The third and final section considers the ecclesial character of the Bible as a book of the covenant, which is to say, the sacred book of the covenant people, Abraham's children by birth and by baptism. For the church's scriptures consist of two testaments—as the shorthand "prophets and apostles" is meant to keep us from forgetting—and inattention to both testaments and the distinct covenants to which they bear witness will inexorably lead to deprivation and atrophy in the doctrine of Scripture.

1. An Ontology of Scripture

The clearest contemporary treatment of this topic comes from John Webster. He uses the work of Wilfred Cantwell Smith as a point of contrast. In the latter's book, *What is Scripture? A Comparative Approach*, Smith writes as a scholar of comparative religion, analyzing the role that texts designated—which is to say, used—*as* "scripture" play in different communities. Late in the book he turns philosophical, making the repeated italicized claim, *"There is no ontology of scripture."*[2] By which he means that the term, considered as a religious universal, "has no metaphysical, nor logical, reference; there is nothing that scripture finally 'is.'" What there "is," instead, is the complex network of convictions embodied in practices of usage of texts thereby set apart *as* "scripture." That altogether human, cultural, and universal (though universally particular) activity is what we mean when we employ the concept of "scripture"; we do not need any extra, possibly spooky essence to justify our (academic) use of the word, much less for concrete communities to do so. So-called "scriptures" are functions of human ontology, which is to say, human dispositions and habits and beliefs (bundle them as "nature" if you prefer), not the other way around.[3]

In response to these claims, Webster simply, calmly, and rightly demurs. Where he agrees is that, played on these terms, the game is predetermined; it cannot be won. For what Smith refrains from doing, and what Webster therefore offers, is "a thoroughly theological ontology of the biblical texts."[4] The point, as we saw in the last chapter, is not that such an ontology—one rooted, that is, in the saving works of the Holy Trinity—repudiates a depiction of the texts' ongoing use and present being and prior coming-to-be in fully human terms. The point, rather, is threefold. First, that such human depiction does not exhaust the nature of the texts. Second, that the antecedent and therefore determinative aspect of the texts' nature derives from the divine will and action,[5] such that God's relation to the canon is not accidental, additive, optional, or epiphenomenal to it. Not every account of the Christian Bible need be theological, or primarily so. But any account that deliberately or definitionally ignores, elides, or rejects the theological component has made a grave error. Such an account is radically incomplete, potentially fatally so, on analogy to a treatment of the human person that

---

2. Smith, *What is Scripture?* 237; cited in Webster, *Holy Scripture*, 7.

3. See the larger discussion in Smith, *What is Scripture?* 212–42.

4. Webster, *Holy Scripture*, 21.

5. In distant analogy, as we will see below, to the divine assumption of human nature, and thus to the precedence of the former over the latter with respect to fundamental identity. Think of the pre-Chalcedonian language used by St. Cyril of Alexandria to describe Jesus: "the one incarnate nature of the Word of God"—a formulation intended not to deny either that the Word remained divine in the incarnation or that he truly became human, but rather to emphasize the persisting dominant factor in the *identity* of the incarnate Word. Jesus is *God* in the flesh; just so, Scripture is *God's word* in human words. For discussion, see Beeley, *Unity of Christ*, 171–223, 256–84, esp. 259–64.

focused solely on her external relations with others and neglected, say, the inner workings of her organs, brain, and cardiovascular system.[6]

The third point is that Smith fails to attend to the particularity of *Christian* Scripture, instead placing the Bible beneath the genus "scripture," of which all religious communities' sacred texts are species, including the church's. Doubtless scholars of religion may learn something from such a move, but it is a fundamental category mistake for Christian theology. For if the Bible is what the church confesses it to be—and the presupposition of the church's faith and worship and therefore of this book is that it is, namely, "the word of the Lord"—then it is not an instance, even the truest or one true instance, of a more general concept. It is an entity, a something-or-other, without peer. For the Bible is *sui generis*. There is nothing else like Holy Scripture.[7] In this sense it is decidedly *not* "like any other book," the slogan of late nineteenth-century biblical hermeneutics. The church's Bible is a book unlike any other.[8]

As we have seen, though, this is not because it lacks any properties common to ordinary human texts. It does not lack those. What sets it apart is the living God's action in eliciting and deploying just these texts for his redemptive and communicative purposes in the economy of grace. They are indexed, annexed, to the divine desire; they serve the purposes of the risen Lord Christ, as he puts them to work as he sees fit, through his Spirit.

We will see in the next chapter what further properties characterize the canon in light of this work. What ought we to say now, though, about Scripture's nature or ontology as such? Let me offer three suggestions.

First, whatever the metaphysics of Scripture's ontology, the principle is one of theological grammar: what Holy Scripture *is*, it is so in virtue of the triune God's sovereign will and work. This is a rule for proper Christian syntax in describing the Bible: *Do not speak as if the canon is limited to its human historical and cultural trappings; so speak, instead, that the origins and defining features of Scripture are the loving designs of the Father, Son, and Holy Spirit as revealed in Israel, Jesus, and the church.*

---

6. The stricter analogy would be a consideration of human beings wholly socially and empirically, to the neglect of their spiritual nature—immaterial soul, created by God in his image, claimed by Christ in baptism, etc.—but I opt here for a more obviously "visible" negligence. Perhaps the *strictest* analogy would be to reading a text as though it had no author, that is, lacking an intentional agent who produced it and who possessed communicative purposes. Neither texts in general nor the biblical texts in particular nor human beings as such are without a telos. Creation is teleological all the way down.

7. In distant analogy to Scripture's author: *Deus non est in genere.*

8. The hermeneutical axiom ("to read Scripture like any other book") comes from Jowett, "Interpretation."

Second, the metaphysics, though secondary, are not unimportant. The question presents a task for the mind, one we should engage with the humility and pleasure proper to theological speculation. It suggests that we treat texts as what they are: creatures, that is, created entities that are, in this case, inanimate. Inanimate entities that are simultaneously cultural products are nevertheless creatures, brought into being and sustained therein by the omnipotent will of God. What a creature is, its ontology, is finally a theological question; it is not reducible to empirical inquiry. So here, the biblical texts are what they are in their relation to God. And what the church confesses in the liturgy is that God's relation to these texts is unique and efficacious: unique, because no other texts stand in the same relationship; efficacious, because the relation itself is what makes the texts to be what God desires that they be. God the Father wills that they be Holy Scripture, the textual mouthpiece of the Holy Spirit in and for the body of Christ. And so they are. For if what creatures are is determined principally by their relation to God and God's will for the role they are to play in the world, in their manifold relationships to other creatures, then it makes no difference in principle whether the creature in question is a tree, a mouse, a quark, an angel, an icon, a planet, or a text.[9] Each, on the view here offered, is what it is—has the being proper to it—as a gift from God, a gift that is not a mere discrete occasion but an uninterrupted relation of love, an ongoing benevolent telos bestowed in every moment without ceasing. Such a gift, such a relation, such a telos is what we mean when we speak of the distinct nature of the church's canon.

This claim, third, raises the question: To what object or objects in the world do we refer when we use the terms "Holy Scripture," "Bible," and "canon" in this context? The only answer can be: *to each and every instance, past, present, and future, of any or all parts of any and all versions of the texts included in the canon of the church's Scripture.*[10] Scripture, then, is no *simple* object. It is not like the Kaaba (a single object persisting in a single place), or a particular pope (an individual person mobile in space but delimited in time),[11] or the Dodo bird (a species no longer located in the present but only

9. To anticipate the eucharistic analogy in the next section, it is worth noting here that the elements of the Lord's Supper are not "raw" elements—mere grain and grapes—but are themselves artifacts, products of human cultural making: bread and wine. This strengthens the analogy, since neither bread nor texts are, strictly speaking, "natural" objects discoverable in the wild. But they remain creatures for all that. And their status before God and in the life of the church is a question, first of all, not of what humans have made them to be but what God wills that they be in and for his people.

10. For what follows, see Griffiths, "Words of Scripture"; "On Radner's *Time and the Word.*"

11. Though perhaps an office, whether papal or presidential, offers a more interesting object for comparison.

in the past), or a Rembrandt (a finite set of authentic paintings locatable and countable at any one time), or a math theorem (neither an entity in the world, at least necessarily, nor tracked by the movement of time). Scripture, by contrast, consists potentially of an infinite and ever-growing set of versions "inscribed" in various ways: in the mind, in oral retellings, in handwritten manuscripts, in printings, in radio, on film, on mainframes, online, in the cloud, on audio books, on smart phones, on e-readers, and more. Not only are such "inscriptions" expanding indefinitely, but even the very words of Scripture increase almost by the day. For if each version of Scripture is itself in unqualified form the Lord's sanctified word to his people—leaving aside the procedure for discerning a faithful from an unfaithful version— then as the canon is translated and re-translated, the words that constitute Scripture themselves multiply. Once upon a time, "in principio erat Verbum et Verbum erat apud Deum et Deus erat Verbum" was not Scripture; nor was "Im Anfang war das Word, und das Wort war bei Gott, und Gott war das Wort"; nor still was "In the beginning was the Word, and the Word was with God, and the Word was God"; nor until quite recently was "Hapo Mwanzo, Neno alikuwako; naye alikuwa na Mungu, naye alikuwa Mungu." Now each and every one of them is. Many languages have yet to receive the imprint of God's word in translation, though it is conceivable that we are within sight of that happy finish line. Even then, languages, customs, and vernaculars change with time, and new translations are called for. Should the Lord tarry, and should the earth and its inhabitants exist long into the distant future, and should we meet rational creatures from another planet, and should they request a translation of the prophets and apostles into an alien tongue, and should we comply: that, too, would be Holy Scripture.

And unless otherwise specified, for example by reference to a particular stage in the canon's formation or to a particular version (e.g., "what St. Paul dictated in AD 55" or "the LXX quoted from memory by Philo" or "St. Jerome's Vulgate" or "die Lutherbibel" or "the dread NIV"), it is to each and to all of these that "Holy Scripture" refers when used in Christian theological speech.[12]

12. An important distinction that will receive discussion in later chapters: Scripture as sacramental vehicle of the saving word of God and Scripture as statutory norm for doctrine (and thus theological disputation). Each and every version of Scripture may be and is a fitting and adequate instance of the former; as for the latter, if argument over some theological controversy is sufficiently fine-grained, then recourse may and must be made to the "original" versions, that is, the most ancient Greek and Hebrew manuscripts. These function as a "control" on theological interpretation of, e.g., the argument of St. Paul regarding Adam and sin in Romans 5 or the meaning of *sarx* in the Gospel of St. John. This works by analogy to the long-standing tradition, rooted in St. Augustine and St. Thomas, that theological argument can appeal only to the literal,

That is what permits us to speak of the ontology of Scripture. Not because Scripture has an "essence," a metaphysical extra hidden within, though inaccessible to empirical investigation. Not because Scripture has an "original," or rather originals, access to which would secure our possession of the one and only object in the world properly designated "the Christian Bible," and of which nothing but copies or translations might be made.[13] No, the infinite translatability—the missionary fecundity—of the canonical texts paired with and supported by a theological account of the texts as communicative signs created, sustained, and ordered toward definite ends by the gracious and lordly will of the triune God, acting in and through ordinary creaturely and cultural processes in history: together, these ground and establish the nature of the canon and our ability to describe that nature theologically. Typically, this is all beneath the surface, the proverbial body of the iceberg unseen in fathomless depths. The visible tip is simply the scriptures themselves: the open volume on the lectern, the family Bible on the shelf, the secret translation sewn into a jacket smuggled into a hostile land. That is all the church needs in its daily life of prayer and devotion, proclamation and adoration. But when the question arises, into the depths we plunge—of which depths I have been able in this section to offer only a glimpse.

2. A Sacrament of Revelation

Holy Scripture is not a sacrament. The reading of Scripture is, however, a sacramental act. For it is a sign—a collection of texts comprising signs—of that which its public and devotional reading makes present and effective. It is thus a reliable creaturely and liturgical act in and through which the Lord acts. It is, in short, a means of divine grace.[14]

These are simply variations on the definition of a sacrament. The words of Scripture are a vehicle for the word of the Lord God; that is why a reading from them can be truthfully described as a hearing from him. The analogy to the Eucharist suggests itself again, for the elements of the meal are changed by God's action upon them, in answer to the prayers of the rite (and God always answers these prayers). While the visible and chemical aspects

---

not the spiritual, sense of Scripture. For more, see chapter 6.

13. Interestingly, the comparison that suggests itself here is not the Kaaba but the Qur'an. The fact that Christians encourage and practice text criticism of their sacred text and that Muslims do not suggests not only the difference of the texts' status between them but a different conception of what versions, especially translations, of the texts *are*. It is that implicit conception I am wanting to draw out here.

14. See further the rich patristic discussion in Boersma, *Real Presence*.

of the elements—the accidents of bread and wine—remain, the elements themselves become—having been made by the hidden work of the Holy Spirit to be—the body and blood of Christ.[15] The analogy fails, though, in at least two important respects. First, though it is supremely fitting to acclaim the words of the prophets and apostles as the Lord's word in the setting of the church's public worship, it is not only there that they are such, nor is there a periodic ritual by which the words become the Word. The analogue to the epiclesis is not the lector's act or the appeal for illumination in the hearts of the listeners; it is divine inspiration. The scriptures' status is settled in a way that the eucharistic elements, by definition, are not.[16]

Second, the elements on the altar are changed in such a way that it is proper to call them (*now*) "the body and blood of Christ," and improper to call them (*still*) "bread and wine." But it is not improper at any time to call the Old and New Testaments the human words of the prophets and apostles. That is what they are, and what they will remain. Their identity as *also* (or even primarily) God's word neither overwhelms their persistent human facticity, nor is it threatened thereby. In this, they resemble not so much the change in the elements as the two natures of Christ.[17] This is a more fraught analogy and only goes so far before running aground, but it can nevertheless prove helpful. Consider the Chalcedonian adverbs: in the personal union of the human nature with the divine in the incarnation of God the Son, the two natures are without confusion, without change, without division, and without separation. So, in a manner of speaking, in the inspiration and confection of the holy scriptures: their human and phenomenal features are

15. "The sacramentality of the word can thus be understood by analogy with the real presence of Christ under the appearances of the consecrated bread and wine. By approaching the altar and partaking in the Eucharistic banquet we truly share in the body and blood of Christ. The proclamation of God's word at the celebration entails an acknowledgment that Christ himself is present, that he speaks to us, and that he wishes to be heard. Saint Jerome speaks of the way we ought to approach both the Eucharist and the word of God: 'We are reading the sacred Scriptures. For me, the Gospel is the Body of Christ; for me, the holy Scriptures are his teaching. And when he says: *whoever does not eat my flesh and drink my blood* (John 6:53), even though these words can also be understood of the [Eucharistic] Mystery, Christ's body and blood are really the word of Scripture, God's teaching. When we approach the [Eucharistic] Mystery, if a crumb falls to the ground we are troubled. Yet when we are listening to the word of God, and God's Word and Christ's flesh and blood are being poured into our ears yet we pay no heed, what great peril should we not feel?' Christ, truly present under the species of bread and wine, is analogously present in the word proclaimed in the liturgy": Benedict XVI, *Verbum Domini* 2.56.

16. Against tendencies toward an episodic or occasionalist account of Scripture; cf. Barth, *Church Dogmatics* I/1, 88–124; I/2, 457–537; Webster, *Holy Scripture*, 5–41; Paddison, *Scripture*, 5–32.

17. See, e.g., Work, *Living and Active*; Enns, *Incarnation and Inspiration*.

not merged with or altered by the divine Spirit's generation or employment of them, even as they are never detached from Christ's loving and sovereign will uniting them to his saving purposes, nor estranged from his binding promise to speak through them in and to his people. On this basis, and in this respect, the scriptures are both human and divine, equally and wholly each together with the other.

The christological analogy breaks down just at this point, though, since the scriptures are not in fact divine, any more than the church is (also often analogized to Christ in this way).[18] All analogies to Christ fail inasmuch as Christ's identity as God lacks any qualification: the relation is one of total identification, without exception or asterisk. It is true that his humanity is not divine[19] inasmuch as his natures are distinct—he is not partially human or partially divine, nor is he some third hybrid thing—but that claim functions precisely to enable unreserved affirmation of the one incarnate Christ's full divinity. Jesus Christ is God in the flesh, full stop. Neither the scriptures, nor the church, nor the Eucharist can say as much. Even in the Eucharist, the consecrated elements are the body and blood of Christ *under the form and aspect of a sign*, that is, identity within non-identity. That is just what it means to be a sacrament: effecting the grace and presence of that which is otherwise not present, or not present to the fullest degree. Neither absence nor total presence, in other words, but *veiled* presence. Scripture is sacramental in this way because it brings to word that which is not a feature of our mundane lives: the *viva vox Dei*. There will come a day when our lives, no longer mundane, *will* feature the intimate and unstinting presence of the living voice of the Lord. Until that day, Scripture is the means of our hearing and hearkening to it. If, on the church's long journey through the wilderness here below, the visible words of the Eucharist are manna for the mouth, the audible words of the scriptures are manna for the ears (cf. John 6:25–69).[20]

In sum: Scripture is and is not God's word; identity within non-identity. The affirmation followed by negation is crucial. Much of this chapter has focused on recalling or retrieving the former, but the latter is no less important. For the words are not the Word as such; the only Word incarnate is Jesus. Not only may we not point at the words of a canonical text and say "that there is the Lord" (even as we *may* do that with the consecrated

18. See, e.g., de Lubac, *Catholicism*; von Balthasar, *Spouse*; Cavanaugh, *Migrations*, 141–69; Lawson, "Apostasy."

19. Though it is divinized.

20. See Jenson, *Visible Words*; both the phrase and the concept comes from St. Augustine. The trope of Scripture, being God's word, as manna or bread, and thus fittingly figured by the Eucharist, is common to the tradition. Peter Leithart refers to the sacred text as "God's verbal bread" in *Deep Exegesis*, 207.

elements); we also may not so identify them with the Lord's speech as to lose sight of their distinction from it. This neglect can take more practical and more theoretical forms. Practically, a sort of *bibliolatry* is one upshot of forgetting the texts' status, not as revelation *simpliciter*, but as a sign and instrument thereof. This involves, for example, relating to the text as if it were divine, or as if it were the one and only means of grace or of access to the divine will and presence. On the one hand, this latter move ignores or subordinates all other forms of fellowship with God (Communion, baptism, prayer, confession, fasting, service, suffering) to exegesis; on the other hand, it mistakes the servant for the master, the sign for the reality, the messenger for the sender. Scripture does not bring us face to face with God: if *in via* we see, then so also do we hear, through a glass darkly (cf. 1 Cor 13:12).

Another practical form is *biblicism*,[21] according to which Scripture is not only the ultimate authority for the church's faith and morals, but a kind of blueprint for a church fixed in amber:[22] more than sufficient, the Bible becomes exhaustive in scope and comprehensive in teaching. Here the Bible provides, not only in substance but even in its syntax and lexicon, an adequate answer to every question (in vitro fertilization, embryonic stem-cell research) and a full account of every human project (eating, business, art, science, politics).[23] Above all it provides in advance the doctrinal point beyond which the church need never progress or develop. Matters like creeds, councils, episcopacy, Trinity, icons: either Scripture is silent about them (which silence speaks volumes); or, to the extent that it does speak about them, what it says is both the first and the final word. Consequently, if Scripture is all there is to say on the matter (unclothed by tradition, it stands naked: *nuda scriptura*), it must be excavated to the utmost.[24] Arguments over ecclesiastical polity, for example, drill down to the interpretation of

21. For blistering critique, see Barth, *Church Dogmatics* I/2, 607–9: "Will those who will have the Bible alone as their master, as though Church history began again with them, really refrain from mastering the Bible? In the vacuum of their own seeking which this involves, will they perhaps hear Scripture better than in the sphere of the Church?" (609). For recent example at the popular level, see Viola and Barna, *Pagan Christianity?*

22. Forgive the mixed metaphor.

23. See the discussion in Smith, *Bible Made Impossible*, 3–89.

24. For *nuda scriptura*, see Stanglin, *Letter and Spirit*, 130–32, 168–74, 222–25. The metaphor of excavation calls to mind the proposal of Smith, "Sacred Persistence," regarding "the necessary obsession with exegetical totalization" that follows from the concept and practice of canonization (48). If all canonical work is a kind of drilling deep into the same textual ground, then the image that presents itself for primitivist-biblicist reading is fracking (or even strip mining). Whereas the figural contemplation of the scriptures never exhausts their spiritual depths; in its sacramental mode, the canon is an infinitely renewable resource.

a single word in the pastoral epistles. If the exact details of local church governance are set out there, and only there, then nothing would be more logical than to read them as if they are the Constitution and believers in the present are strict originalists—albeit lacking both jurisprudential precedent and judicial authority.[25]

On the theoretical side, the twin claims of perspicuity and inerrancy—that the Bible is clear (because God's word is not opaque) and without error (because God's word does not lie)—produce, all too predictably, a radically individualized form of *sola scriptura*. To each believer a Bible and a miter. In more sophisticated form, this view affirms sacred tradition as the necessary matrix within which to understand Scripture.[26] Yet Scripture's non-identity with revelation can still be neglected in matters of interpretation: treating its words not as irreducibly human signs marked by historical and cultural properties but as timeless ciphers of communicative immediacy. The non-identity of Scripture with divine revelation, however, entails that its words *mediate* the Lord's word: God's word is not immediate. Webster writes of the "pathos" this situation produces for the church, since we are forbidden to "resolve scriptural mediacy into revelatory immediacy."[27] Accordingly, to attend to the biblical texts as if they are God's *immediate* word is to mistake their nature, and therefore the nature of God's revelatory speech. Faithful hearing of the word of the Lord through the embassy of the prophets and apostles means close attention to their words, *as* their words. For it is only as their words that they are the word of Another. An ambassador speaks for her sovereign: but her words, though they stand for his, remain her own.

The principal error to avoid in all these examples is a flattening of the text.[28] Biblical scholars are right to worry that the scriptures' sanctification, like the canonization of a saint, ends up ironing out all that makes them interesting. Voice, tone, genre, perspective, emotion, hard edges: these are

25. In the words of Alexander Campbell, "I have endeavored to read the Scriptures as though no one had read them before me, and I am as much on my guard against reading them today through my views yesterday as I am against being influenced by any foreign name, authority, or system whatever" ("Reply," 204). See further Hatch, *Democratization*, 67–81; "Christian Movement." For the connection to American jurisprudence, see Pelikan, *Bible and the Constitution*.

26. See, e.g., Gerhard, *Interpreting Sacred Scripture*; Allen and Swain, *Reformed Catholicity*; Webster, *Works of God*, 195–210; Vanhoozer, *Biblical Authority*, 109–46.

27. Webster, *Domain*, 9: "we are instructed to receive the divine Word in these contingent forms—to hear, not God's own voice in unmediated force and power to persuade, but God's voice as it has been heard and then repeated by other creatures."

28. A predominant example of such flattening is so-called "proof texting" (see, e.g., the critique in Vanhoozer, *Drama of Doctrine*, 270–72), but see Allen and Swain, *Reformed Catholicity*, 117–41, for a considered defense of the practice.

what give a text recognizable life; they are the reason we read in the first place, why we return to a text over and over. Ecclesiastes is not Deuteronomy is not Ruth is not Ezekiel is not Acts is not Revelation: on that much the position of this book and that of biblical scholarship agree.

The negative task, then, is to avoid Scripture's flattening, to resist the homogenization that results from imagining that the unity rooted in the Bible's single source and end—one divine *auctor*, one divine *res*—is the sort of unity found in a book written by a single *human* author. Framed positively, the goal is to predicate of the Bible that it is a sign and instrument of divine revelation, that it is in fact the word of the Lord, without losing in this identification its role as a mediator of that which it is not.

In the twentieth century Karl Barth suggested a biblical concept for just this quandary: *witness*.[29] The Bible bears the saving word of God exactly insofar as it witnesses to it. As testimony to divine revelation it just thereby communicates it. In bearing witness, in its human words, to the divine word, the latter shines forth in the former. This is the pattern of prophetic and apostolic speech in Scripture, not least in the book of Acts. Christ commissions his apostles to be his witnesses to the ends of the earth (Acts 1:8). And so they offer testimony, and through their words the word of God is spoken (e.g., 4:31; 6:2; 13:5)—that word being one and the same as the message of the gospel (e.g., 11:1; 13:48–49; 15:7). The biblical canon, set apart by the Spirit through the church's activity in history, now functions in textual form as once the living words of the apostles did in the early decades of The Way. In testifying to the one living word of God the written words of the prophets and apostles set forth that word in the world for all to hear. In their attesting it, it draws near; borne to us by them, the word comes alive, is made present in and through their testimonies.

The plural "testimonies," moreover, is important: though Scripture as a whole testifies, it consists of any number of discrete witnesses.[30] That is one of the reasons why for most of the church's history the Bible has been known in the plural as "the scriptures." The sacred writings were multiple objects in a literal sense, but more to the point, they were multiple *kinds* of documents, breathed into human life by multiple voices. The testimony of Scripture is in fact the testimonie*s* of the scriptures. And the church has no

---

29. Barth, *Church Dogmatics* I/2, 457–72.

30. These are not only the distinct books of the Bible. Distinct books often contain multiple witnesses. Think, for example, of the different characters in the Gospels or in the Deuteronomic history. Or of the different singers in the Psalter. Or of the different friends in Job. Or of the different sources woven into a single text in the Torah. Or indeed of interpolations in the New Testament, such as John 8:2–11 or Mark 16:9–20 or even 2 Cor 6:14—7:1.

interest in artificially reducing or silencing the plurality of those testimonies. Just as there are four evangelists, so there are dozens of prophets and apostles besides. The Word speaks through the words: it does not make the words a single word. The church bows before the fourfold Gospel; it kneels before the hundredfold Scripture. Each and every voice matters. The voice of the Lord speaks through all of them, severally and jointly. If they did not speak, just as they are, then something would be lacking, too, in our hearing him in and through them.[31]

The plurality of Scripture's witness, in short, is a feature and not a bug. But a plurality is not a chaos; diversity is not incoherence. There is a unity in difference rooted in an order internal to the canon.[32] That order is historical and covenantal. For the scriptures are not only the church's book but the synagogue's. That external duality, which persists into the present—a painful reminder of division, rejection, and violence—is a function and reflection of Scripture's inner duality. It is to this ordered unity-in-difference, across and between the old and new covenants attested in the Old and New Testaments, that we turn now in the next section.

3. A Book of the Covenant

The church's Holy Scripture is a two-testament book.[33] A seemingly obvious observation, it often goes unremarked in contemporary treatments of Scripture, at least with respect to its significance for understanding the nature of the canon. I will open and close my reflections on this feature with discussion of "covenant" as a central concept both within Scripture and for the doctrine of Scripture. In between I will offer a series of propositions regarding the church's reception of the Law, the Prophets, and the Writings as part of its own sacred canon.

In Exodus 24, after receiving the laws and ordinances from YHWH for the people Israel (20:1—23:33), there is a ritual of covenant ratification. Moses reads the words of the Lord to the people, and the people respond with a promise to obey the Lord's commands (v. 3). Moses writes down all the Lord's words and erects "an altar at the foot of the mountain, and twelve pillars, according to the twelve tribes of Israel" (v. 4). The people make sacrifices and offer burnt offerings (v. 5). Half the blood Moses splashes against the

31. I mostly avoid recourse to the metaphor of the canonical texts as "voices," since its widespread usage in contemporary theological hermeneutics tends to forget that it *is* a metaphor, and so functions as often to mystify as to clarify the issue.

32. See further the discussion that closes chapter 5.

33. I take this language from Seitz, *Christian Scripture; Elder Testament*.

altar, half he places in basins (v. 6). "Then he took the book of the covenant, and read it in the hearing of the people; and they said, 'All that the LORD has spoken we will do, and we will be obedient.' And Moses took the blood and threw it upon the people, and said, 'Behold the blood of the covenant which the LORD has made with you in accordance with all these words'" (vv. 7–8). At which point Moses, together with his three closest companions and the rest of the leaders of Israel, ascends the mountain and sees the Lord, at table with him (vv. 9–10): "they beheld God, and ate and drank" (v. 11).[34]

The book of the covenant to which the text refers is the set of laws and commands found in the prior four chapters of Exodus. It is presumably this document—or a similar section from an early recension of Deuteronomy—that is later rediscovered by King Josiah and read aloud to the people in a covenant renewal ceremony (2 Kgs 22:1—23:25; 2 Chr 34:1—35:19; cf. Sir 24:23–29; 1 Macc 1:41–64). The book of the covenant is at once a kind of microcosm of the Law—the Torah in miniature—and the means of establishing a binding relationship between the Lord God and the people he delivered from bondage through the waters of the Red Sea (Exod 14:1—15:21). The spoken words, the liberating lawgiver functioning as mediator, the leaders representing each of the tribes of Israel, the sacrifices, the blood, the promises made, the vision of God, the eating and drinking: all of it, together, enacts and certifies the covenant by which the people now belong to the Lord, and vice versa. The Lord speaks to his people through the mouth of his prophet, and in so doing effects their union with him—thus confirming and fulfilling the oath he swore in covenant to Abraham centuries before (Gen 12:1–9; 15:1–21; 17:1–27; 22:1–19). This union will endure as long as the word of the One making it: and "the word of our God will stand forever" (Isa 40:8).

If these few chapters are the law within the Law, a synecdoche for the whole Torah; and if the Torah, for Israel, was the scripture within the scriptures, that is, the privileged heart around which the rest was organized and to which the rest was ordered; then it is fitting to use this passage to stand in not only for the rest of the Law but for Tanakh as a collection. The Hebrew scriptures are, considered as a single entity, the book of the covenant of the people of God. They are the words the reading and hearing of which, and obedience in response to which, constitute and renew and revivify the children of Abraham as the elect, that is, as the Lord's beloved covenant family. In this, too, we see the Lord's gentle and generous grace: he provides the words of Moses and David and the other prophets for all time as provision for his

---

34. See Jenson, *Triune Story*, 182: "they saw the One who would become visible flesh, and they celebrated a figure of the Eucharist." Cf. St. Gregory of Nyssa, *Life of Moses*.

people in dispersion. By this they will remember and the gentiles will know that they are the Lord's and the Lord is one (Ezek 13:23; 20:33–44; 36:1–38).

Josiah's discovery of the book of the covenant is not the only recapitulation of this all-important scene in Exodus 24. On the night when he was betrayed (1 Cor 11:23), Jesus ate a final Passover meal with his disciples (Matt 26:17–19; Mark 14:12–25; Luke 22:7–23). He, a prophet of the Lord (Matt 13:57; 21:11; Luke 24:19; John 4:44), issued commands to The Twelve (Matt 26:20), who represent all Israel. Having taken bread and blessed it, he broke it, and said, "Take, eat; this is my body" (Matt 26:26). After the meal (Luke 22:20; 1 Cor 11:25) he took a cup of wine and, having given thanks, he gave it to them, saying, "Drink of it, all of you; for this is my blood of the covenant, which is poured out for many for the forgiveness of sins" (Matt 26:27–28). Other witnesses report his words as saying, "This cup which is poured out for you is the new covenant in my blood" (Luke 22:20; cf. 1 Cor 11:25). Within hours this same man would offer himself as a sacrifice upon a cross (Matt 26:47—27:54; John 10:14–18; 9:23–28), and within days the same men who had abandoned him would be proclaiming not only that he was alive (Luke 24:1–53), but that in his death and resurrection God had acted once for all to liberate his people from sin and death (Acts 2:14–42; 3:11–26; 4:8–12), held as captives for so long to that great liar and tyrant, the devil (Heb 2:14–15; 1 John 3:5). He, the Anointed, a prophet and deliverer like Moses (Acts 3:22–23), would lead the people through the waters of baptism (1 Cor 10:1–4; Rom 6:1–11) to the promised new creation (Gal 6:15; 2 Cor 5:17) in which God would dwell with mortals (2 Pet 3:11–13; Rev 21:1–4), peace would abound (Rom 5:1; 8:6; 14:17; Eph 2:14–17; Phil 4:7–9; Col 1:19–20), and gentiles would have a share in the Lord's eternal covenant with Abraham (Gen 17:7, 13; 1 Chr 16:17; Ps 105:10; Sir 17:8–14; cf. Heb 13:20), renewed now in Jesus his seed, through faith in him (Gal 3:6—4:7). So would God be faithful to his friend (2 Chr 20:7; Isa 41:8; Jas 2:23), to his people Israel (Rom 11:1–2, 25–32), and to all the families of the earth (Gen 12:3; 28:14; Amos 3:2; Acts 3:25; Gal 3:8).

Consider now the replayed scene in summary form. Words of the Lord spoken aloud by a liberating prophet and teacher functioning as mediator to his companions, leaders who represent the twelve tribes of Israel; a sacrifice, a deliverance, the giving and shedding of blood to establish a covenant (itself the fulfillment of an older covenant), promises offered and received, eating and drinking in the presence and sight of the Lord himself: in the Upper Room we are again at the foot of Mount Sinai.[35] And again we see the nucleus

35. Even as they are also literally at the foot and spiritually at the feet of Mount Zion, the incarnate site of God's holy temple, bound for destruction and rebuilding in just three days: "But he spoke of the temple of his body" (John 2:19–22). Cf. Gal

of the whole. This is the gospel within the gospel, the book of the covenant standing in for the wider book of which it is a part. It is fitting, therefore, for the collection of apostolic writings to receive its name from this momentous occasion. Whereas the scriptures of Israel are the book of the old covenant, the scriptures of the church are the book of the new covenant. Each is a text—a compendium of texts—*of* the covenant, bearing the words of the covenant God in, for, and to God's covenant people. They are an item in that intimate relationship, as well as a product of it. They cohere within it, and disintegrate apart from it. The prophets and apostles are, in short, covenantal writings in the one covenantal history of the one God of Israel.

But as it stands, this isn't quite right. For "the scriptures of the church" include not merely the book of the new but also the book of the old covenant. The scriptures of the church consist, that is, of both Old and New Testaments, while the scriptures of the synagogue consist solely of the Old (that is, Tanakh, or in our terms, the first book of the covenant).[36] As we said at the outset, the church's Bible is a two-testament book. So far I have elaborated the character of those testaments as covenant writings, rooted in the paradigmatic scenes of covenant-ratification found in the Sinai and institution narratives, respectively. Now I want to offer a series of fundamental—I am inclined to call them nonnegotiable—claims regarding the Old Testament as Christian Scripture, considered especially in its relation to the New Testament.

1. The sacred scriptures of Israel are part of the Christian canon. Any and all attempts to expunge them are repudiated in advance. Marcion is the arch-heretic, the anathematizing of whom ought to be reiterated anew in each generation.

2. Israel's scriptures are an *equal* part of the Christian canon. They are not second-class citizens in the Bible. They are not functionally

---

4:21–31; Heb 12:18–29.

36. There are various proposals of alternatives to "Old Testament" for the church's designation of Israel's scriptures, to which the apostles' writings are appended. I am not persuaded that "Old Testament" is either derogatory or theologically deficient, or that the alternatives are better; but nor am I opposed in principle to different terminology being supplied. The issue is the church's own usage, however, not academic jargon. The liturgy is the control, in other words, not scholarship. Cf. Seitz, *Elder Testament*; Goldingay, *First Testament*; Soulen, *God of Israel*; Davis, *Opening Israel's Scriptures*.

deuterocanonical.[37] They are in fact primocanonical:[38] first both in sequence and in precedence.[39] The One incarnate in Jesus of Nazareth is the Lord of Israel; the God who raised up Jesus from the grave is one and the same as he who earlier raised up Israel from Egypt.[40]

3. The New Testament is incomplete without the Old.[41] Quite plainly nothing in the gospel of Jesus proclaimed in the writings of the apostles makes any sense apart from the Law, the Prophets, and the Psalms. St. Gregory of Narek, in a litany for St. Gregory the Illuminator, writes that when the latter was but "a nursling infant," he was "brought to the edifice of light where [he] suckled the twin breasts extending from Sion: the New and the Old Testament for a spiritual drink, with which [he was] amazingly nourished, growing to mature manhood in Jesus, the Savior of all."[42] The metaphor is exact. The city of God is a mother to her many children; gentiles hailing from as far as Armenia stream to Jerusalem to be nourished by the saints of Israel, apostles and prophets alike. Each collection of texts thus offers its own milk—but the one milk of mother Zion—for the nourishment and growth of Abraham's children. The children would be undernourished, or rather malnourished, in the absence of either.

4. The Law and the Prophets are no less the word of the Lord for the church than they were for Israel prior to Christ.[43] Their reception in the eschatological assembly of the baptized—Jews and gentiles united by faith in Jesus—is differentiated, but then, this is equally true in the exilic synagogue, which interprets commands about sacrifices and the

37. For prominent examples, see Schleiermacher, *Christian Faith*, 62, 115, 608–11; von Harnack, *Marcion*; Bultmann, "Old Testament." At the popular level, see most recently Stanley, *Irresistible*.

38. This term is not meant to trade on the technical distinction between proto- and deuterocanonical texts.

39. Robert Jenson consistently presses this point; see, e.g., *Triune Story*, 187–219; *Triune God*, 26–33: "the canon of Israel's Scripture is for the church a sheer *given*" (30).

40. Jenson, *Triune God*, 63.

41. "For the law was given through Moses; grace and truth came through Jesus Christ" (John 1:17). This is not, as it is sometimes taken to be, a disparagement of Israel or its scriptures. Rather, it is a statement of the distinction between two divinely wrought covenants or ages *within* their inseparability. That is: no Messiah without Torah, of which he is the telos; no Law apart from Jesus, toward whom it points.

42. St. Gregory of Narek, *Festal Works*, 112.

43. Few figures in Christian history exemplary commitment to (and practical enactment of) this principle more than John Calvin. See, e.g., his discussion in the *Institutes* 2.9–11. See also McKim, *Calvin and the Bible*, 1–130; Puckett, *John Calvin's Exegesis*; Holmes, "Calvin on Scripture."

monarchy and the priesthood and life in the land not "literally" but rather in accordance with the Talmud and the long-standing traditions of Rabbinic Judaism. A differentiated word from the Lord is still a word from the Lord. There is no asterisk set next to a reading from the Old Testament in the church's liturgy: Moses and David, Isaiah and Ezekiel, Ruth and Esther speak to Christ's body in the power of the Spirit, and their words are rightly received as what they are: God's word.

5. The ancient scriptures of Israel were not stolen or otherwise appropriated "from" Judaism (or Jews) "by" Christianity (or gentiles). To say they were is both historically and theologically inaccurate. Any number of rival nascent Judaisms were in contest with one another in the powder keg of the first century. In the wake of the destruction of the Jerusalem temple in AD 70 (and, later, the aftermath of the failed Bar Kochba rebellion in the 130s), two distinct, mutually hostile, coeval Judaisms emerged from the wreckage. One was Pharisaic, the other messianic. The former interpreted the scriptures as a sort of portable Shekinah—Torah enframed by narrative and prophecy—set within the life of the synagogue, the teaching of the rabbis, and the exile of the Jews from the land. The latter interpreted the scriptures as the great drama of God's works in Israel and creation at once foretelling and culminating in the advent of a crucified Messiah, the dawning of the new age, and the in-gathering of the gentiles to the covenant people. Each was a fundamentally Jewish movement founded on interpretation of the Jewish scriptures; the claim of each to Israel's scriptures and to continuation of the life of old Israel was equally aboriginal. That messianic Judaism did not follow Pharisaic judgments regarding Torah observance; that it came to admit gentiles into its covenantal fold without requiring their being circumcised; that, within a century or so, it became predominantly gentile; that, within three centuries, it became the official cultus of the Roman Empire: these historical facts, regrettable though some of them may be, are irrelevant to the matter at hand. The notion of a wholesale gentile "religion" created *de novo* arbitrarily arrogating the Jewish scriptures to itself is as fanciful as it is anachronistic. The Christian church may be wrong in its interpretation of Tanakh. But it is not wrong per se to read them as Scripture for itself. Were it to stop, it would cease to exist.

6. The new covenant wrought in Jesus is the climax and consummation of God's work in Israel and of the Law and the Prophets that attest it. As St. Paul writes, "Christ is the end of the law, that everyone who has faith may be justified" (Rom 10:4). That is, the telos of the Torah is

Jesus the Messiah. In him all the scriptures have their aim and fulfillment. Note well: fulfillment is not abolition: "Think not that I have
come to abolish the law and the prophets; I have come not to abolish
them but to fulfill them" (Matt 5:17). Neither is God's covenant with
Abraham's seed according to the flesh abolished: "I ask, then, has God
rejected his people? By no means! . . . God has not rejected his people
whom he foreknew" (Rom 11:1–2). For "as regards election they are
beloved for the sake of their forefathers. For the gifts and the call of
God are irrevocable" (vv. 28–29). Whatever the relationship of fulfillment that obtains between new and old covenants, and thus between
New and Old Testaments, it does not entail supersessionism,[44] that is,
the claim that God has either canceled his covenant with the biological
descendants of Abraham or replaced them with the gentile *ekklesia*.[45]

7. Just as Mishnah and Talmud function as hermeneutic controls on Rab-
    binic Judaism's interpretation of Tanakh, so do the apostolic writings
    function for Christian exegesis. The church rightly reads the Law and
    the Prophets and the Psalms through the lens of the Gospels, the Epis-
    tles, and the Apocalypse. This is no more anachronistic or eisegetical

44. Against the view articulated by Walter Brueggemann: "We Christians are learning, albeit belatedly, how much supersessionism is inscribed in our liturgical cadences
and our interpretive habits. We are becoming aware that our habits of reading the two
biblical testaments as 'promise and fulfillment' are inherently supersessionist as the
Hebrew Bible (Old Testament) functions then as an anticipatory text that culminates
in the reality of Jesus. We know, moreover, that such renditions of the biblical text in
supersessionist categories inescapably lead to anti-Semitism based on the unspoken
premise that the theological claims of Judaism no longer pertain" ("Foreword," xi).
Such a view sweepingly and unqualifiedly dismisses the hermeneutic of apostolic and
indeed of all premodern ecclesial exegesis as essentially supersessionist, unavoidably
anti-Jewish, and thus unworthy of imitation. I fail to see how this position is distinct
from the claim that the gospel is untrue. See further the comments in the next footnote.

45. Let this stand as my shorthand definition of supersessionism, here and in the
following. The slipperiness of the term has led to its being wielded as little more than an
epithet: whatever one thinks, one doesn't want to be labeled *that*. For it to serve a useful
purpose, however, it must have clearly defined content and, from a theological vantage,
it cannot mean "whatever Christianity is." In other words, the term fails to differentiate
forms of Christian faith and practice if it is true that Christianity as such is convertible with supersessionism; for in that case the call for non- or post-supersessionist
Christianity would be nonsense. Partly the divergence in meaning comes from separate
academic discourses that deploy the term in overlapping but distinct contexts. In any
case, see, e.g., Soulen, *God of Israel*; Nanos, *Reading Paul*; Kinzer, *Israel's Messiah*; Mc-
Dermott, *New Christian Zionism*; Jennings, *Christian Imagination*; Jenson and Korn,
Covenant and Hope; Braaten and Jenson, *Jews and Christians*; D'Costa, *Jewish People*;
Novak, "Supersessionism"; Roberts, "Rethinking Israel"; Tapie, *Israel and the Church*;
Levering, *Torah and Temple*; Levering, "Aquinas and Supersessionism"; Marshall, "Reli-
gion and Election"; Marshall, "Christ and Israel"; Marshall, "Jewish Election."

than Talmudic commentary on Torah. Moreover, the church believes, following the apostles, that the New Testament sheds *light* on the Old: such reading is illumined and not led astray by following the examples of St. Matthew, St. John, and St. Peter. The oddity would be if Christians did *not* read in this way (try as the historical critics might to persuade them of its perils). For with what other justification would a gentile, living more than two and a half millennia after the fact, have for reading the sacred texts of the Jews? Must she pretend that it is not because she confesses Jesus as Israel's Messiah? Is she supposed to believe that, though Jesus has grafted her into Abraham's family, she should read these texts as alien to herself? Ought she to suspend such belief and read these texts as nothing but ancient reports of a distant people in a faraway time and place that bear in no way on her own life and are in no way altered by the knowledge that Messiah has come and she, a gentile, is party to the covenant? The answer to all three questions is *no*.[46]

8. The scriptures of Israel prophesy Jesus's coming, and the church is right to read the Old Testament as prefiguring the mystery of the gospel. "If you believed Moses, you would believe me, for he wrote of me," says Jesus to the crowds: "You search the scriptures . . . and it is they that bear witness to me" (John 5:45, 39). Risen from the dead, sitting at table with two disciples who earlier mistook him for a stranger, Jesus scolds them for being "'slow of heart to believe all that the prophets have spoken! Was it not necessary that the Christ should suffer these things and enter into his glory?' And beginning with Moses and all the prophets, he interpreted to them in all the scriptures the things concerning himself" (Luke 24:25–27). For, as he says later to the rest of his disciples, "everything written about me in the law of Moses and the prophets and the psalms must be fulfilled" (v. 44). There are other warrants for the church's long-standing practices of spiritual interpretation of the Old Testament, but these apostolic testimonies to Jesus's own teaching are sufficient on their own.[47]

9. It follows from all the foregoing that, just as the New Testament is incomplete without the Old, so the Old is incomplete without the New. This is a more controversial claim. The former is an easy enough rejection of Marcionism (though perhaps easier said than done). The latter

46. Against, e.g., Goldingay, *New Testament*.

47. See further my "Reading the Trinity," as well as chapter 5 below. In biblical scholarship, see the disagreement between Longenecker, *Biblical Exegesis*, xiii–xli, and Hays, *Letters of Paul*; *Gospels*.

verges on dangerous ground. It seems to suggest that non-messianic Jews—which is to say, the vast majority of observant Jews past and present—not only err in their reading of Tanakh but are by definition unable to avoid such error, given their rejection of Jesus's messianic identity and the writings that bear witness to it. I do not think this is a necessary conclusion, but I accept that something like it is the almost inevitable concomitant of strong Christian claims to the inseparability of, and reciprocal interpretive relationship between, the Old and New Testaments. Such claims are unavoidable in honest Christian or Jewish theology.[48] The faith of the church is that the God of the Jews became incarnate in the man Jesus,[49] and that those who reject this claim are, to say nothing else, lacking something essential in their understanding of the one true God.[50] Yet most Jews today do reject this claim.[51] From the church's side, this is a source of pain and a cause for lament. It is only deepened by the church's long history of exclusion, ostracization, polemic, and violence toward the synagogue and toward Jewish families, neighborhoods, and communities. It is up to gentile Christians to demonstrate, across the long haul, that such behavior does not follow,

48. See, e.g., Wyschogrod, *Abraham's Promise*; Ochs, *Another Reformation*; Novak, *Talking with Christians*. For recent theological treatment of Scripture from a Jewish perspective, see Sommer, *Revelation and Authority*.

49. One of the most beautiful yet succinct ways of formulating the truth of the Incarnation *as* the incarnation of Israel's God is found in the polemic of St. Theodore the Studite against the iconoclasts. The theological question that exercised the controversy over iconographic depiction of Christ was whether the infinite could be written in a finite artistic medium; how could he who is uncircumscribable be circumscribed in an image? Yet the human Christ was circumscribed in his body, if in fact he was God in the flesh, fully human yet fully divine. St. Theodore: "Some bodies may only be divided in thought; for instance, some cannot be touched, and as such are uncircumscribable; others bodies, instead, can be cut in actuality; for instance, some are solid, because they can be touched, and as such they can be circumscribed. If, then, Christ assumed a body that cannot be cut, then this body is also uncircumscribable. But Christ's body can be cut; indeed, Luke of blessed speech says, 'And when the eight days were passed of his circumcision' [2:21]. And if he was circumcised, then he was circumscribed—and this is the truth" (*Third Refutation* 46, in *Writings on Iconoclasm*, 102). *If he was circumcised, then he was circumscribed*: no formulation could express with greater clarity or brevity the confession of the church that in Jesus of Nazareth the God of Abraham became a human being.

50. For nuanced comment, see McFarland, *Word Made Flesh*, 22.

51. Not all: see, e.g., the essays gathered in Rudolph and Willitts, *Messianic Judaism*. See also the impressive historical and exegetical arguments set forth in Rudolph, *A Jew to the Jews*.

logically or theologically, from the scriptural commitments outlined in this section. If it does, then plainly the commitments are wrong.[52]

10. The canon of the church's two-testament Scripture is closed. This means that no additional books may be added to the canon. For, as Luke Timothy Johnson rightly observes, if the canon is a ruler meant to measure the life of the church in accordance with the witness of the prophets and apostles, the ruler must be common to the church of all generations. It must, in other words, be *catholic*.[53] Once the writings to be included are judged canonical, they are in for all time; those that are not, are out for all time. Let us imagine that humanity as a species and the church within it endure for tens of thousands more years— a doubtful proposition, that—and the church finds itself on another planet, in this or another solar system. The canon's closure means that, if the church has been faithful to its charge in the Spirit, the Bible will have one and the same set of books as it does today: no more, no less.[54]

Such a claim raises the question: Which canon? Of whose church? I have no easy answer in reply. It seems to me that those reforming traditions that rejected the so-called deuterocanonical books in the sixteenth century erred, inasmuch as that corpus was and is common to catholic Christianity East and West.[55] If we submit to the church's mind on that particular matter, then the remaining disagreements are relatively minor.[56] That does not resolve the ecclesiological problem—and it is a problem: that of the impossible possibility of the church's division—but then, the topic of this book is the doctrine of Scripture, not of the church.[57]

One aid in this regard is the practice, prominent in the East, of privileging certain books over others. In one respect, the practice and teaching of the West is correct here: canonical status it not a matter of degree; canonicity is not a series of gradations on a spectrum. Rather, it is binary: either a text is canonical, or it is not. The flexibility of the East may be construed

---

52. See Fredriksen, *Augustine and the Jews*. See also my "Specter of Marcion," and the powerful reflection by Hill, "Death at the Tree of Life."

53. See Johnson, *Scripture and Discernment*, 35–38.

54. Though we should hope that the Lord will *not* delay his appearing, it is an interesting exercise to imagine future believers reading Leviticus and Judges, Job and Hosea, Acts and Revelation on Mars in the year 3500.

55. I.e., Maccabees, Wisdom of Solomon, Sirach, Tobit, Judith, Baruch, and the additions to Esther and Daniel.

56. I.e., Esdras, Manasseh, Jubilees, Enoch, Clement.

57. As Jenson writes, "theology may be impossible in the situation of a divided church, its proper agent not being extant" (*Triune God*, vii).

in another way, however. Instead of creating a continuum of canonicity, the practice of the East firmly locates (or, as the case may be, *re*locates) the canon, not in doctrinal disputes or tomes of the learned, but in the life of the church's liturgy. For Holy Scripture, as this book will continue to insist, has its home in the liturgy. The verbal heartbeat of public worship is the word of the Lord according to the prophets and apostles. That means the canon is first of all a practical matter; its nature is discovered as it is used in the oral readings of the gathered assembly. And there, certain texts are privileged: not as "more" canonical than others, but as more *central* to the canon than *other* (equally) canonical texts.[58] Thus, for example, in Eastern Orthodox churches the gold-laden *Euangelion* (the book of the Gospels) rests on the center of the altar table at all times. Venerated as an icon itself, it is not bound together (between leather or other signs of death) with the rest of the scriptures, for it is first among equals there: being the written account of the birth, life, ministry, teaching, suffering, death, resurrection, and ascension of God incarnate. The binary of the canon remains intact, but the functional differentiation enacted in liturgical practice displays how we might understand diverse parts of the canon as *differently* canonical. To show especial honor to the fourfold Gospel is not to dishonor the other scriptures. It is simply to render "honor to whom honor is due" (Rom 13:7).

Perhaps, in some heretofore unimagined future in which God has healed the rifts in his church, while some texts that the Spirit has not in fact set apart to mediate Christ's word to his people have been excised from the lists, others—Baruch? Judith? Enoch?—have been received as canonical but survive on the margins of the liturgy. Or perhaps, as I said above, because the canon is closed, such an event is neither possible nor desirable, and the canon we have—one of the canons we have—is it, set in stone. I think the latter makes more sense, both theologically and historically. But God has done stranger things before.

I want to close by returning to the concept of covenant with which this section began. Scripture is the book of the covenant, consisting of the testimonies of both the old and the new covenants. This chapter has taken up the nature of Scripture, and we have traversed quite a bit of ground: ontological, sacramental, covenantal, canonical. One last component is an analogy to the threefold office of Christ. This is rooted in covenantal history because it is an application to Jesus in the context of the New those public roles in the Old

---

58. In this way there *is* a canon within the canon, but it is a function not of individual predilection but of the church's liturgical use.

that are set apart by anointing: priests, prophets, and kings. As John Calvin taught, Jesus in his mission from the Father fulfills and executes each of these "offices."[59] He is the eternal priest of the new covenant (Heb 7:3; 13:20) who makes the perfect offering of his own body on the cross (10:10–14), entering into the heavenly sanctuary there to effect our salvation (9:23–28) and abide as our advocate forever (7:23–28). He is the great prophet to rise up in Moses' stead (Acts 3:22–23), announcing the good news of God (Mark 1:14), speaking the word of the Lord (Luke 5:1; 8:11; 11:28), casting out the servants of Satan (Matt 8:16; 9:33; 10:8; 12:28), rebuking the corrupt leaders of Israel (23:1–36), serving the poor and vulnerable (Luke 4:16–21; 6:20–26), healing the sick (Matt 4:23–24; 8:13; 9:35; 12:15; 14:14), and performing other mighty works and signs in the name of YHWH (John 2:23; 3:2; 6:2; 11:47; 12:37). He is the royal seed of David (Matt 1:2; Rom 1:3), the Messiah of Israel and King of the Jews (Matt 2:2; 16:16; Mark 15:1–26), heir to the throne and triumphant victor over the enemies of his people (1 Cor 15:54–57; 1 John 3:8; Heb 2:14–15), exalted in glory to God's right hand and sovereign over all the nations of the earth (Heb 1:1–4; 2:5–10; Phil 2:9–11; Acts 2:29–36; 5:31; 7:55; 17:6–7; Rom 8:34; Eph 1:3–23; Rev 11:15).

The sacred scriptures, for their part, are inspired by the Holy Spirit. That inspiration is a kind of anointing, not unlike the descent of the dove on Jesus in the Jordan (Mark 1:10) or the appearance of flaming tongues resting on each of the apostles at Pentecost (Acts 2:3).[60] The Bible is already bound up with the living agency of the person of Jesus. What if we conceive of Scripture in terms of his threefold office?

---

59. Calvin, *Institutes* 2.15.

60. Or, as I proposed at the end of the last chapter, the anointing of the scriptures is a function not so much of their inspiration as of their chrismation by the Spirit. In *Of Water and the Spirit*, Alexander Schmemann makes the connection between the Holy Chrism and the *munus triplex* explicit: "Being thus the fulfillment of Baptism, the rite of the white garment inaugurates the next act of the liturgy of initiation. We are vested in this 'shining robe' so that we may be anointed. In the early Church there was no need to explain the organic and self-evident connection between the two rites. The Church knew the three essential connotations of this double action, revealing the three fundamental dimensions of man's 'high calling' in Christ—the *royal*, the *priestly*, and the *prophetic*. . . . Born again in the baptismal font, 'renewed after the image of Him Who created him,' restored to his 'ineffable beauty,' man is now ready to be 'set apart' for his new and high calling in Christ. Baptized into Christ, having put on Christ, he is ready to receive the Holy Spirit, the very Spirit of Christ, the very gifts of Christ the Anointed—the King, the Priest, and the Prophet—the triune content of all genuine Christian life, of all Christian 'spirituality'" (75). The subsequent discussion (75–108) spells out how baptized believers share in Christ's threefold office through their anointing in his Spirit; what follows is my application of that chrismatic character and vocation to Holy Scripture.

As the word of the Lord, the Bible is a book of *prophecy*. More than that, the community in which it is read is a prophetic community (1 Cor 12–14), filled with the Spirit of prophecy (Rev 19:10), the Spirit who makes its members prophets (Acts 2:14–21). When the text is read, it is a prophet of the Lord reading aloud to fellow Spirit-filled prophets eager to hear the Lord speak in the present tense through the ancient prophetic text. What they hear is the words the Spirit inspired in the women and men who wrote, revised, and collected these texts. What they hear is the voice of Jesus.[61]

As the word of the Lord, moreover, the Bible is a mediating entity, standing between the people and the Lord. As such, it is *a priestly document*. Like the "one mediator between God and men, the man Christ Jesus" (1 Tim 2:5), Scripture is at once divine and human. Or rather, unlike Christ, but like his mother, Scripture bears the Word of God in itself, not by any merit of its own, but by sheer divine miracle—even by a kind of retroactive or anticipatory sanctification. Like Mary, the Bible mediates salvation to the world.[62] Like Mary, too, and the church she figures, the Bible births ever more sons and daughters by faith, giving sinful men and women, through nothing but the name and gospel of Jesus, "power to become children of God" (John 1:12). Scripture's status as intermediary suggests that, when the End comes, we will not only see face to face, but hear with perfect sweetness and crystalline clarity the voice of the high priest—who even now intercedes for us before the Father, himself the head of the priesthood in which all believers partake. Until that day, we hear him borne to us by the mediate and mediating reality of the text.

As the word of the Lord, finally, the Bible is the *herald of the king*. Isaiah 52:7, quoted by St. Paul in Romans 10:15, offers a lovely image by which to understand the royal nature of Scripture: "How beautiful upon the mountains are the feet of him who brings good tidings, who publishes peace, who brings good tidings of good, who publishes salvation, who says to Zion, 'Your God reigns.'" The canon of Scripture publishes the gospel of the Lord, the Lord who saves—"you shall call his name Jesus, for he will save

61. On the prophetic office of Jesus, see Barth, *Church Dogmatics* IV/3.1; Webster, "Prophetic Office."

62. Mary is also the arch-prophet (cf. Jenson, *Works of God*, 200–204), who receives and bears to the world the one Word of God, as well as the Queen Mother, that is, the mother of Israel's king. In this way Mary, through the grace of her Son, shares in, prefigures, and testifies to the threefold office of Christ the prophet, priest, and king (hers and ours). Like her, the church preaches the word, begets by baptism children of God the Father, mediates and intercedes through prayer and Eucharist for God's children and the world, and rules God's people on Christ's behalf through his word and by his Spirit—a royal rule Christ will one day share with his sisters and brothers in glory (cf. Rev 1:1–3; 11:15–19; 20:4–6; Matt 19:28; 1 Cor 6:3; 14:1–40; Acts 2:16–21).

his people from their sins" (Matt 1:21)—the Lord who establishes shalom, the Lord who reigns as king: of Israel, of earth, of heaven. Scripture is thus at once the royal summons to the great victory feast (Matt 22:1–4; Rev 19:6–9) and the king's ambassador announcing that the victory has already been won (2 Cor 2:14–16; Rom 8:37). Recall St. Irenaeus: In Scripture we find outlined the peerless mosaic of the royal son.[63] In Scripture, then, we hear the voice of the king. High and lifted up (Isa 6:1; John 3:14–15; Phil 2:9; Acts 2:33; 5:31; Heb 7:26), he draws all people to himself (John 12:32). But we, whom he addresses by name, do not remain his subjects. No, we—we for whom he lays down his life (John 10:18; Rom 14:15; 1 Cor 8:11)—he addresses no longer as servants, but as friends (John 15:15). In a word: we are friends of the king, for the Bible tells us so.

63. St. Irenaeus, *Against Heresies* 1.8.1.

3

Attributes

Forever, O LORD, your word is firmly fixed in the heavens. . . . Your testimonies are wonderful. . . . The unfolding of your words gives light. . . . You have appointed your testimonies in righteousness and in full faithfulness. . . . Your testimonies are righteous forever. . . . The sum of your word is truth. . . . I rejoice at your word like one who finds great spoil.
—Psalm 119:89, 129, 138, 144, 160, 162

Sanctify them in the truth; your word is truth.
—John 17:17

Because Scripture comes from God, it has an ontology, a particular character. It is not like any other book in this respect, though it is like other books in all other respects. Its unique nature is not indeterminate, however. Scripture is characterized by attributes that are proper to it in light of its special relationship to the divine will and work. God makes it to be what it is, and what it is may be described: it is not opaque to us. But it is crucial to clarify that these properties are not natural features of the text. On the one hand, they do not belong to the text in and of itself, but wholly in virtue of God's antecedent and continuous action in and upon it. (If inspiration is akin to creation, then the analogy here is to concurrence.) On the other hand, Scripture's properties are not susceptible to empirical investigation or phenomenal observation. They do not admit of falsification, at least from outside the circle of faith, that is to say, on the basis of arguments that exclude revelation or reject reference to God. From within the domain of the gospel, there is certainly contestation, regarding both how to understand Scripture's attributes and which attributes do or do not obtain. Some of that contestation will be on display below. But that Scripture bears certain attributes and that these are discerned spiritually is a matter of ecumenical conviction, because it is a matter of common confession.

Attention to the attributes of Scripture is largely a function of post-Reformation theological reflection, and flourishes above all in Protestant thought. The reason for that is obvious enough: if Scripture is not only the final but the sole authority for the church, then the nature of Scripture is a question of prime importance. Extraordinary insight into Scripture's being and ends is the long-ripening fruit of this Protestant turn. Of the many glories of Protestant dogmatics, its sophisticated treatment of Scripture is arguably chief. Such treatment has naturally generated parallel, often alternative, proposals on the Roman side of the divide. In either case, both seek to draw lines not just from the Bible's internal testimony about its contents but from patristic and medieval commentary. These latter sources have much to say about Scripture, to be sure, but usually as asides, as unquestioned givens, or as pertaining to exegesis. In most respects the essential character of Scripture—its veracity, its unity, its authority, its purposes—is simply taken for granted in premodern theology.[1] The depths of the doctrine come to the surface only once some aspect of it is called into question, thus requiring clarification. That is just what happened in the sixteenth century and the era that followed.

In this chapter I will attempt, in accordance with the *modus operandi* I outlined in the introduction, to affirm and appropriate post-Reformation concepts in service of claims that were either implicit in the pre-divided church or would have found ready reception there. I will begin with a brief reflection on the terminology of attributes, properties, characteristics, and perfections. The subsequent four sections will each be devoted to two attributes, for a total of eight. On the one hand, I will discuss the classic Reformed properties of Scripture: necessity, sufficiency, clarity, and veracity. With these, on the other hand, I will pair the creedal attributes of the church (though out of order): apostolicity, holiness, catholicity, and unity.[2] This is

---

1. For samples of patristic reflection, see Origen, *On First Principles*, Book 4; St. Augustine, *De Doctrina*.

2. I have left aside authority, since it will be treated separately in chapter 6; and I have included unity as one of the ecclesial properties of Scripture, whereas it is often included in the other group. Theologians offer different lists, and within those lists, discuss different aspects of Scripture under different headings (e.g., apostolicity under veracity, or infallibility under authority, etc.).

fitting given Scripture's character as the church's book, so that we do not lose sight of the fact that the Bible does not drop from heaven but has a double source: God (ultimate) and God's people (proximate).[3] My hope is that, when combined in this way, the attributes mutually illuminate one another as well as the book of which they are the divinely bestowed perfections.

1. Properties and Perfections

That last word is a provocation, or at least a question. Are the attributes of Holy Scripture rightly designated as "perfections"? Let me say more about the notion of Scripture bearing properties as such before I venture an answer to that query.

Most of what is necessary to say about the metaphysical status of Scripture I have already outlined in chapter 2. If all that is not God is created and thus a creature; and if what any creature is—its nature—is defined by its relation to God and God's will concerning it; then even a complex object or set of objects like the church's canonical scriptures may be said to have a nature, and a determinate nature at that. To say, as we will below, that Scripture *is* one, holy, or sufficient, is to predicate of the text a property that, if true, is independent of—though not abstracted from—my (individual) or the church's (communal) subjective judgment of the claim. Just as the name I received from my parents is independent of my acceptance of it, and just as the earth's roundness is independent of human knowledge of it, so Scripture's properties obtain apart from and prior to their acknowledgement on the part of believers, theologians, or others. Whatever Scripture is, by God's will, it is in fact. That is the ontological claim. The epistemic question is separate and secondary: How is Scripture's nature discerned? How do we come to learn of its attributes? For our purposes, nothing much hangs on the answers to these questions, except to say that the work of the Holy Spirit in the company of the faithful is ingredient in the process. This work in God's people by the same God who inspired and sanctified the scriptures is crucial to keep in mind, since, though their attributes are antecedent to and independent of the church's recognition of them, they are not divorced from such recognition, for the scriptures only exist by, within, and for just this community. The Bible, that is, exists in a constant twofold relationship:

---

3. I drafted this chapter before I read the similar proposal in Castelo and Wall, *Marks of Scripture*, which also applies the four marks of the church to the Bible. There is some overlap, especially in our shared concerns about using the incarnation as the principal analogy for Scripture. But in terms of substance, our treatments are mostly different, though not necessarily divergent or contradictory.

with God, and with the church. The first relationship is ultimate and definitive, but it remains true that there is no Bible apart from the church—being,
in proximate terms, both its *terminus a quo* and its *terminus ad quem*. The
Old and New Testaments have their genesis as well as their telos in the life
of God's covenant people. It is both from and for *them*. So although the particular properties that characterize the books of the old and new covenants
obtain wholly in virtue of God's will, they do so as the properties of the
books of a particular people: the Israel of God.

The danger to be avoided, then, is an account of Scripture's attributes
that reifies their independence from the church, making them free-stand-
ing, as it were, as though Scripture were a magical book lacking human
origins or human reception. Such a volume—homeless, timeless, naked, yet
enchanted—is not the embassy of the apostles and prophets borne across
time in the liturgy and tradition of the one holy catholic and apostolic
church. It is a talisman, a sacred object full of mysterious power, but *not*
the archive of the Lord and of his saints.[4] The danger, in other words, is to
forget the eschatological character of Scripture,[5] as if we did not still long to
hear and see the Lord face to face, and in that forgetfulness to divinize it, on
analogy to the Qur'an. The holy book of Islam is itself the eternal word of
Allah; it is therefore lauded as perfect and, in principle, untranslatable from
the original Arabic. The gospel, by contrast, confesses that the eternal Word
of God is himself one and the same God as the Lord of Israel, and that this
Word became flesh in Jesus Christ. The words of the apostles of Jesus mediate, by the Spirit's grace, the word of the Word in sacramental form. But they
are not the Word as such. They are not *perfect*.

Comes the question: Ought we to describe the attributes or properties
of Scripture as "perfections"? The practice of so naming them has its source
in Aristotelian grammar as baptized by and incorporated into Christian theology. "Perfect" here is an analogous term: creatures are not perfect, do not
acquire or achieve perfection, in the way that God is perfect. Rather, their
perfections are in accordance with their several given natures: to realize or
to enact most fully what it is they are meant to do or to be. Perfection here
pertains to excellence, to flourishing as the sort of thing one is. The term
need not be limited to living creatures but extends to a range of activities
and inanimate entities: music, architecture, logic, worship, and so on. In the
doctrine of Scripture, the label is applied to the Bible in virtue of its ontology, its divinely willed what-ness. If part of *what* God wills Scripture to be is

---

4. Not to deny in principle the liceity of talismanic deployment of Scripture. See the
suggestive comments of Johnson, *Scripture and Discernment*, 46.

5. More on this below, in the next section.

clear, then (a) clarity is one of the properties that constitute Scripture's nature (b) the fullness of which, considered discretely and in sum, constitutes Scripture's perfection: its unhindered and unqualified fulfillment of what God desires it to be. Each of the attributes is itself a perfection of Scripture, on this view, and in their totality they authorize the analogical predication: namely, that Scripture is perfect.[6]

On its own terms, this is a legitimate way of discussing Scripture's attributes. I will not follow it in this chapter, however. The main reason I have already offered above: the distinction between God's Word incarnate and God's word written is absolute and therefore absolutely crucial to a well-ordered doctrine of Scripture.[7] Rhetoric and substance are not so easily distinguished in the mind that *calling* Scripture perfect but *meaning* something different than ordinary usage of that term is a simple affair. If theology follows from and serves the life, worship, and mission of the church, then its rhetoric ought not to mislead where it can help it. The Bible and the liturgy typically—not exclusively—reserve the language of perfection for the one and only recipient worthy of the name: God.[8] If there are other terms ready to hand that will do the same work as "perfections," and there are, I see no reason not to prefer them, all things being equal.

Context also matters. Anglophone doctrine of Scripture in the last century, especially in the United States, lies in the shadow of fundamentalism. Christians in this context have been liable to think and to speak of Scripture as if it were univocally, and not merely analogically, perfect. The radical biblicism on offer—a biblicism this book rejects—finds itself drawn, in rhetoric and popular piety if not in technical substance, toward

---

6. See, e.g., Gerhard, *Nature of Holy Scripture* 18.367–93; Turretin, *Institutes* 16.1–36; Bavinck, *Reformed Dogmatics*, 449–94; Swain, *Trinity, Revelation, and Reading*, 72–93; Webster, *Domain*, 59–60. It should be noted that sometimes "perfection" is used interchangeably with "attribute" and sometimes with the particular attribute of "sufficiency," since the latter implies that Scripture is wholly suited to its task, and thus perfect in that sense.

7. But see Radner, *Time and the Word*.

8. Cf. Deut 32:4; 2 Sam 22:31; Ps 18:30 (the psalm is simply quoted in the 2 Sam passage). It is telling that Scripture attributes holiness to God far more commonly than perfection, at least in terms of bare terminology (since perfection can be rendered and narrated and described without the word itself). Moreover, I grant the biblical idiom of applying variants of "perfect" to, e.g., the Law, the city of Jerusalem, the temple and its sacrifices, and other objects of the divine largesse (cf. Lev 22:21; Ps 19:7; 50:2; Lam 2:15; Ezek 16:14). This usage, however, at least as received in canonical Christian grammar, ought to be controlled by Matt 5:48; Phil 3:12; and 1 Cor 13:9–10. According to these passages, perfection is indeed a gift of God to human beings through Christ by the Spirit, but the form it takes is that of an eschatological seed or deposit whose full fruition or completion will not come in this life but only in the next.

an implicit bibliolatry. I am more worried about that danger in what follows than I am its opposite, namely, undervaluing Scripture. That too is a
problem, but in my view, it is not a problem in a doctrine of Scripture such
as the one I am proposing here. Christians in the contexts with which I am
familiar, who are at all interested in a theological account of the Bible, are
more likely to think of the Bible as Muslims do the Qur'an than to treat it
"like any other book."[9] Calling it "perfect" and its attributes "perfections"
can only contribute to that tendency, or so it seems to me.

Now to the attributes in question. Allow me to remind the reader that
she or he is not reading a multivolume monograph on the doctrine of Scripture. Each of the following attributes could receive—has received—book-
length treatment; yet no more than a few pages will be allotted here. Much
will go unmentioned: space allows only for a representative summary, from
a certain catholic slant. *Caveat lector.*

2. Apostolic Necessity

Holy Scripture is, in the most literal terms, a medieval book. It is a book
at "the ends of the ages" (1 Cor 10:11), a text stuck in the middle, in the
time between the times. The Bible—that is, in the form we have it—has no
existence prior to the resurrection of Christ, which inaugurated the new age
of God's reign in the cosmos, and it will have no existence after the return
of Christ, which will consummate the kingdom's coming.[10] In this way, the
Bible is at once eschatological and missionary, each because the other, and
both because these features first characterize the church. Put it this way:
theologically speaking, the "middle ages" are not an epoch stretching from
St. Augustine to Martin Luther. They are coterminous with the church mili-
tant, that is, the apostolic community sent by the risen Christ in his Spirit to
bear witness to the gospel to the ends of the earth, until his public appearing
(Acts 1:8). Time itself is set and marked by this twofold advent of Christ:
from Mary's womb and Bethlehem's manger through Golgotha and Easter
morning to the ascension and exaltation at the Father's side, on the one
hand, to the parousia of the selfsame Messiah, on the other: for "Jesus, who

---

9. I recognize that this is context dependent. But the larger cultural claim stands, it
seems to me; fundamentalism is but the obverse of Protestant liberalism, and both are
a failed response to the crisis that modernity presents for ecclesial claims to authority.
I fail to see, however, how the risk of semantic confusion and of amplifying a certain
kind of individualist American biblicism is worth the trade-off, when equally apposite
terms are available.

10. See the perceptive proposals in Behr, *Mystery of Christ*; Behr, *John the Theologian*, 99–131; Behr, "Introduction."

was taken up from you into heaven, will come in the same way as you saw him go into heaven" (v. 11). The coordinates thus marked out by Christ's bodily presence on earth are the window of the church's mission and therefore its life *in via*. And the same is true for the church's book.[11]

If the time of mission is delimited by the bodily absence of Jesus, it is filled with his sacramental presence and voice through the indwelling power of the Holy Spirit. The time of the church is the time of the ascension, the purpose and fulfillment of which is not solely Christ's reign from the Father's right hand but the outpouring of the Spirit upon all flesh.[12] Shift focus among the persons of the Trinity, and the role of Scripture in the economy of grace becomes just as much a function of Pentecost (a positive *gift*) as of Christ's departure (a negative *lack*). For the Bible, as the word of God written, is the sword of the Spirit (Eph 6:17) in his execution of the *missio Dei*. It is thus the resurrection *paired with* the ascended Christ's outpouring of the Holy Spirit from heaven—thinking especially of the Spirit's presence in the community as a sign, pledge, and foretaste of the new creation—that makes the overlapping of the ages at once the time of the church, the time of the Spirit's mission, and consequently the time of Holy Scripture.[13] The word of God that is the announcement of the gospel (Acts 4:31; 8:25; 13:5; 1 Thess 2:13; 1 Pet 1:25) is the new thing the apostles enjoy in virtue of the Spirit's presence: in their speech, the Lord speaks; as the Lord speaks, Jews and gentiles across the empire flock to The Way in startling numbers (Acts 2:47; 5:14; 9:31; 16:5).

In terms of Scripture's attributes, a number of things follow.

First, it is proper to say that Scripture is *necessary*, but this necessity is derivative in at least two ways. On the one hand, what is necessary is the proclamation of the gospel: "faith comes from what is heard, and what is heard comes by the preaching of Christ" (Rom 10:17). It is possible to come to faith ignorant of whole swaths of Scripture. It is not possible to come to faith ignorant of the gospel, for what faith grasps is the good news of Jesus. On the other hand, only a portion of the scriptures, strictly speaking, are truly necessary for the life, faith, and mission of the church: the book of the old covenant.[14] The communities of faith in Christ scattered across the

11. For "the mission of Scripture," see Work, *Living and Active*, 125–213.

12. For theological reflection on the significance of the ascension, see Farrow, *Ascension and Ecclesia*; for a recent accessible treatment, see Schreiner, *Ascension of Christ*.

13. The language of Pentecost as paired with, or peer to, Easter comes from Jenson, *Triune God*, 146.

14. See, e.g., Jenson, *Triune Story*, 120–26, 146–62, 183–219; Griffiths, *Catholic Theology*, 57. For a complementary but somewhat different perspective on the notion of "canons" in the life of the church, see Abraham, *Canon and Criterion*; Abraham, *Divine Agency and Divine Action, Vol. 3*, 9–38.

Mediterranean basin (and south into Africa and east into Asia and . . .) did not, for the most part, have writings from the apostles to guide them. They lived under the guidance of Christ's Spirit, tradition handed down from the apostles or their deputies, and the testimony of Israel's scriptures. Most such communities lived this way into the early second century, and even once writings attributed to the apostles began to be shared and distributed widely, neither their authority nor their exact number nor their status as a collection was settled for at least one or two more centuries. So while it is true that there is no church apart from the Old Testament or the preaching of the apostles, it is not true that the Christian Bible of Old and New Testaments is a *sine qua non* of the church's being.[15]

What this means, second, is that Scripture in its final form is a *contingent* matter. It could have been otherwise. Had the Lord willed for the time between the times to be shorter than it turned out to be—had he, in the old formulation, not tarried—there would have been no need for a New Testament. That there is a New Testament is (humanly speaking) a response on the part of the church to an unexpected historical situation: life without apostles. But if neither the Lord's swift return nor the apostles living to see it is essential to the faith, then the church had better make preparations for the long haul. And so it did. It passed on unwritten traditions, not least in the liturgy; it perpetuated forms of leadership, especially the episcopacy; and it collected and republished and commented upon the teaching of the apostles in the form of letters, histories, homilies, and an apocalypse.[16] Both in the moment and looking back, the church has judged this historical stock-taking and consolidation of apostolic authority not merely as a historically contingent matter, but as a Spirit-led response to the Lord's will. It turns out that the Lord meant what he said when he referred to the ends of the earth: he desired that all peoples, generation upon generation, hear the good news. "The Lord is not slow about his promise as some count slowness, but is forbearing toward you, not wishing that any should perish, but that all should reach repentance" (2 Pet 3:9). The New Testament is necessary in *this* sense, for it is the divinely willed addendum to Israel's scriptures—in

---

15. For Reformed reply, see, e.g., Calvin, *Institutes* 1.7; Schaff, *Principle of Protestantism*, 119–24; Warfield, *Inspiration and Authority*, 411–16.

16. See, e.g., St. Ignatius of Antioch, *Epistles*; St. Justin Martyr, *First and Second Apologies*; St. Irenaeus of Lyons, *Against Heresies*; Origen, *On First Principles*. For later comment, see Eusebius, *History*, or St. Basil the Great, *On the Holy Spirit*. A lovely wide-angle view may be found in Wilken, *First Thousand Years*; for theological comment, see Jenson, *Canon and Creed*; for historical, exegetical, and theological woven together, see Young, *Biblical Exegesis*; Young, *God's Presence*; Young (with Teal), *From Nicaea to Chalcedon*.

the words of Robert Jenson, an *aide-memoire* in the absence of the apostles' living voice—so long as the church's mission lasts.[17]

Third, then, Scripture is *apostolic*. In simplest terms, it teaches faithfully the deposit of faith entrusted to those to whom the risen Christ appeared, whom he commissioned to go into all the world bearing his authority and his saving message (Matt 28:18–20; Acts 1:8; John 20:21–23). Scripture is thus a book for the mission, a portable library of trustworthy samples of gospel speech. Whatever the church in its ongoing encounters with new questions, challenges, and cultures elects to say in its attempts to announce the gospel, such attempts must be tested by the records contained in the New Testament. Moreover, those records are themselves missionary documents: *in media res*, they offer neither a blank slate upon which to construct the gospel nor a final word definitively closing this or that matter. They are experiments in improvisation on the way from Pentecost to parousia. Gentiles are coming to faith, women are prophesying with heads uncovered, ex-pagans are eating idol meat, traveling teachers are suggesting Jesus didn't come in the flesh, scoffers are claiming Jesus isn't coming back, others are saying he's already returned, Jewish apostles aren't eating with gentile believers, a church member is sleeping with his stepmother: what to do?[18] These aren't perennial issues in philosophy, and the apostolic writings are not treatises in systematic theology. They are makeshift answers, sometimes on the fly, to pressing questions of lived faith. That haphazard character may be a thorn in the flesh of theologians, but it is a boon to the church's life among the nations. For what it offers is not timeless answers but snapshots of the apostles in action, a model for discernment of the Spirit in real time. And when further questions arise—Should we worship Jesus? Is Mary God's mother? May icons be venerated? Is the Spirit fully God?—the church turns to Scripture not only for divine instruction but for exemplary patterns of sound judgment exercised on the mission field and captured, in the moment, for future generations of believers.[19]

It is important to see that Scripture's apostolicity is not juxtaposed to its contingency but rather is the shape its contingency takes. For apostolicity itself is a limited, missionary office. There are no apostles after the originals depart, and the status of an apostle in glory will be like motherhood: a function of what one was on earth, in time, not a continuing office that might

---

17. Jenson, *Triune Story*, 122.

18. Acts 10:1—15:35; 1 Cor 5:1–13; 8:1—11:16; 1 John 4:1–6; 2 Thess 2:1–12; Gal 2:1–21.

19. Commenting on the work of John Howard Yoder, especially his *To Hear the Word* and *Priestly Kingdom*, I expand on this theme in *The Church's Book*, chapter 5.

be expanded or continued in a heavenly fashion.[20] What this means, fourth and last, is that, in light of Scripture's particular apostolic necessity and, as we noted in the last chapter, its sacramental character, Scripture is *eschatological*. Though this is implicit in all that has been said so far, it is worth making explicit. For sacraments are themselves functions of the ascension and Pentecost: modes of the Lord's presence and intimacy to his people on earth, made possible by his Spirit, employing creaturely media until such time as intermediaries are no longer needed. As we saw, Scripture is one such intermediary, which is why we may deem its liturgical and devotional use as sacramental in character. But sacraments come to an end. There is no need for manna after crossing the Jordan. Just so, there is no need for Scripture once the Lord, face to face, speaks unveiled to his beloved. The bridal veil, as it were, hides the ears as much as the face. But in the marriage of heaven and earth, in the consummation of Christ's love for his people, his voice will ring loud and clear, no longer brought from afar by his many servants. "Oh my dove, in the clefts of the rock, . . . let me see your face, let me hear your voice, for your voice is sweet, and your face is comely" (Song 2:14).[21] The Lord's granting of that figural petition—one of the many promises that are all Yes and Amen in Christ (2 Cor 1:19–20)—means that Scripture, like the sacraments, will pass away too.[22] Scripture is thus provisional: an eschatological gift that, once it has fulfilled its purpose, will be necessary no more. In this respect as well, to call Scripture "perfect" is a theological misnomer, inasmuch as "when that which is perfect is come, then that which is in part shall be done away" (1 Cor 13:10 KJV). What is perfect is the vision of the Lord "face to face," and what is partial is all forms, signs, and instruments through which we see and hear him now, as "in a mirror dimly" (v. 12).[23] The church loves and clings to Scripture here below,

20. This may be an overstatement; after all, the apostles judge the nations and sit around the throne (cf. Matt 19:28; Rev 4:4; see also the depiction of apostles, martyrs, saints, and doctors in Dante's *Paradiso*), and the church's tradition of Marian piety suggests her office as Queen Mother is more than nominal in heaven. Either way, though, my point is that the exercise of apostleship is temporally bound, and the office of apostleship is limited to the first generation of the church.

21. This passage is potent for the point made here, since its reference to "the clefts of the rock" locates us lover-readers, figurally, with Moses on Sinai, capable in this life of only the briefest glance at the Lord's back as he passes before us in liturgical proclamation and sacramental participation (cf. Exod 33:18—34:9). To hear his voice and to see his face, however, is to be released from the clefts of the flesh and lifted to "the Jerusalem above" (Gal 4:26).

22. Paul Griffiths is lucid on this point: see *Catholic Theology*; *Decreation*; *Song of Songs*.

23. I note the irony of cessationist-biblicist interpretation of this passage in "Standards of Excellence."

but so too does it long for Scripture's end. For "while we are at home in the body we are away from the Lord," and so "we groan, and long to put on our heavenly dwelling . . . so that what is mortal may be swallowed up by life" (2 Cor 5:6, 3, 4). The church looks with joy to the end of Scripture because it looks with hope to the coming of Christ.

3. Holy Sufficiency

Scripture is holy as the church is holy: set apart through the Spirit by the Father's gracious act in Christ to form for himself a people from all the nations—and within that people, a book to light the way. St. Peter writes of the prophets who spoke of the saving grace to come in the Messiah as foretold by the Messiah's Spirit (1 Pet 1:10–11).[24] "It was revealed to them that they were serving not themselves but you": that is to say, the writings of the old covenant are servants of the saints in advance of the gospel's advent. Now in these last days that which they anticipated has "been announced to you by those who preached the good news to you through the Holy Spirit sent from heaven" (v. 12). Exhortation follows: "As obedient children, do not be conformed to the passions of your former ignorance, but as he who called you is holy, be holy yourselves in all your conduct; since it is written, 'You shall be holy, for I am holy'" (vv. 14–16, quoting Lev 19:2). Such holiness comes, on the one hand, from having set one's "hope fully upon the grace that is coming to [the saints] at the revelation of Jesus Christ" (v. 13); and, on the other hand, from being "born anew, not of perishable seed but of imperishable, through the living and abiding word of God" (v. 23). "That word," he adds, "is the good news which was preached to you" (v. 25).

The grace of holiness, therefore, is at once ecclesial and evangelical. Its source is the Holy Trinity, the God who sanctifies his people: "Once you were no people but now you are God's people": "a royal priesthood, a holy nation, a people for his own possession" (vv. 10, 9). The proclamation of the gospel is itself the instrument of God's holy-making action, while the two-testament scriptures—comprising the prophets and apostles—attest the good news in prospect or retrospect.[25] But the instrument of God's sanctification must be holy as well, and so it is. God sanctifies the texts of Old and New Testament alike to be, for his holy people, the unique medium of his saving speech: that, like the angels, the people of God might "hearken[] to the voice of his word" (Ps 103:20).

24. This is my paraphrase, though the messianic phrasing is found in the CJB, ISV, Message, and NTE translations.

25. See the discussion in Barth, *Church Dogmatics* I/2, 45–121, 481–85.

Rendered fit for service, Scripture is sufficient to the task.[26] To speak of sufficiency as a divinely bestowed attribute of Scripture is simply to affirm that what God has ordained it to do it is capable of doing. God has not, as it were, brought a knife to a gun fight. The next chapter will speak of the multiple ends, primary and secondary, of Scripture: befriending, following, imaging, and knowing Christ; or put differently: saving us, edifying us, sanctifying us, and drawing us into fellowship with the Lord. The Bible, this attribute claims, is adequate to *that*. In the communion of saints, in the power of the Spirit, the scriptures will accomplish the Lord's purposes because the risen Jesus has endowed it with the capacity to do so. God has not asked of the text something it cannot achieve; God has not given the church a book that cannot deliver on his promise.

The challenge is specifying more exactly the nature of Scripture's sufficiency. Here the heirs of Luther and Calvin depart from their catholic forebears (East and West). All agree that Scripture is *materially* sufficient: one ought, with St. Timothy, to be "acquainted with the sacred writings, which are able to make you wise for salvation through faith in Christ Jesus" (2 Tim 3:15 ESV). There is no revelation *in addition to* Scripture; the one and only deposit of faith is that found in and announced by the embassy of the apostles and prophets. The canon contains and proclaims the gospel of God. If someone wants to hear the gospel, the church points to the canon, or better, opens it up and reads it aloud.

Where reformers and catholics differ is Scripture's *formal* sufficiency.[27] To deny formal sufficiency is to deny *sola scriptura*: so that not only Scripture but also sacred tradition and the living teaching office of the church are necessary for the proper understanding and teaching of the apostolic faith across time. To affirm formal sufficiency is to agree with the Westminster Confession of Faith: "The whole counsel of God concerning all things necessary for his own glory, man's salvation, faith, and life, is either expressly set down in Scripture, or by good and necessary consequence may be deduced

---

26. For discussion, see Turretin, *Institutes* 16.1–36; Bavinck, *Reformed Dogmatics*, 481–94; Muller, *Holy Scripture*, 327–40; Barrett, *God's Word Alone*, 332–71; Ward, *Words of Life*, 106–15.

27. John Webster also draws attention to what he calls the rhetorical sufficiency of Scripture: "The prophets and apostles are appointed by God, dogmaticians are not; prophetic and apostolic speech is irreducible; the sufficiency of Scripture includes its *rhetorical* sufficiency. . . . *Sermo* is certainly subject to *res*; but *paradeigmata* are subservient to *sermo*, and the prophetic and apostolic *sermo* remains the governor of theological discourse, not simply that which we pass through on the way to the *res*" (*Domain of the Word*, 131, 131n.34). This argument has implications not only for theology's self-understanding but for liturgical practice as well.

from Scripture:[28] unto which nothing at any time is to be added, whether by new revelations of the Spirit, or traditions of men."[29] Partly the disagreement is semantic: all are at one that the revelation of Christ is complete and final; neither new revelations from God nor more books of the Bible may be added to the canon or to "the faith which was once for all delivered to the saints" (Jude 1:3). Moreover, no one disputes the fact that Scripture requires readers for its implementation: if the text is a blueprint, an architect is called for.[30] The question is the status of the altogether human architect under God and the consequent status of her construction attempts. The reformers protest that all interpretation of the Bible is necessarily fallible and subject to the distortions and imperfections of fallenness and finitude. The catholic reply is that if ordinary believers—not universally literate Westerners in the twenty-first century, but all too often illiterate peasants, laborers, servants, nursemaids, and caretakers from the third and sixth and ninth and twelfth and fifteenth and eighteenth centuries—cannot trust the teaching of the church as reliable, has not God left his people ill equipped for its mission? All agree that ministers and teachers are beneficial. The question is whether, apart from them, Scripture alone is sufficient.[31]

This book sides with the older view. It would have been unthinkable for the church fathers to consider the scriptures sufficient apart from the requisite matrix of sacred tradition and episcopal, synodal, and conciliar exercise of interpretive authority.[32] Arius and Sabellius, Apollinaris and Nestorius could affirm the formal sufficiency of Scripture: Does the text not report Jesus's teaching that "No one is good but God alone" (Mark 10:18) and "'The Father is greater than I'" (John 14:28)? Does it not say that "The Lord created [wisdom] at the beginning of his way, the first of his acts of

28. Though even here, such deduction is the rub. May the perpetual virginity of Mary be rightly deduced from the material witness of Scripture? What of her bodily assumption into heaven? (See, e.g., Pitre, *Jewish Roots of Mary*.) Or to focus on a less disputed question, consider the divinity of the Spirit. Both St. Basil of Caesarea (*On the Holy Spirit*) and St. Gregory of Nazianzus (*Theological Orations*), who labored strenuously for the church's confession of the Spirit's full and co-equal deity along with the Father and the Son, admitted that part of the case was post-apostolic (not to say *non-apostolic*) tradition, not least as embodied in liturgical practice.

29. Westminster Confession of Faith 1.6. Cf. the Thirty-Nine Articles of Religion: "Holy Scripture containeth all things necessary to salvation: so that whatsoever is not read therein, nor may be proved thereby, is not to be required of any man, that it should be believed as an article of the Faith, or be thought requisite or necessary to salvation" (6).

30. Cf. Turretin, *Institutes* 16.28.

31. See further chapter 5 for Scripture's interpretation and chapter 6 for the church's authority.

32. From the East, e.g., see Ware, *Orthodox Church*, 193; Louth, *Discerning the Mystery*, 107; St. Philaret of Moscow, *Longer Catechism* 10–61.

old" (Prov 8:22), that Jesus is "the wisdom of God" (1 Cor 1:24), and that he is thus "the firstborn of all creation" (Col 1:15)? In practical terms, should the teaching of the ecumenical councils be a perennial issue for disputation? Should each generation redraw the battle lines and hash out whether Jesus is subordinate to the Father, whether the Spirit is himself a divine hypostasis?[33] The answer is both that this should not happen and that it will not happen. It will not happen because the divided branches of the church cannot turn back the clock: if the church erred *there*, then the gospel was lost—or rather, cast away in a fit of blasphemy—long before we came on the scene.[34] And it should not happen because the Lord's provision of the canon of Scripture is at once coextensive with, and the mutual implication of, his provision of the Rule of Faith as well as authoritative teaching on central matters of dispute through the church's ordained leadership.[35]

Think back again to the image of the mosaic from St. Irenaeus. The Rule of Faith, eventually codified in the creeds and canons of the ecumenical councils, is the key to ensuring that the tiles of Scripture form the image of the living Christ and not a simulacrum of him, much less a false god. For the truth is that the meaning of the biblical texts, considered in themselves, is largely underdetermined. They admit of many readings. They are patient of heresies. And heretics are neither stupid nor deluded nor malicious. They are usually well-intentioned, doing their level-headed best. Consider an exchange in one of G. K. Chesterton's Father Brown stories:

> "Is that all?" asked Flambeau after a long pause. "Have we got to the dull truth at last?"

---

33. Cf. St. Francis de Sales, *Catholic Controversy* 4.2–3. "Once let the canons of Councils be submitted to the test of private individuals, as many persons, so many tastes, so many opinions": "Everything must be done over again, and posterity will never trust antiquity but will go ever turning upside down the holiest articles of the Faith in the wheel of their understandings" (4.3).

34. "We become Christians by becoming members of the Church, by *trusting* our forefathers in the faith. If we cannot trust the Church to have understood Jesus, then we have lost Jesus: and the resources of modern scholarship will not help us to find him": Louth, *Discerning the Mystery*, 93. Jenson concurs: "If, for example, the decision of Nicea . . . was false to the gospel, the gospel was thereby so perverted that there has since been no church extant to undo the error" (*Triune God*, 17).

35. For a recent impressive case for the magisterial Protestant position, see Allen and Swain, *Reformed Catholicity*, esp. 49–116. See also Allen and Swain, *Christian Dogmatics*, both the essays within (esp. Vanhoozer, "Holy Scripture," 30–56) and the enacted project of reformed catholicity more broadly; cf. Allen, "Reformed Retrieval." See finally Vanhoozer, *Biblical Authority*; Ortlund, *Theological Retrieval*; Collins and Walls, *Roman but Not Catholic*.

> "Oh, no," said Father Brown. . . . "Ten false philosophies will fit
> the universe; ten false theories will fit Glengyle Castle. But we
> want the real explanation of the castle and the universe."[36]

Ten false teachings will fit the Bible; ten heresies will fit the scriptures. What we want is the *real* explanation of the canon. We want the mosaic of the Son: nothing more, nothing less. And we cannot have it apart from the reliable interposition of the church, which by the gift of Christ's Spirit is both *mater* and *magister* of the faithful.

4. Catholic Clarity

The question of Scripture's formal sufficiency is closely related to the question of its clarity, or perspicuity.[37] Like the former, the latter is an adjunct of the doctrine of *sola scriptura*: if the Bible is the exclusive source and authority in the church with respect to faith and morals—if the community of faith across time does not in principle need the authoritative exercise of the church's teaching regarding how to read the text rightly or wrongly—then the meaning of the text must be plain. It must be evident to all, at least to all who make "due use of ordinary means," in the words of the Westminster Confession. See the larger context:

> All things in Scripture are not alike plain in themselves, nor alike
> clear unto all; yet those things which are necessary to be known,
> believed, and observed for salvation, are so clearly propounded,
> and opened in some place of Scripture or other, that not only the
> learned, but the unlearned, in a due use of the ordinary means,
> may attain unto a sufficient understanding of them.[38]

Let me also instance here two recent discussions of Scripture's clarity by Reformed evangelicals. First, Daniel Treier lays down the negative premise: "If Scripture were not clear, then Tradition . . . would be necessary to avoid interpretative chaos."[39] He goes on:

36. Chesterton, "The Honour of Israel Gow," in *Father Brown*, 82.

37. For discussion, see Callahan, *Clarity of Scripture*; Barrett, *God's Word Alone*, 302–31; Muller, *Holy Scripture*, 340–57; Ward, *Words of Life*, 115–27; Webster, *Holy Scripture*, 91–101; *Confessing God*, 33–68; Gerhard, *Nature of Holy Scripture* 20.414–36; Turretin, *Institutes* 2.17.1–22; Bavinck, *Reformed Dogmatics*, 475–81.

38. Westminster Confession of Faith 1.7. As with Treier below, "may" does a good deal of work here, not least if ordinary means include wise, orthodox teachers to guide both the learned and the unlearned.

39. Treier, *Evangelical Theology*, 315. The ellipsis contains the phrase "and/or an infallible pope."

> Tradition plays an inevitable, often helpful, and "ministerial" role in Protestant interpretation, but is never a magisterial necessity for communicating the biblical gospel. The Spirit can use ordinary reading of the literal sense to help people hear this Word. . . . [T]he Bible's central message . . . can be understood personally and faithfully, through reading vernacular translations, with the Holy Spirit's help and without necessary interpretive reliance upon the institutional church.[40]

Second, Scott Swain writes that perspicuity "refers to the fact that Scripture so clearly reveals the central truths of Christianity, the gospel of Jesus Christ, and the path of godliness, that the regenerate mind can, under the Spirit's tutelage, perceive and receive that revelation."[41] Both authors deny that this means that each and every passage of Scripture lacks ambiguity or opacity; both agree that the work of the Holy Spirit in illuminating the reading of the baptized is essential. Indeed, Swain argues that "Scripture's teaching is not finally clear to unaided natural reason."[42]

Each theologian goes on, however, to offer qualifications or clarifications regarding the role of tradition and the church's authority vis-à-vis Scripture. Treier issues "a series of nuances." In reading the text, believers (a) "need the Holy Spirit," (b) "need teachers," (c) "need" to engage in conventional practices of reading (i.e., the scriptures are not runes for divination), and (d) "need the creedal, trinitarian 'Rule of Faith' and the wider biblical 'analogy of faith' to guide their reading."[43] Swain initially takes a

---

40. Treier, *Evangelical Theology*, 313, 314. As with Westminster's "may," Treier uses the auxiliary "can" twice to stipulate the possibility of ordinary personal reading of Scripture leading to basic understanding of God's word. So far as I know, no one denies that such a thing *can* happen (or has happened). The question is whether that possibility justifies the claim of formal sufficiency, and thus of perspicuity. A person can be saved without baptism, but baptism is nevertheless the ordinary means by which God saves us. Just so, a person can read the Bible correctly apart from the church's worship, tradition, pastoral guidance, and/or instruction, but those are nevertheless the ordinary—indeed the normative, because divinely instituted—means by which believers reach an accurate understanding of Scripture.

41. Swain, *Trinity, Revelation, and Reading*, 87. Note that Swain is not discussing reading apart from faith, but reading by "the regenerate mind." Such a person is baptized, however, clothed with Christ through faith. Which means that such a person is both catechized and a participant in the sacramental life of the church. That would suggest that "the Spirit's tutelage" to which Swain refers *is always already ecclesially mediated*, which is just the point of the catholic denial of a strong account of clarity rooted in Scripture's formal sufficiency: the Christian reader ordinarily needs, indeed by definition already has, the church to teach her the truths of Scripture in order to understand it.

42. Swain, *Trinity, Revelation, and Reading*, 92.

43. Treier, *Evangelical Theology*, 313–14. Two more in the list include (e) focusing

harder line, writing that "we should not seek a vantage point beyond the New Testament—whether in church tradition [or other things]—to shed further light upon biblical teaching."[44] Having said that, he goes on not only to affirm the use of the Rule of Faith in exegesis, but denies that "the rule of faith is open to endless revision," for dogma, understood as "the church's public and binding summaries of scriptural truth," is irreversible.[45] In this way ecclesial "dogmas provide . . . a divinely authorized interpretive key for unlocking the treasures of God's word."[46] In sum, "Reading Scripture in light of the rule of faith is a way of acknowledging that, when it comes to biblical interpretation, *sola Scriptura* (Scripture's status as the sole supreme author-ity for faith and life) cannot function appropriately as an interpretive norm apart from *tota Scriptura* (Scripture's teaching in its entirety)."[47]

I have quoted extensively from these recent forays into the attribute of perspicuity in order, first, to present it in its fullest, most positive, most com-plex form; and, second, to show, in the words of its proponents, the subtlety and scope of its claims. There is a baseline sense in which any Christian can affirm a certain clarity to Scripture's basic teachings: that God is one, that Jesus is Lord, that God raised Jesus from the dead, and so on. Moreover, the laudable unwillingness on the part of magisterial Protestants to forsake the tradition of the church, however they subordinate its authority, separates them from other, more radical Protestant branches. At times this move makes their teaching appear more like a matter of emphasis, compared to the catholic view, than a matter of fundamental disagreement; a difference in degree, not in kind. Ecumenical opportunities are rife here.

The denial of tradition's ongoing interpretive authority, however, though attached to the affirmation of tradition's goodness and even necessi-ty, makes rapprochement difficult to realize. Consider that final quote from Swain, which says that Scripture's exclusive status as norm cannot operate as it should apart from "Scripture's teaching in its entirety." To which one must

---

upon the gospel and (f) encountering unclear passages. The analogy of faith "applies clearer teaching [from the rest of the canonical scriptures] to understanding more dif-ficult passages."

44. Swain, *Trinity, Revelation, and Reading*, 92. I have replaced in brackets the phrase "another holy book, or supposed cultural progress."

45. Swain, *Trinity, Revelation, and Reading*, 110–11, 111.

46. Swain, *Trinity, Revelation, and Reading*, 111.

47. Swain, *Trinity, Revelation, and Reading*, 113–14. Cf. the summary later on the same page: "Reading Scripture in light of the rule of faith thus involves reading Scrip-ture from within the context of our trinitarian faith, aided by the church's good confes-sion, for the sake of the church's continuing growth in this trinitarian faith. To read Scripture in any other way is to read against the grain of its authority." With this elegant formulation I could not agree more.

ask: How does one *know* "Scripture's teaching in its entirety"? No more than the catholic tradition will Swain answer that each believer needs to read the whole canon and make up her mind for herself. We return, once again, to the issue of trust. Practically speaking, most believers past and present put their trust in the church to which they belong to provide them with the truth of God in a reliable manner: the contents of the canon; its basic message; creeds and confessions from the past worth upholding in the present; essential doctrines like the Trinity, sacramental efficacy, salvation, election, and so on. What the catholic perspective adds is that this unavoidable human, communal, temporal situation is as it should be, for God has willed it thus. And, accordingly, that he has provided the means by which to ensure its success in history.

Treier and Swain are right, in short, that the trinitarian faith articulated and established—humanly speaking, one might say created[48]—in the fourth century is the *sine qua non* of both the Christian faith and (therefore) Scripture's interpretation. It is the key that unlocks the text. What then keeps us from adverting to Swain's repudiated metaphor: namely, that it sheds light upon the canon? The light in question is not the light of revelation. It is the illuminating light of the Holy Spirit, guiding our path across admittedly murky terrain; or, to switch metaphors again, guiding our hands in the sometimes dimly lit task of mosaic assembly. But the channel of the Spirit's light is not merely my own soul or mind. It is the communion of saints.

48. Perhaps the core theoretical issue in dispute is the status of the fourth century as a contingent event. Humanly, historically, politically, philosophically, and exegetically speaking, the achievement of the fathers from Nicaea to Chalcedon was not a foregone conclusion. Wise, brilliant, and faithful Christian leaders and teachers thought otherwise than what came to rule the day. Settled orthodoxy was not settled in advance. Chalcedon itself split the church (and not without reason). It is easy enough, in hindsight, to trace the lines that lead from the Gospel of St. John and the letters of St. Paul to the judgments issued in Nicene faith; but they were not inevitable, and there are other lines that could be drawn with good support from other biblical texts and other church thinkers. If we, the inheritors of Nicene faith, ultimately defer to what the fathers accomplished, it is because we trust that in and through them the Spirit worked an undeniable and nonnegotiable settlement in, of, and for the faith: the identity of God and of the persons of the Godhead. We trust that settlement no less than we trust either the contents of the canon or the *content* of the canon: and rightly so. To subject that settlement theoretically (but not practically) to the naked authority of Scripture apart from catholic teaching is to want to have our cake and eat it too. We must decide. And those radical traditions of restoration and restitution—Anabaptists, Stone-Campbellites, certain Baptists, Pentecostals, and evangelicals—see the dilemma with perhaps greater clarity than magisterial Protestants: they consistently (which is not to say coherently or justifiably) reject the authority of the councils and, on occasion, upon a rereading of the canon, reject the doctrine of the Trinity, or some aspect thereof. I see no reason why an heir of Calvin or Luther may think them *in principle* wrong to do so. See further chapter 6 on Scripture and dogma.

"When the Spirit of truth comes, he will guide you into all the truth" (John 16:13). That "you" is plural (*hymas*), and the means of the Spirit's guidance is the graces he bestows on different members of the body, some of whom he calls and equips to be teachers (Rom 12:7; 1 Cor 12:28; Eph 4:11). Such teachers are figured in both testaments: first by Ezra and his companions who, as the book of the Law was read aloud to all Israel, stood among them "making it clear and giving the meaning so that the people understood what was being read" (Neh 8:8 NIV); and second by St. Philip and the Ethiopian eunuch, who in reply to Philip's question, "Do you understand what you are reading?" answered, "How can I . . . unless someone explains it to me?" (Acts 8:30–31).

Above all the need not only for interpretation but for Spirit-enabled authority in interpretation is signaled by Jesus's response to the lawyer who tested him by asking, "Teacher, what shall I do to inherit eternal life?" (Luke 10:25). Jesus's two questions in reply stand at the head of all Christian interpretation of Scripture and, indeed, of the question of its clarity: "What is written . . . ? How do you read?" (v. 26). For what is written does not determine its reading; it may be read any number of ways. It is rather the catholicity of Scripture that controls or establishes its clarity. Scripture is *katholikos*, universal or common, to the church; that is what makes it a *kanon*, a ruler or measure for the beliefs and behavior of all believers. But it is not Scripture *understood in any way*—canonical texts arranged, for example, contrary to the faith passed down from the apostles and their successors—but Scripture *as received and interpreted in accordance with catholic teaching that functions as the norm for the church's life and mission*. Treier is correct: reading Scripture with Nicaea and Constantinople as guides is not optional; it is a necessity.[49] To read otherwise is bound to lead astray. Whereas when Scripture is read with and under and through them, it will shine with dazzling radiance, serving God's people as God's word always has: as "a lamp to my feet and a light to my path" (Ps 119:105). The clarity of Scripture, in short, is *liturgical* clarity: the power of the incarnate Word, in the gathering of his corporate body to hear and adore him, to enlighten minds and set hearts afire with "the love of God shed abroad in our hearts through the Holy Spirit who has been given to us" (Rom 5:5).[50]

49. How or why this excludes "the institutional church"—who else met in councils or produced the creeds?—I am unsure.

50. The translation is a mixture of the KJV, RSV, and NIV.

5. One Truth

The unity of Scripture is partly a historical claim, but ultimately it is a confession of faith. It is true that, humanly speaking, the community that arose in the first and second centuries in the wake of the crucifixion of Jesus of Nazareth and the destruction of the Jerusalem temple began to gather writings of its founding leaders and thence to pair their public reading with that of the scriptures of ancient Israel held in common with the synagogue. But whether or not these two collections cohere in a single volume is a theological question. The church believes that indeed they do. Which is to say, that together they bear witness, in all their diversity and complexity and internal differentiation, to the one God of Israel revealed by the Spirit in the person and work of Jesus Christ. And as we have seen in the preceding chapters, this foundational belief is an orienting one: the doctrine of Scripture then works backwards so as to discover how it is that this testimony is one. Having done that work, the church thereupon confesses that Scripture speaks of one *res* because it speaks with one voice, the voice of the triune Lord: it not only points toward him but comes from him. The unity of Scripture is a function of the unity of God and of his mighty acts in creation, Israel, and the church. "There is one body and one Spirit, just as you were called to the one hope that belongs to your call, one Lord, one faith, one baptism, one God and Father of us all, who is above all and through all and in all" (Eph 4:4–6). *Because* of these prior and persisting unities, Holy Scripture is one.

To say that Scripture is one is not only to affirm that it holds together but also to clarify that the story it tells, the truth it teaches, is one. The unity of Scripture's truth is analytic in the unity of Scripture as such. This unity is partly narrative and historical: the biblical story is not fictional, and the events it reports are in principle locatable in space and time. Its places and characters bear names—God included. More to the point, there is no fundamental break or rupture in the story: God's work is consistent and continuous; the work of the one *God* means God's one *work*, however multifarious or unexpected from our perspective. Scripture's alethic unity is also doctrinal. What it teaches is true, and the truth it teaches does not contradict itself. It is trustworthy regarding the most precious of things: the knowledge of God and eternal salvation.

Consider a representative statement: "since everything asserted by the inspired authors or sacred writers must be held to be asserted by the Holy Spirit, it follows that the books of Scripture must be acknowledged as teaching solidly, faithfully, and without error the Truth which God wanted to be put in Sacred Writings for the sake of our salvation."[51] The ambiguity here is a useful example of the questions that divide Christian accounts of Scripture's truth. Granting issues of genre and cultural convention, are there errors of any kind in the canon? If there were—if a date or a location or a number or a plain fact were inaccurate—would that obviate Scripture's truth?[52] Or is the truth of Scripture limited to what it "asserts"? If so, what counts as an assertion? Perhaps a further qualification is in order: Only what Scripture asserts that pertains, directly or indirectly, to *salvation* is without error; anything else, either non-assertions or non-salvific matters, may or may not contain errors, but the essential attribute of Scripture's veracity remains intact.

This is neither a modern nor a Protestant concern. No less an authority than St. Augustine saw the vexed issues it raises and cut to the heart with a passionate defense of total inerrancy:

> the books of later authors are distinct from the excellence of the canonical authority of the Old and New Testaments, which has been confirmed from the times of the apostles through the successions of bishops and through the spread of the churches. It has been set on high, as if on a kind of throne, and every believing and pious intellect should be obedient to it. If something there strikes a person as absurd, it is not permissible to say, "The author of this book did not have the truth," but, "Either the manuscript is defective, or the translator made a mistake, or you do not understand." . . . [Therefore as regards] that excellence of the canonical sacred writings, even if the canon shows and confirms that only a single prophet or apostle or evangelist is found to have put something in his writings, it is not permissible to doubt that it is true. Otherwise there will be no writing to govern the weakness of human ignorance if the most salutary authority of the canonical books is either completely destroyed through contempt or subjected to interminable confusion.[53]

51. *Dei Verbum* 3.11. Serial comma added. The translation, slightly altered from the Vatican's, comes from Farkasfalvy, O Cist, *Christian Bible*, 132. Here is the Latin: *Cum ergo omne id, quod auctores inspirati seu hagiographi asserunt, retineri debeat assertum a Spiritu Sancto, inde Scripturae libri veritatem, quam Deus nostrae salutis causa Litteris Sacris consignari voluit, firmiter, fideliter et sine errore docere profitendi sunt.*

52. For a sample of a vast literature (ranging from academic to popular), see Muller, *Holy Scripture*, 318–26; Warfield, *Inspiration and Authority*, 419–42; Henry, *God, Revelation, and Authority*; Noll, "Inerrancy"; Burtchaell, CSC, *Biblical Inspiration*, esp. 164–229; Vanhoozer, "Inerrancy"; Rogers and McKim, *Authority and Interpretation*; Woodbridge, *Biblical Authority*; Barrett, *God's Word Alone*, 223–63; McGowan, *Divine Spiration*; Pinnock with Callen, *Scripture Principle*; Boyd, *Inspired Imperfection*; Carson, *Enduring Authority*.

53. St. Augustine, *Contra Faustum* 11.5. See also, e.g., the correspondence with St. Jerome in his *Letters* 28, 40, 67–68, 71–73, 75, 81–82.

In the last century a distinction has been drawn by some writers on this topic between inerrancy and infallibility.[54] Whereas the former concept denies any and all errors in the canon,[55] the latter has to do less with the presence or absence of inaccuracies in the text (factual, theological, or otherwise) and more with Scripture's empowerment for the tasks to which the Spirit has ordered it. In this way Scripture's infallibility is a corollary of its sufficiency.[56] It will not fail to execute that for which the Lord has purposed it. Through Scripture God's word does not fail to be communicated; his saving grace does not fail to be received; his wise instruction does not fail to edify; his truth does not fail to be heard and believed. What factual or historical errors may or may not obtain in the texts are neither here nor there to the material point. We might draw a parallel to the pious silence of some Anglicans regarding the real presence of Christ in the Eucharist: here too the veil is drawn across the question of error in the canon; what is affirmed is the real presence of the true word of the living Christ in and through the texts of Scripture. Understood in this way, the infallibility of Scripture is an attribute commonly presumed or confessed across denominational and other lines.

In response to these options, let me begin with two observations. First, it is not the uninterpreted text, but the text understood to be making determinate claims, that is or is not without error. For example, does Genesis 1–3 "assert" either a "young earth" or an original human pair without evolutionary ancestors? Answer: it depends. That is, it depends on how it is read. If *homo sapiens* has an evolutionary prehistory, and the relevant passages in Genesis are interpreted so as to confirm or at least not to contradict that, then those passages are without error. A less heated example is whether Jesus cleared the temple at the outset or the conclusion of his career (see John 2:13–22; Mark 11:15–19). A *prima facie* harmonized reading would say both: he did the same act twice, forming a kind of prophetic *inclusio* for his public ministry. An alternative would be that St. John has moved the one climactic clearing to the beginning of his narrative to make a theological point. But the text, in its reticence, does not say this. It is up to the reader to decide. So even the status of the question, "Does the canon err in its assertions?" is imprecise, constituting at best a moving target and at worst a shell game. For if we say, "The canon *rightly interpreted* does not err," such a claim opens the possibility to certain seemingly evident errors being read out of the text, perhaps against the plain sense of the text; such a strategy might

54. See, e.g., Davis, *Debate*.

55. That is to say, in the original autographs. See the "Chicago Statement."

56. Think of this as a kind of canonical analogue to ecclesial indefectibility (cf. Matt 16:18).

then preserve the text's truth at the potential expense of what the attribute of veracity wants to secure: the *objective* truth of Scripture.[57]

Second, the claim of inerrancy does not pertain to the authorial intentions of the text's human authors and redactors but only to the text as it stands as authored and intended by God. Doubtless ancient Israelites both maintained and intended scientifically false assertions about, say, cosmology, and assertions along those lines saturate the scriptures. But neither the presuppositions nor the intentions of such factual assertions are themselves spelled out: what we have is just the text. There we find mention of "the heavens" and of waters above the "firmament," for example, but usually in poetic formulations and always without hermeneutical marginalia specifying their fixed meaning. How we interpret these terms is thus up for grabs. One aspect of such interpretation involves distinguishing between sense and reference: the historical, grammatical, contextual, and intra-canonical signification of the words, phrases, and passages in conjunction with one another, on the one hand, and that to which they refer, on the other—whether that be an object in the world or an event or a time or a person or a spiritual being or what have you.[58] The upshot here is that, to recur to Genesis, the *ruach Elohim* (1:2) may be taken to refer to the Holy Spirit poured out on Pentecost without that reference being in any way intended, much less knowable, on the part of the Israelite who penned or revised those words. Furthermore, whether or not the referent of a term or sentence may gainsay its humanly intended sense is itself a question of interpretation. Stipulate that the humanly intended *sense* of the opening verses of Genesis is that Israel's God overcomes the preexistent chaos by his powerful creative speech, but that to which it *refers* is the same God's creation of all that is not God from nothing at all.[59] If the latter is true while the former, understood literally, is not (though it bears witness to an important theological aspect of

57. To be clear, this is only a problem (a) when the plain sense is equated with a *prima facie* historical reading or (b) in the absence of an authoritative teaching office, which recognizes the underdetermined nature of much of the text (and its "assertions"). The trouble arises, in other words, in the Protestant need for a clear canon apart from interpretive authority. Whereas the catholic view *presupposes* that the Bible admits of non-self-evidently false readings that would, on their face, entail textual errancy—on matters both indifferent and essential. See again Behr, "Introduction," for a brilliant rendition of Origenist-patristic hermeneutics regarding the enigmas and truths of Scripture brought to light by the cross of Christ.

58. Ordinary examples of identical referents with different semantic meaning (or sense): "water" and "H2O," or "Abilene Christian University" and "my alma mater."

59. Note well that this is only a stipulation, and what is stipulated is not even that the plain sense of the text is identical to the humanly intended sense. For a different but compatible (and quite brilliant) approach to theological interpretation of this passage, see Ticciati, "Anachronism or Illumination?"

divine sovereignty and the spiritual forces that threaten creation), in what sense is the text as it stands inerrant? Finally, even apart from the distinction between sense and reference, historic Christian exegesis distinguishes between what God may be intending to communicate in, with, and through the biblical texts—then and there or here and now[60]—over against their human authors and tradents.[61] The question of the texts' proper interpretation, therefore, is not settled by what the available options for meaning were at the time of their original composition.

All this and more will be discussed at length in chapter 5. What I mean to show here is the sheer complexity of the question of whether Scripture "contains" errors. But let me be more direct. With respect to what we are, I think, forced to label with appropriate obliqueness "rightly interpreted scriptural teaching[62] regarding theological matters"—the identity, character, and activity of God; the economy of salvation; the person and work of Jesus; the election, faith, and conduct of God's people—it is well and fitting to say that Scripture is *sine errore*. It tells us the truth about such things. Accordingly, we may rely on its telling for knowledge and for salvation.

Whether this carefully qualified affirmation entails the further claim of inerrancy *simpliciter* is, in my view, doubtful. Though I understand the logic that impels both St. Augustine and many contemporary evangelicals to the stricter view, it seems to me both that it is unnecessary in order to ensure the truthfulness of Scripture's testimony and that modern historical criticism has demonstrated beyond a reasonable doubt that the canon contains plenty of examples of what any fair-minded person would call a factual error. St. Augustine himself recognized that there were discrepancies between the Hebrew scriptures and the Septuagint.[63] But since he held, with the ancient church, that the latter translation was no less inspired than the original, he

60. See Volf, *Word of God*, 15–22.

61. Consider the provocative proposal of Gundry, *Peter*, namely that St. Matthew's Gospel originally meant to depict St. Peter as a "false disciple and apostate." I am not persuaded by Gundry's argument, though his exegetical observations are quite interesting and worthy of serious engagement. But even if he were right that the author(s) or editor(s) of the first canonical Gospel *did* intend to present Simon son of John as an accursed blasphemer who denied Jesus and fell under the divine curse, that would not settle the interpretive question for the church: both because the canonical texts' human authorial intention is not decisive in that way and because the Gospel does not assert this view plainly; the text must be read *as* asserting it. And that is just the business of interpretation; the meaning does not announce itself as such, nor is it known prior to the act of reading.

62. We could keep the phrase "assertions by Scripture," but *doctrina* seems a more fitting designation than *assertum*, as does making Scripture adjectival rather than agential, not least since so much of what the church understands Scripture to teach is rendered in narrative and poetic form, not in propositions.

63. See St. Augustine, *City of God* 18.42–44.

suggested that we take one version of a historical account to be literally true and the other to be a spiritual truth that God wanted to communicate to his people in just this way.[64] Whether or not we opt for similar hermeneutical gymnastics,[65] the desire for Scripture to be perfect in this particular form— free from discernible error of any kind—is, I submit, itself an error and one to avoid in the doctrine of Scripture. God is Truth itself, and Scripture by consequence is true: God does not lie, and neither does Scripture. But Scripture is a servant of the truth, not *the* Truth itself. The Truth is a person, Christ incarnate (John 14:6). He does indeed speak through Scripture, but not *as* it. I therefore see no reason in principle why the various (in my view, quite minor and usually uninteresting)[66] historical inconsistencies and factual inaccuracies in the canon should in any way undermine the credibility of Scripture's truthful testimony regarding "the gospel . . . [that] is the power of God for salvation for all who believe" (Rom 1:16).

For the credibility of a witness concerns, not an unrestricted scope of knowledge, much less omniscience, but reliability *with respect to that to which the witness offers testimony*.[67] Here, as with sufficiency, the veracity of the Bible is duly ordered to a purpose, or rather multiple purposes: it is not indeterminate or undefined. So far, however, we have left those ends unspecified. To the many *teloi* of Holy Scripture, then, we turn in the next chapter.

64. If I may be permitted to quote a tweet—the only time in this book, and from a scholar who studies the church's interpretation of Scripture—Erin Risch Zoutendam (https://twitter.com/erinleigh28/status/1113439003464929280) captures the sentiment nicely:

—Future employers: Do you believe Scripture is inerrant?

—Me, a latent Origenist who will never get hired by anyone: Oh yes, definitely. All the mistakes are there for a reason.

65. The worry here being not so much the proverbial wax nose as a sort of exegetical Mottramism. The term takes its name from a scene in Evelyn Waugh's *Brideshead Revisited* in which Rex Mottram, a schemer eager to swim the Tiber under false pretenses, supplies absurd answers to a priest's questions. One of these regards papal infallibility. Suppose the pope predicted it would rain tomorrow, and it didn't rain. Mottram: "I suppose it would be sort of raining spiritually, only we were too sinful to see it" (192).

66. Or rather, since they are often quite interesting when considered theologically, they are uninteresting as "gotcha" defeaters in anti-apologetics from former evangelicals and fundamentalists. See, e.g., Enns, *Bible Tells Me So*; Ehrman, *Jesus, Interrupted*.

67. See McFarland, *From Nothing*, xvn.9.

4

Ends

But as for you, continue in what you have learned and have firmly believed, knowing from whom you learned it and how from childhood you have been acquainted with the sacred writings, which are able to make you wise for salvation through faith in Christ Jesus. All Scripture is breathed out by God and profitable for teaching, for reproof, for correction, and for training in righteousness, that the man of God may be complete, equipped for every good work.
—2 Timothy 3:14–17 *ESV*

The first and final cause of Holy Scripture is the will and glory of God. But in the words of St. Irenaeus, "the glory of God is a living human being; and the life of the human consists in beholding God."[1] God's glorious, everlasting life as Father, Son, and Holy Spirit is not closed in on itself. It is infinitely open, for there is no loss in God's gifts to creatures of existence and grace or in their participation in his being and life. Holy Scripture is ultimately about those gifts, liberally bestowed one after another. Indeed, Scripture is one of the principal means of receiving such gifts from the Lord. As a means to those ends, it is itself a gift of grace, provided for our blessing and nourishment in the long exile from paradise. As Christ is both the destination and the way,[2] his word in Scripture is a glimpse of heaven and, just thereby, offers

1. The translation of *Against Heresies* 4.20 comes from Behr, *Irenaeus of Lyons*, 156.

2. Cf. John 14:6; Rom 10:4. See also St. Augustine, *City of God* 11.2; St. Thomas Aquinas, *Summa Theologica* I, Q2; Calvin, *Institutes* 3.2.1. Cf. Gerhard, *Interpreting Sacred Scripture* 8.140: "The aim of all Scripture is Christ."

a taste of it in the present. As George Herbert writes, addressing Scripture in the second person, "heav'n lies flat in thee, / Subject to ev'ry mounters bended knee."[3]

Scripture, in short, has a purpose, a telos. This telos is a function of its nature as the inspired and sanctified witness of the prophets and apostles to the good news of Israel's Lord. Like its nature and properties, Scripture's telos has its source in God. It is not first of all a matter of the church's uses of Scripture; rather, the church's uses of Scripture follow from and are dependent upon Scripture's divine telos. That is a matter of ontology. In terms of our knowledge, we—the church as a body, ordained pastors, individual believers, even theologians—come to learn of Scripture's telos through the church's ongoing life with Scripture. Texts in the canon speak of the purposes and effects of God's word. But these are neither systematic nor exhaustive. Nor do we have in the New Testament (because we could not have) a picture of a richly developed post-apostolic church with one and the same canon as we have today, putting it to use in multifarious liturgical and devotional and other practices. Such a thing takes time. As ever, the doctrine of Scripture is not a matter of applying *a priori* judgments to the text before our encounter with it or our experience of its role in the corporate worship and daily piety of the faithful. Rather, the doctrine of Scripture is a set of posterior investigations into the origins and conditions and character of what we *already find to be the case* in the life of God's people with the canonical books. In the order of knowing, we work backwards. Working backwards, we arrive at judgments in the order of being: what the canon is, whence it comes, what it is for. This chapter concerns what Scripture is for.

The first section expands briefly on this question of the end, or rather ends, of Scripture. The subsequent four sections consider the work that Scripture does in and among believers in terms of their relationship to Christ—which is to say, in terms of the activity of Christ in their lives, bodies, and souls. Through Scripture Christ acts as savior, teacher, archetype, and lover. So that Scripture's ends may be distinguished in terms of befriending Christ (beatitude and conversion), following Christ (instruction and edification), imaging Christ (sanctification and perseverance), and knowing Christ (communion and contemplative delight).[4] Scripture is not merely christocentric, however. If Scripture is here a created means of our union with Christ, the Holy Spirit is the uncreated: "The Holy Spirit is the bond by which Christ effectually unites us to himself," in the words of

---

3. Herbert, "The H. Scriptures I," in *English Poems*, 76–77.

4. Scripture's role as norm or rule governing the church will be considered in chapter 6 under the heading of its authority.

John Calvin.[5] The Spirit has other means at his disposal: baptism, Eucharist, proclamation, prayer. As one of the Spirit's tools, therefore, Scripture is an instrumental cause of our being "in Christ," whereas the Spirit is himself the efficient cause. For in the school of Christ, the Spirit is principal. He would not only have us learn of the Lord. He would make us his friends. Throughout in what follows, whether named or not, the ultimate agent of Scripture's work on us, the One who brings its purposes to fulfillment in us, is "the Spirit alone."[6]

A word about method before we begin. Though this book is not a sustained argument in the form of providing, say, necessary and sufficient reasons to justify every assertion, it has willy-nilly contained arguments *in nuce*, or represented the arguments of others. This chapter, however, is a different animal altogether. Think of it as a kind of midrashic meditation or figural rumination on the Bible's teleology. I am wanting here to display the kind of bounded freedom in theological exegesis made possible by the doctrine of Scripture this book propounds; I am seeking to follow the way the words run within the Rule of Faith, with the questions of Scripture's ends before me. The final criterion, as chapter 5 will show, is not so much logical correctness as fittingness, an aesthetic judgment about the way the parts hold together in light of the whole. I leave you, the reader, to judge.

1. Ends

Although the nature of Scripture obtains independently of our recognition of it, we saw in the previous two chapters that it is not a static or phenomenal feature of the text. Rather, the nature of Scripture consists in its relation to God and, in turn, the role God has given it to play in the economy of salvation. In its role, Scripture is ordained to an end: it is purposive. The modern reduction of causality to creaturely efficient causes and the resulting austerity in talk of teleology is foreign to Christian theology and therefore to the doctrine of Holy Scripture.[7] Scripture is not what we make of it, or what we take it to be for. It is for what God intends of it in the life and mission of the church. Our use of it will correspond to that intention more or less

5. Calvin, *Institutes* 3.1.1. John Webster uses this and the next quote from the *Institutes* in *Culture*, 89, where he calls Calvin "arguably the first and last great Protestant theologian of the Spirit."

6. Calvin, *Institutes* 3.1.3. To *solus Christus* is paired, in Calvin, *solus Spiritus*: only by union with Christ are we saved, a union effected by none but the Spirit, whose "principal work" is faith (3.1.4).

7. See, e.g., Dupré, *Religion*; Dupré, *Enlightenment*. For polemic, see Feser, *Last Superstition*.

faithfully, as the case may be. Our less than faithful usage bears not at all on the actual telos of Scripture, only on ourselves.

The relationship between scriptural teleology and scriptural usage runs deep, however. The reception of Scripture—that is, our modes of interpreting it—ordinarily and rightly follow upon our understanding of its purpose. If Scripture's *raison d'être* is the communication of discursive knowledge and our proper reception of it is correct apprehension of that knowledge, then procedures for reading will be directed to that end above all others, perhaps exclusively. But if the communication of such knowledge is only one among Scripture's multiple ends, and not even its primary end, then exegetical practice centered on accurate excavation of information derived from the biblical text will mislead or distort the church's overall relationship to the Bible.

For now, let me stipulate my use of the term "telos" or "end" in the singular and the plural. The upshot of this chapter is that Scripture has not one end, but many. It is helpful, however, to use "telos" in the singular to signify the unified horizon of Scripture's varied purposes. They conduce to a single point; they are not haphazard, disordered, or wayward. The canon is from and for God, ultimately, just as it is from and for the church, proximately. It conducts the covenant people in its exilic mission to the nations in a kind of circle: from its sending in the presence of the risen Christ back to the selfsame Lord, now enthroned, glorious, and manifested for all creation to behold. Scripture is the sword of *his* mouth (Rev 19:15) on the journey through the wilderness: and that word, which does not return to him empty (Isa 55:10–11), will indeed bring with it "a great multitude that no one [can] count" (Rev 7:9 NIV). The gospel announced by the prophets and apostles will prepare a way for the people of the Lord; "the mountains and the hills . . . shall break forth into singing, and all the trees of the field shall clap their hands" (Isa 55:12); there, "before the throne of God," they will "serve him day and night within his temple," and "the Lamb in the midst of the throne will be their shepherd, and he will guide them to springs of living water; and God will wipe away every tear from their eyes" (Rev 7:15, 17). That is the end for which God has appointed the Bible.

Within that single horizon, there are diverse needs and tasks. Continuing the figural imagery of exodus: the mighty word of the Lord (a) accomplishes salvation, liberating the captives from slavery to demonic powers and false gods; next it (b) draws the freed slaves to the holy Mount, where *torah* outlines the terms of covenant life and offers instruction for the sake of wise living and just order within the covenant people; it then (c) sets the people apart unto the Lord and feeds them from heaven, for "man does not live by bread alone, but . . . by everything that proceeds out of the mouth of the LORD" (Deut 8:3); and finally, it (d) establishes fellowship between the Lord and his people, communing intimately in the sacrifices and in the tent of meeting and, proleptically, in the promise of what is to come: a place for God's name to reside, in the midst of the land sworn on oath to the fathers long ago; there too the people will dwell, at peace at last, living under the reign of the Lord, whose word is true. These four acts of the Lord's saving word, figured in and by Israel's deliverance and journey from the Red Sea to the River Jordan, are the four tasks or ends of Holy Scripture within the church: to save, to instruct, to sanctify, to consummate. Together, they accomplish the work of mercy in sinful women and men. From start to finish—from the fleshpots of Egypt to the milk and honey of the promised land—the scriptures elicit, accompany, sustain, and conclude the redemption of the seed of Adam, by the grace of the seed of Abraham. Their purpose is his purpose, for their work is his work, and their word is his word. He will not fail or forget his covenant (Deut 4:31).

As the church waits, it begs of the Lord: "Make haste, my beloved!" (Song 8:14).[8] He answers: "Surely I am coming soon." With "eager longing" and "groaning" (Rom 8:19, 22), the Spirit and the bride reply: "Amen. Come, Lord Jesus!" (Rev 22:20). Scripture keeps us company in the interim. Its work endures until it unites the bride with the bridegroom. Then it is finished.

2. Befriending Christ: Beatitude and Conversion

Of the principal end of Holy Scripture, Johann Gerhard wrote in the early seventeenth century:

> With respect to God, the goal of Scripture is the salutary knowledge and glorification of God. It is for this purpose that God revealed himself in his Word that was first spoken orally and later was committed to writing: So people, having understood him correctly according to his essence and will, might praise him in this life and in that to come. When we learn from the Word of God his goodness, power, and wisdom and when we meditate devoutly on the mystery of our salvation that has been planned from eternity and revealed in time, then we cannot help but be stirred by that knowledge and meditation into a love for God. From this there immediately arises in our hearts a celebration and glorification of that great good.[9]

8. The exclamation point is mine.

9. Gerhard, *Nature of Holy Scripture* 17.362. In the next section he uses 2 Tim 3:16

Note that this goal is "with respect to God," although it still concerns Scripture's role *in the church* with respect to God. The threefold end here articulated is the praise and knowledge of God on the part of human beings, which praise and knowledge are, by their nature as revealing grace, salvific. The damned do not glorify God, or rather, do not worship God with the grateful joy and glad freedom of the blessed. "What profit is there in my death, if I go down to the pit? Will the dust praise you? Will it tell of your faithfulness?" (Ps 30:9). "For Sheol cannot thank you, death cannot praise you; those who go down to the pit cannot hope for your faithfulness" (Isa 38:18). To glorify God is to have been glorified (Rom 8:17, 30); to know God is to be known by God (Gal 4:9): such acts on earth, in and by the church, are meet and right inasmuch as they are foretastes of heaven. The knowledge Scripture imparts is salutary.

Scripture, therefore, is above all soteriological in purpose. Not the Word of God but the word of God written is a postlapsarian phenomenon. Like the incarnation, we may speculate about whether there would have been "Scripture anyway," but the reticence of the premodern doctors of the church regarding the former is a model for us regarding the latter.[10] The Law and the Prophets and the Psalms, the Gospels and the Epistles and the Apocalypse: these are documents of a fallen world. They are conditioned by sin, as medicine is conditioned by illness. The Eucharist is indeed the bread of heaven (cf. John 6:32–35), yet Jesus during his temptation also restates the teaching of Moses that fallen humanity lives not by bread alone but by "every word that proceeds from the mouth of God" (Matt 4:4). Not for the mouth alone, therefore, but also for the ears does the Lord provide the medicine of immortality: supersubstantial bread (6:11), on the one hand, and the Lord's saving word (Jas 1:21), on the other. This connection, noted in previous chapters, is worth reiterating: the body and blood of Christ are visible words that proclaim the gospel and communicate grace just as the public reading of Scripture in the assembly of believers does the same in the form of audible words. For the ears are the way to the heart (e.g., Matt 13:15), and "what comes out of the mouth proceeds from the heart" (15:18), whether good or evil.[11] In this twofold form of receiving God's word, that is,

---

and Rom 15:4 to discuss the "intermediate goals" of Scripture, that is, those goals that pertain to this life, short of the ultimate horizon of salvation in the world to come.

10. See van Driel, *Incarnation Anyway.*

11. One wants to extend the reflection to all the modes of the body's, and thus the heart's, and thus the soul's reception of external "inputs." If "the lamp of the body" is the eye, as Jesus teaches in Matt 6:22, and the soundness of one's eye means one's "whole body will be full of light," perhaps we may find here recommended the veneration of icons—those mirrors of heavenly light. For icons themselves prefigure the vision of the

eating it and hearkening to it—combined most memorably in St. John the Seer's consuming of "the little scroll, . . . bitter to [the] stomach, but sweet as honey in [the] mouth" (Rev 10:9)—Christ bestows a double grace, filling and feeding us till our hearts run over.

It is important to see how, in describing the Bible's purpose, there is a constant toggling back and forth, namely, beyond and before the eschatological horizon set by Christ's return. For the ultimate end of Holy Scripture is *beatitude*. That is what it is for; every one of its other ends conduces to that final goal. Scripture exists for the sake of our happiness: "I consider that the sufferings of this present time are not worth comparing with the glory that is to be revealed to us" (Rom 8:18). But what it means to be happy, to enter into the final "sabbath rest for the people of God" (Heb 4:9), is at once a matter beyond telling and simply put: "Through Holy Scripture, the Holy Trinity makes friends with us."[12] The good news of Jesus is that, in his all-surpassing love, he died for his friends, and that you and I are among them: "You are my friends if you do what I command you" (John 15:14). And what is his command? Answer: "that we should believe in the name of his Son Jesus Christ and love one another" (1 John 3:23). In and through Scripture Christ befriends us, granting us faith in his name, the very faith that, working in love, will effect our salvation (Gal 5:6).

Love will last, but faith, like Scripture, will pass away (cf. 1 Cor 13:13). For faith concerns that which is not seen (Heb 11:1; Rom 8:24). If Scripture is a book for the time between the times, a text for a fallen world awaiting redemption, then in the meantime, until we reach beatitude, Scripture's primary soteriological purpose is *conversion*. This is the work of the Spirit. As Jesus teaches, when the Spirit comes "he will convict the world concerning sin and righteousness and judgment" (John 16:8). This is evident at Pentecost in the people's response to the sermon preached by St. Peter:

> Now when they heard this they were cut to the heart, and said to Peter and the rest of the apostles, "Brothers, what shall we do?" And Peter said to them, "Repent, and be baptized every one of you in the name of Jesus Christ for the forgiveness of

---

Lord face to face, when in his light we shall see light (Ps 36:9). The Bible is less concerned with smell (ours at least; the Lord's is a different story), though the use of incense in worship attends to that creaturely sense; whereas those parts of our body dedicated most intimately to union and life, waste and death, although there is no formal use of them by analogy to other religious traditions (e.g., temple prostitutes), the Bible has *much* to say about their proper deployment and enjoyment; and the church, following St. Paul, has long taught that their use or non-use is sanctified in Christ, even constituting, within marriage, a sacrament of the Lord's love for the church (Eph 5:21–33).

12. Swain, *Trinity, Revelation, and Reading*, 60.

> your sins; and you shall receive the gift of the Holy Spirit. For
> the promise is to you and to your children and to all that are
> far off, every one whom the Lord our God calls to him." And
> he testified with many other words and exhorted them, saying,
> "Save yourselves from this crooked generation." So those who
> received his word were baptized, and there were added that day
> about three thousand souls. And they devoted themselves to the
> apostles' teaching and fellowship, to the breaking of bread and
> the prayers. (Acts 2:37–42)

The word of God "cuts to the heart" (v. 37), eliciting repentance and "the obedience of faith" (Rom 1:5), enacted in "baptism . . . which saves you" (1 Pet 3:21). This salvation announced in the gospel and proclaimed by the apostles is one and the same word of God attested in Holy Scripture. And as it is written in Hebrews, "the word of God is living and active, sharper than any two-edged sword, piercing to the division of soul and spirit, of joints and marrow, and discerning the thoughts and intentions of the heart" (4:12). The previous chapter outlined how, so long as the apostles and their deputies lived, the preaching of the gospel as the living word of God continued without obstacle. In the wake of their passing, however, the need arose for apostolic proclamation to continue; and not only to continue, but to endure for all generations. As St. Peter says elsewhere in Acts, "there is salvation in no one else, for there is no other name under heaven given among men by which we must be saved" (4:12). Yet St. Paul asks the right questions:

> But how are men to call upon him in whom they have not be
> lieved? And how are they to believe in him of whom they have
> never heard? And how are they to hear without a preacher? And
> how can men preach unless they are sent? As it is written, "How
> beautiful are the feet of those who preach good news!" But they
> have not all obeyed the gospel; for Isaiah says, "Lord, who has
> believed what he has heard from us?" So faith comes from what
> is heard, and what is heard comes by the preaching of Christ.
> (Rom 10:14–17)

Faith comes from what is heard, and what the church hears in its mission, now, is the voice of the apostles committed to writing. Together "with the sacred writings" of Israel, these "are able to make you wise for salvation through faith in Christ Jesus" (2 Tim 3:15 ESV). In all the many centuries since, the church, like the Jewish believers of Phoenicia and Samaria hearing the testimony of St. Paul and St. Barnabas, has celebrated with wonder and thanksgiving "the conversion of the nations" (Acts 15:3 YLT).[13] This

---

13. The response is not limited to believers. Orthodox Jewish theologian Michael

Spirit-wrought miracle is the triumph of that great missionary volume, the scriptures of Old and New Testament. Repurposing the summative words of the Gospel of St. John: "these [were] written that you may believe that Jesus is the Christ, the Son of God, and that believing you may have life in his name" (20:31). Life in Christ's name is "eternal life" (3:14–16, 36; 4:14, 36; 17:2), for Christ just is "the eternal life . . . made manifest to us" (1 John 1:2). By the power of the Holy Spirit, the church's canon of Holy Scripture offers and confers this very life,[14] not only in the age to come (John 6:40; 10:28; 12:25; cf. Mark 8:36; 10:30; Heb 6:5) but here and now, in the present age (John 6:47; 5:24; 17:3; cf. Acts 2:47; Eph 1:21; 1 Cor 1:18; 2 Cor 1:21–22; 2:15; Gal 1:4).

3. Following Christ: Instruction and Edification

St. Mark narrates the calling of the first disciples with characteristic economy:

> And passing along by the Sea of Galilee, he saw Simon and Andrew the brother of Simon casting a net in the sea; for they were fishermen. And Jesus said to them, "Follow me and I will make you become fishers of men." And immediately they left their nets and followed him. And going on a little farther, he saw James the son of Zebedee and John his brother, who were in their boat mending the nets. And immediately he called them; and they left their father Zebedee in the boat with the hired servants, and followed him. (1:16–20)

But the passage, broken off at this point in some Bibles by a separate chapter heading, continues: "And they went into Capernaum; and immediately on the Sabbath he entered the synagogue and taught. And they were astonished at his teaching, for he taught them as one who had authority, and not as the scribes" (vv. 21–22). What follows is a demonstration of Jesus's power to cast out unclean spirits (vv. 23–28) and to heal the sick (vv. 29–31). The amazement of onlookers finds expression in the question, "What is this? A new teaching! With authority he commands even the unclean spirits, and they obey him" (v. 27). Jesus's instruction is inseparable from his power; his

---

Wyschogrod writes, "Can anything but joy fill the heart of Israel as it observes the mysterious way in which the God of Israel begins to be heard by the nations?" (*Abraham's Promise*, 183).

14. Inasmuch as the scriptures "bear witness to" Christ, of whom St. Peter confesses, "You have the words of eternal life" (John 5:39; 6:68). Offered this gift, all those who ask for it will be "given . . . living water," becoming by faith "a spring . . . welling up to eternal life" (4:10, 14). For "he who hears my word and believes him who sent me, has eternal life" (5:24), since the One who sent the Son is the Father, and "his commandment is eternal life" (12:50).

authority to teach is one and the same as his authority over malign forces that threaten the life of Israel. His authority, in other words, is divine: this rabbi is the Son of God (1:11), who on earth does what only the Father in heaven can do: forgive sins (2:5–11).[15]

The authority Jesus has from the Father he confers upon his disciples, sending first the Twelve (Matt 10:5—11:1) then the Seventy (Luke 10:1–24) into all Israel to proclaim the kingdom in word and deed. After his resurrection from the dead, the Lord then deputizes his apostles once for all until his return: "All authority in heaven and on earth has been given to me. Go therefore and make disciples of all nations, baptizing them in the name of the Father and of the Son and of the Holy Spirit, teaching them to observe all that I have commanded you; and lo, I am with you always, to the close of the age" (Matt 28:18–20).[16] Baptism initiates believers into the life of Christ through the gift of his Spirit, and teaching guides them in the way of Christ as they journey from death to life beyond death. The opening chapters of Acts depict this dynamic of baptism, instruction, and fellowship in Christ's Spirit. The first to respond to St. Peter's preaching "devoted themselves to the apostles' teaching and fellowship, to the breaking of bread and the prayers" (2:42). The apostles arouse the ire of the priests and the Sadducees "because they were teaching the people and proclaiming in Jesus the resurrection from the dead" (4:2). So threatened were they that "they called them and charged them not to speak or teach at all in the name of Jesus" (v. 18). But this would be to forsake the apostolic mandate; thus St. Peter and St. John answer them, "Whether it is right in the sight of God to listen to you rather than to God, you must judge; for we cannot but speak of what we

15. The ongoing concern with Jesus's authority in the opening chapters of St. Mark's Gospel pairs well with similar passages in St. John's; the latter offer a more extended theological gloss on the former. See, for example, the following passage spoken by Jesus: "Truly, truly, I say to you, the hour is coming, and now is, when the dead will hear the voice of the Son of God, and those who hear will live. For as the Father has life in himself, so he has granted the Son also to have life in himself, and has given him authority to execute judgment, because he is the Son of man. Do not marvel at this; for the hour is coming when all who are in the tombs will hear his voice and come forth, those who have done good, to the resurrection of life, and those who have done evil, to the resurrection of judgment" (5:25–29; cf. vv. 30–47; 7:14–24; 8:21–30). The authority of Jesus is derivative, inasmuch as it comes from the Father; but this derivation speaks not to the subordinate or incomplete quality of Jesus's authority but rather to its source in God and thus its completeness in Jesus's person and work: for the life of the Son comes from the Father, but as "from" him, it is the gift of having life—divine life—"in himself." It is the unity, perfection, and transparency of the Son's relationship to the Father that defines both who he is and what he does on earth. The same, *mutatis mutandis*, goes for Jesus's identity and ministry in the Synoptics.

16. See further chapter 6, in which I develop this line with respect to apostolic and ecclesial authority.

have seen and heard" (vv. 19–20). Undeterred by threats and beatings, the apostles "every day in the temple and at home . . . did not cease teaching and preaching Jesus as the Christ" (5:42).

This ceaseless instruction in the knowledge and way of Jesus Messiah is one of the ends of Holy Scripture. For Scripture consists of the apostles and prophets, who together tell of the gospel. The former hand it on by word of mouth and by writing (cf. 1 Cor 15:1–11); the latter foretell of it in advance, as St. Paul writes, having himself been "set apart for the gospel of God which [God] promised beforehand through his prophets in the holy scriptures" (Rom 1:1–2; cf. 3:21). In the wake of the apostles' passing, the church depends upon their teaching in every generation, across vast expanses of time and place. That is what the Bible is for: to teach the gospel anew to the church, to maintain its faith in the good news of Christ. But as we have seen, the scriptures are not *merely* the written record of now-long-dead human beings, however great and esteemed they might be. Those departed souls—not dead but alive in Christ (Phil 1:21; 2 Cor 5:1–10; 1 Thess 4:13–18), for the God of Abraham, Isaac, and Jacob is the God not of the dead but of the living (Matt 22:32)—were and, by grace, remain the servants and instruments of the living word of God.

The prophets and apostles are therefore the church's teachers in perpetuity. What of the One whose word they teach? Who is the divine pedagogue of the Lord's people?

On the one hand, it is Jesus himself. He whom the apostles saw alive after death confirms that he is indeed both "Lord and Teacher" (John 13:13–14). Yet as St. Paul says, "the Lord is the Spirit" (2 Cor 3:17). On the other hand, then, it is also the Spirit who teaches. Jesus expands on this matter in his final discourse with the disciples before being handed over to the authorities: "These things I have spoken to you, while I am still with you. But the Counselor, the Holy Spirit, whom the Father will send in my name, he will teach you all things, and bring to your remembrance all that I have said to you" (John 14:25–26). Both Jesus and the Spirit act as teacher, therefore, since the Spirit of Jesus only speaks what he hears from the Son, just as the Son only speaks what he hears from the Father (5:19–20; 12:49; 15:15; 16:13–15). This dynamic continues in the life of the church across time through the collection of Old and New Testaments. Scripture is thus the medium—not the exclusive but the principal and unassailable medium—of the unified teaching of Christ and the Spirit, themselves the two hands of God the Father.[17] He, the triune Lord, is the sovereign teacher of the church; the canon is the embassy of his manifest will.

---

17. See, e.g., St. Irenaeus, *Against Heresies* 4.20.1; 5.28.4.

It is for this reason that we find over and again the insatiable refrain of the Psalms: "Teach me" (25:4–5; 27:11; 51:6; 86:11; 143:8, 10). Psalm 119 is nothing if not one long sustained plea that "he who teaches men knowledge" (94:10; cf. 1 Sam 2:3) would draw near to this student of Torah—and hence to Israel—and reveal to him, tutor him in, the wise ways of the Lord (119:12, 26, 29, 33, 64, 66, 68, 108, 124, 135, 171). This petition, notably, is not for direct or immediate instruction, but for the Lord to teach the student *in* and *by means of* Torah; the implement of doctrine is "your law," "your statutes," "your ordinances," "the way of your statutes," "good judgment and knowledge" (vv. 29, 26, 108, 33, 66). The divine pedagogy, in short, is mediated: to know the Lord is to know his *torah*; to learn *torah* is to be instructed by the Lord from whose mouth *torah* proceeds. From, not apart from, knowledge of the law comes "good judgment" (v. 66). Consider a telling couplet. The psalmist prays, "Make your face shine upon your servant." How? He continues: ". . . and teach me your statutes" (v. 135). That is, "make your face shine upon me *by* teaching me your statutes." We read elsewhere in the Law that the Lord's blessing—the bestowal of his grace and peace—means his face turned, radiantly, toward a person (Num 6:24–26). But here, in the Psalmist's prayer, we learn that the shalom of God comes by means of studying the Law of the Lord: "Blessed is the man . . . whom you teach out of your law" (Ps 94:12). The light of the Lord's face shines from, in, and through the signs of the sacred page that bear the Lord's word to his people. To attend with care, humility, and prayer to those signs, therefore, is not only to find the Lord there, to hear his voice. It is to be taught by him, and thus to be blessed by him. Making the necessary changes, the same goes for the Christian reader of Holy Scripture.

The teaching of Scripture is itself directed to a particular end. On the one hand, as we saw above, the knowledge we receive from Scripture is saving knowledge, for it is knowledge of the Lord God. (In the final section below we will discuss further the nature of this knowledge as intimate communion with the Holy Trinity.) On the other hand, if the ultimate end of Scripture's pedagogy is beatitude, its proximate end is defined by St. Paul as *edification:* the building up of the church in faith, hope, and love. This is why St. Augustine can propose that any interpretation of Scripture that does not lead to love of God or neighbor is, just in virtue of that fact, a reading to be spurned. The converse holds as well: no interpretation that *does* lead to such love is to be scorned, though it may be gently guided toward a more preferable exegetical procedure that sublates the original interpretation without rejecting it.[18] Over all the activities of the church, not least

18. See St. Augustine, *De Doctrina* 1.36.41. See my qualification and extension of

in the liturgical assembly, St. Paul provides the governing rule: "since you are eager for manifestations of the Spirit, strive to excel in building up the church" (1 Cor 14:12). But "the most excellent way" (12:31 NIV) is that of love, which surpasses even faith and hope (13:13). And since "he who loves his neighbor has fulfilled the law," for "love is the fulfilling of the law" (Rom 13:8, 10), the measure of behavior in the church is that which builds up one's sister or brother in Christ: "Let all things be done for edification" (1 Cor 14:26). The church is the family of Jesus whose God is his and their *abba*: "Everyone who believes that Jesus is the Christ is a child of God, and everyone who loves the parent loves the child" (1 John 5:1). But "he who does not love his brother whom he has seen, cannot love God whom he has not seen. And this commandment we have from him, that he who loves God should love his brother also" (4:20–21).

This, too, is what Scripture is for. More precisely, it is what the knowledge that comes by Scripture's teaching is for. Scriptures makes us disciples of Christ. It keeps us as disciples, too, by the Lord's word continually venturing forth from his sacred temple, that is, the canon of Old and New Testaments. In this respect we listen to Numbers and Job and Hebrews, Habakkuk and Esther and Colossians, with a single aim in mind: as the company of disciples—as pupils in the school of Christ—to follow him more faithfully. As individuals, however, we listen and read not only to walk more closely "in step with the Spirit" of Christ (Gal 5:25 ESV), but to help our sisters and brothers in their walk, too. For we are "the household of faith" (6:10) and thus "the household of God" (Eph 2:19; 1 Tim 3:15; 4:17). The canon contains the house rules, the parental will for the children's flourishing. If we use it against our siblings, we are not only contradicting the purpose of the scriptures, abusing them to gratify ourselves while hurting those "for whom Christ died" (Rom 14:15; 1 Cor 8:11). Even more, we are provoking the Lord's anger (cf. Deut 9:1–29; 1 Cor 10:1–22). For judgment begins with the house of God (1 Pet 4:17). Doubtless this is why those "who teach shall be judged with greater strictness" (Jas 3:1). As Jesus warns, "whoever causes one of these little ones who believe in me to sin, it would be better for him to have a great millstone fastened round his neck and to be drowned in the depth of the sea" (Matt 18:6).

"All scripture is . . . profitable for teaching" (2 Tim 3:16), therefore, but it is for the sake of love that Scripture teaches at all. That is, it teaches "the truth in love, [that we may] grow up in every way into him who is the head, into Christ" (Eph 4:15). Scripture requires living teachers, however, to transmit it to the faithful. That is why Christ gifts "some" to be "pastors and

---

this principle in "Standards of Excellence."

teachers," namely, "to equip the saints for the work of ministry, for building up the body of Christ, until we attain to the unity of the faith and of the knowledge of the Son of God" (vv. 11–13). Woe to them, accordingly, who forsake the end of love and misuse their office to harm even one hair on the head of Christ's beloved. For his beloved is his bride and body (Eph 5:25–32). Though it is not ours to avenge, it is his (Rom 12:19). Not in vain does Israel name him a "God of vengeance" (Ps 94:1).

4. Imaging Christ: Sanctification and Perseverance

Scripture is salutary: it converts us by God's saving grace, which in turn draws us onward to the vision of God, the telos of our redemption. Scripture is edifying: it teaches us, on the journey, how to conduct ourselves as the people of God prior to our arrival at the city of God. But between our conversion and our destination—from our verbal instruction, in the present, to our final transformation, in the end[19]—what role does Scripture play? Or rather, how does the Spirit use Scripture not only to keep us on the path or to guide us in knowledge but to remake us, to render us fit as citizens-in-the-making for God's kingdom? We have seen how Scripture elicits faith and hope, salvation and wisdom. In what follows I will discuss its power to sanctify, and how in doing so, the love thus produced enables the saints to persevere to the last day.

This end of Scripture is no more separable from that of instruction than is justification from sanctification proper. But likewise a distinction is useful for the sake of understanding. Both the unity and the difference are most clearly seen in the canon by noting the role accorded the Lord's teaching, either spoken or written. Whether in Israel or in the church, the word of God acts at once extrinsically, as a kind of fence or guard for behavior, and intrinsically, as the inner renewal of the soul in undivided obedience to the divine will.[20] Let me sketch how this works across the testaments, before and after Christ, attuned to both the differences (the gift of the Spirit) and the similarities (the need for the scriptures) between them.

Consider Jeremiah 31, which proclaims the coming of "a new covenant," one unlike the Mosaic covenant (vv. 31–32). According to this new covenant, "says the LORD: I will put my law within them, and I will write

---

19. Or, in sacramental and therefore eschatological terms, from the baptismal circumcision of the soul to the final circumcision of the body: resurrection from the dead. For incisive theological reflection on circumcision as a practice and trope across the covenants, see Roberts, "Rite of Circumcision."

20. See the discussion of the uses of the Law in Calvin, *Institutes* 2.7.1–17.

it upon their hearts; and I will be their God, and they shall be my people" (v. 33). The same prophet, earlier in the book, calls on Israel to "remove the foreskin of your hearts" (4:4), which echoes the promise spoken at the end of Deuteronomy. There Moses foresees that, after the deliverance from exile, "the LORD your God will circumcise your heart and the heart of your offspring, so that you will love the LORD your God with all your heart and all your soul, that you may live" (30:6). For Jeremiah, there is a further epistemic consequence to this inward renewal: "no longer shall each man teach his neighbor and each his brother, saying, 'Know the LORD,' for they shall all know me, from the least of them to the greatest, says the LORD; for I will forgive their iniquity, and I will remember their sin no more" (31:34).

These prophecies are fulfilled in Jesus Christ, as St. Paul writes: "For all the promises of God find their Yes in him. That is why we utter the Amen through him, to the glory of God" (2 Cor 1:20). But while the new covenant has been established and the messianic age inaugurated, the latter is not yet consummated. So, on the one hand, the Corinthian believers "are a letter from Christ delivered by [the apostles], written not with ink but with the Spirit of the living God, not on tablets of stone but on tablets of human hearts" (3:3). For the apostles have been commissioned and empowered by God "to be ministers of a new covenant, not of letter but of spirit; for the letter kills, but the Spirit gives life" (v. 6 NRSV). So radical is the difference between old and new covenants that the former, apart from Christ, veils the mind from beholding the Lord's glory (vv. 12–16). But freedom comes through Christ's life-giving Spirit (v. 17): "And all of us, with unveiled faces, seeing the glory of the Lord as though reflected in a mirror, are being transformed into the same image from one degree of glory to another; for this comes from the Lord, the Spirit" (v. 18 NRSV).

On the other hand, St. Paul writes here to a community beset by every kind of backsliding, temptation, foolishness, and sin. They are not Joshua in the promised land. They are the disobedient generation in the wilderness, liberated from slavery but begging to turn back (cf. 1 Cor 10:1–13). The apostle does not mince words:

> I feel a divine jealousy for you, for I betrothed you to Christ to present you as a pure bride to her one husband. But I am afraid that as the serpent deceived Eve by his cunning, your thoughts will be led astray from a sincere and pure devotion to Christ. For if someone comes and preaches another Jesus than the one we preached, or if you receive a different spirit from the one you received, or if you accept a different gospel from the one you accepted, you submit to it readily enough. (2 Cor 11:2–4)

Now the experience of Israel in the wilderness "happened to them as a warning, but they were written down for our instruction" (1 Cor 10:11), as he says elsewhere: "whatever was written in former days was written for our instruction" (Rom 15:4).

In sum, the fulfillment of the Lord's promise to write his will on the hearts of his people in a new and final covenant is eschatologically differentiated. It is present in Christ here and now, but will be concluded upon his return: "I am sure that he who began a good work in you will bring it to completion at the day of Jesus Christ" (Phil 1:6). This is why the church needs more than "merely" the presence of the Spirit in its midst for knowledge and guidance. It needs all that was written formerly together with what was written by Messiah's emissaries. These writings become tools in the hand of the Spirit to enlighten the mind and, furthermore, to begin to refashion the soul in conformity to Jesus. Scripture, that is, contributes to our transformation into the image of Christ: "being renewed in knowledge after the image of [the] creator" (Col 3:10), "we shall . . . bear the image of the man of heaven" (1 Cor 15:49). This connection, between the seed of justifying faith and our final eschatological sanctification, is explicit in the closing prayer that St. Paul offers for the Thessalonians: "May the God of peace himself sanctify you wholly; and may your spirit and soul and body be kept sound and blameless at the coming of our Lord Jesus Christ" (1 Thess 5:23).[21]

Scripture is ingredient in this work. The Lord speaks in Scripture, and what he speaks is peace (Ps 85:8). This word of peace is at once the justice and the truth of God: "righteousness and peace will kiss each other" (v. 10); "your word is truth" (John 17:17b). By this truth, which is nothing else than the word God speaks in Scripture, Jesus prays that his disciples might be sanctified (v. 17a). His prayer is not limited in scope, either with respect to God's word or with respect to the disciples of whom he speaks. His prayer, rather, is for all his disciples: in the beautiful phrasing of the old Revised Standard Version, Jesus says, "I am not praying for the world but for those whom thou hast given me, for they are thine; all mine are thine, and thine are mine, and I am glorified in them" (vv. 9–10). Later he adds, "I do not pray for these only, but also for those who believe in me through their word" (v. 20). He prays for all of us.

---

21. This prayer, for the holiness of those called among the gentiles to belong to Israel's Messiah, echoes Rom 15:15–16, where the apostle writes "of the grace given me by God to be a minister of Christ Jesus to the Gentiles in the priestly service of the gospel of God, so that the offering of the Gentiles may be acceptable, sanctified by the Holy Spirit." In this way Scripture's end of sanctification implies its priestly nature as discussed in the final section of chapter 2 above.

Similarly, Jesus's prayer regarding God's word (*ho logos ho sos*) in or by which his disciples might be sanctified applies by extension to the canon as a whole: speaking of his disciples and of the apostolic message entrusted to them, Jesus prays, "thine they were, and thou gavest them to me, and they have kept thy word. Now they know that everything that thou hast given me is from thee; for I have given them the words which thou gavest me, and they have received them and know in truth that I came from thee; and they have believed that thou didst send me" (vv. 6–8). The word of the Lord thus forms a kind of sacred chain extending from the triune life into the ongoing life of God's people: from the Father to the Son in the Spirit, from the Son to the apostles by the Spirit, from the Spirit to future believers by the apostles, from the apostles to future generations by the Spirit's inspiration of the scriptures, from the scriptures to the faithful by the Spirit's work in the liturgy—and so on. The links in the chain are the moments at once of *traditio*, handing-on, and *missio*, sending (cf. v. 18). As the Son is set apart by the Father and the Spirit by the Father and the Son, so the church is set apart by the word of the blessed Three-in-One. That word resounds in the church's canon, and its efficacy is not limited to either the beginning or the end of our life in Christ. It accompanies us at every step, continuing the work of baptism, or rather, returning us to our baptism, the site of our cleansing from sin, the indwelling of the Holy Spirit, and the Lord's consecrating us for his purposes and his people (cf. Eph 5:25–27).[22] The holy word of the Holy Trinity proceeds from Holy Scripture, and by its power we are made holy, too.[23]

Our holiness—proleptic now, perfect then—is like a series of steps by which the Spirit, wielding the word of God, draws us upward to "the things that are above, where Christ is, seated at the right hand of God" (Col 3:1). For in Christ, "we who first hoped in Christ have been destined and appointed to live for the praise of his glory" (Eph 1:12). Our ascent up the ladder is not a matter of our effort or ability, however; it depends entirely on the promise and power of God: "In him you also, when you heard the word of

22. "Returning to one's baptism" is a distinctly Lutheran theme; see Luther, *Large Catechism* 4.1–84; Jenson, *Large Catechism*, 37–46.

23. "For this reason the baptism of our regeneration takes place through these three articles, granting us regeneration unto God the Father through His Son by the Holy Spirit: for those who bear the Spirit of God are led to the Word, that is to the Son, while the Son presents [them] to the Father, and the Father furnishes incorruptibility. Thus, without the Spirit it is not [possible] to see the Word of God, and without the Son one is not able to approach the Father; for the knowledge of the Father [is] the Son, and knowledge of the Son of God is through the Holy Spirit, while the Spirit, according to the good-pleasure of the Father, the Son administers, to whom the Father wills and as He wills": St. Irenaeus of Lyons, *On the Apostolic Preaching* 1.1.7.

truth, the gospel of your salvation, and believed in him, were sealed with the promised Holy Spirit, who is the guarantee of our inheritance until we acquire possession of it, to the praise of his glory" (vv. 13–14 ESV). The Spirit who sanctifies is the pledge of our perseverance, and the scriptures once again are ready to hand for the Spirit's use toward this end. When Hebrews 12:1 exhorts believers to "run with perseverance the race that is set before us," the "cloud of witnesses" to which it refers as those who surround us is as much a *textual* entity as it is a historical and spiritual group of persons. The preceding chapter, after all, which so famously recounts Israel's heroes of faith, is nothing but a series of midrashic glosses on the sacred scriptures (cf. 11:1–29). Knowledge of the communion of saints, memory of the great forebears in the faith, is dependent upon the canon, which preserves their memory and transmits that knowledge across time, to each new generation of the Lord's people.

St. John offers a comparable exhortation, drawing similar connections between perseverance, suffering, and written testimony. After an emboldening glimpse of the Lamb, triumphant on Mount Zion with his ranks of undefiled men (Rev 14:1–5), followed by a terrifying sight of angels announcing divine judgment and the torment of idolaters (vv. 6–11), the text pauses: "Here is a call for the endurance of the saints, those who keep the commandments of God and the faith of Jesus" (v. 12). The Seer goes on: "And I heard a voice from heaven saying, 'Write this: Blessed are the dead who die in the Lord henceforth.' 'Blessed indeed,' says the Spirit, 'that they may rest from their labors, for their deeds follow them!'" (v. 13). The voice of the Father joins with the voice of the Spirit to encourage the holy ones of Jesus in their long-suffering trials on earth. And how are they encouraged? *Graphon*, "write this": inscription. The opening chapter of Revelation confirms this purpose of the book: "I John, your brother, who share with you in Jesus the tribulation and the kingdom and the patient endurance, was on the island called Patmos on account of the word of God and the testimony of Jesus. I was in the Spirit on the Lord's day, and I heard behind me a loud voice like a trumpet saying, 'Write what you see in a book . . .'" (1:9–11). The Spirit of Jesus speaks to the prophet, who thereupon writes what he hears and sees for the sake of the church's perseverance among the nations, until the return of the One "who testifies to these things [and] says, 'Surely I am coming soon'" (22:20): no other summary could better encapsulate the nature and purpose of Scripture. It is thus fitting that Revelation concludes the New Testament and the Bible as a whole, for it is a microcosm of the canon itself. As a work of the Spirit, the canon, like Revelation, is shot through with the Spirit's breath (cf. 2 Tim 3:16), which is the power of God for "wisdom[and] righteousness and sanctification and redemption" (1 Cor 1:30). Scripture is thus the Spirit-breathed medium of our transformation in Christ, from "the womb of the font" to the womb of the tomb.[24] Through Scripture, in the awakening of faith, the Spirit presents us with Christ. Through Scripture, across the course of our lives, the Spirit forms us into Christ. Through Scripture, at the end, as a kind of verbal viaticum, the Spirit brings us to Christ. In each and every moment, the word of God in Scripture not only lights the path before us but renovates our hearts within us, ensuring our arrival. And lest we fear, wondering whether we will fall away, we have the witness of the Spirit for consolation. He testifies, through the written testimony of the beloved disciple regarding the spoken testimony of Jesus the Messiah, that none will be lost: "I give them eternal life, and they will never perish, and no one will snatch them out of my hand" (John 10:28).

5. Knowing Christ: Communion and Contemplative Delight

The end of Scripture, as we have seen, is the knowledge of Christ. But what it means to know Christ is neither simple nor self-evident. It is certainly not a matter of mere information: knowledge *about*; objective, third-person knowledge. No, the knowledge of Christ is *conjugal knowledge*.[25] As a man who is joined to his wife becomes one flesh with her, so a believer "who is united to the Lord becomes one spirit with him" (1 Cor 6:17). In this way marriage is a figure and sacrament of Christ's love for his church, who is the bride to his bridegroom and thus, through the mystery of their union, his own body (Eph 5:25–32): "bone of my bones, and flesh of my flesh" (Gen 2:23). To speak of knowing Christ, or rather of being known by him (Gal 4:9), is to evoke a scriptural grammar that goes back to Eden: "Now Adam knew his wife, and she conceived . . ." (Gen 4:1). Unlike that first pairing, however, the eschatological wedding is not east of Eden but is itself the marriage of heaven and earth, the union of divinity and humanity, the nuptial feast of the Lord and his people in a transfigured creation on the far side of our presumptuous desire for the knowledge of good and evil (Rev 19–22). Life in this new and unsurpassable Eden means the perpetual dwelling of Immanuel in the form of a new Adam and a new Eve: that is, Jesus together with his bride, the latter comprising the innumerable multitude of Jews and gentiles betrothed to the Lord by faith in his name. (These in turn are

24. The phrase, a common patristic trope, come from St. Gregory of Narek, *Festal Works*, 115. For liturgical and artistic discussion, see Jensen, *Baptismal Imagery*.

25. For wider discussion, see Johnson, *Knowledge by Ritual*; Johnson, *Scripture's Knowing*.

personified by Mary, virgin mother of God and man alike, and therefore spiritual mother "of all the living" [Gen 3:20 NIV], namely, of all God's children adopted by grace; see John 19:25–27; Rev 12:1–6.)

If the Apocalypse of St. John comprehends the canon's form or rationale, then the Song of Songs that is Solomon's contains its matter or heart. Like the Holy of Holies, the Song of Songs is the inner sanctum of Holy Scripture: the canon within the canon, the book of books, the *typos* of that book which is unlike all others. It is the textual site of the conjugal knowledge of Israel's God. As the site of that knowledge, it is also the means thereof. We learn the Lord there, even as we learn there how to learn the Lord elsewhere. We follow the sequences of passion, desire, yearning, satisfaction, frustration, all disordered and cyclical, and thereby we glimpse the way of sinners with a holy and jealous God. The beloved speaks for us, even as the song is sung by the Holy One himself; or perhaps we should say, with St. Augustine, that like the Psalms, it is always Christ who speaks in the Song, either as the head or as the body—either, that is, as the bridegroom-lover, or as the bride-beloved.[26] This is the way of Scripture writ large, the voice of Christ reaching out to us, his chosen, his treasured possession, through the words of others, of fellow beloveds like ourselves. What we are for is what Scripture is here revealed to be for: intimate, total, exclusive, and delightful communion with the triune God of Israel.

This is one way of describing the final beatitude toward which Scripture conducts us. But communion with the Trinity is not only far off. It is available today, at least in part, through those eschatological transparencies we call sacraments. Scripture functions similarly, as we have seen. And so it is wholly appropriate to say that Scripture is a means of our fellowship with the Lord Christ: through our hearing and reading of the text, Christ establishes not only a master-servant or teacher-student relationship, but above all a lover-beloved relationship as well. We commune with him when we hear his voice, and we hear his voice when we give ourselves over to the sacred words of his servants. This is what the Song invites us to see: the rapture of sheer pleasure that ought to characterize our reception of Scripture. Using the figural language of the Song, Paul Griffiths describes the Bible as "the Lord's verbal kiss," that is, "a complex verbal caress with which the Lord delights and instructs his people, a kiss that he places upon his people's lips."[27] Griffiths goes on, in a comment on the book's opening verses, to gloss the work of Christ using the idiom of the Song while reinterpreting

26. See St. Augustine, *Expositions on the Psalms*; for discussion, see Byassee, *Praise Seeking Understanding*. See also Origen, *Song of Songs*; St. Gregory of Nyssa, *Song of Songs*; and Turner, *Eros and Allegory*.

27. Griffiths, *Song of Songs*, xxvii.

the crucifixion in connection with Communion: "The Lord's death on the cross is the deepest kiss of humanity's unclean lips . . . extending to all the embrace given to Abraham. Christians reciprocate this kiss most fully here below in drinking the blood-red wine of the Eucharist. The stain of that wine on our lips is the mark of the Lord's blood on our bodies; it is also the mark of his lips on ours, cleaning them with the purifying flame of his passion."[28]

It is no accident that monastic life is the location and model of unguarded intimacy with Christ through the Song and, in turn, through the rest of Scripture. In the lives of monks and nuns—those we later come to call mystics[29]—we come to see that Scripture is not primarily a didactic, discursive, or scholarly text. It is a spiritual book for spiritual persons: those given to know the mind of the Spirit of God (cf. 1 Cor 2:6–16). The way to know Scripture, therefore, is one and the same as the way to know the Song: saturation, meditation, solitude, silence. Spiritual exegesis, in other words. For in the case of the Song, there is no proposition waiting at the end of the interpretive task,[30] no doctrinal payoff.[31] It is just the Lord. The ecstasy of contemplation is finding him—finding *him*—and delighting in nothing else. In this way the faithful reader of the Song exemplifies faithful reading of Scripture as a whole: defined, from beginning to end, by the acclamation, the exultation, the unashamed exclamation: "Whom have I in heaven but you? And there is nothing upon earth that I desire besides you. My flesh and my heart may fail, but God is the rock of my heart and my portion forever" (Ps 73:25–26).

The voice of the Song speaks for all God's people. "I am my beloved's, and his desire is for me": thus the Christian soul, thus the bride of Christ (Song 7:10). "Come, my beloved, let us go forth into the fields. . . . There I will give you my love" (v. 12). The Psalmist is equally breathless, approaching the Lord with a famished heart: "As a deer pants for flowing streams, so pants my soul for you, O God. My soul thirsts for God, for the living God" (Ps 42:1–2 ESV). It is just this posture on the part of Israel, one of commingled need and unsated desire, that ought to mark the baptized before the Bible. From the text they—we all—hear the summons announced by the Lord: "Come, everyone who thirsts, come to the waters; and he who has no

28. Griffiths, *Song of Songs*, 8; cf. 10–11. I quote these two sentences to similar effect in "Reading the Trinity," 473.

29. E.g., St. Hildegard of Bingen, *Scivias*; Julian of Norwich, *Revelations*; St. Catherine of Siena, *Dialogue*; St. Thérèse of Lisieux, *Story of a Soul*.

30. Not a proposition, but a proposal: the betrothal of the Lord's beloved to himself.

31. Not least as a coded handbook for the ideal Christian marriage in the late modern West.

money, come, buy and eat! Come, buy wine and milk without money and without price" (Isa 55:1 ESV); and again: "whoever drinks of the water that I shall give him will never thirst; the water that I shall give him will become in him a spring of water welling up to eternal life" (John 7:14); and once more: "let him who is thirsty come, let him who desires take the water of life without price" (Rev 22:17). It is with these glad tidings ringing in our ears that we run to the scriptures, drinking our fill at the trough of Christ,[32] longing to be sated but knowing we never will be in this life.

For now, here below, Holy Scripture is for the church a figure—a sacramental anticipation—of "the tree of life with its twelve kinds of fruit" growing "on either side" of "the river of the water of life" (Rev 22:2, 1).[33] The fellowship that awaits us, in the city where the river flows from "the throne of God and of the Lamb . . . and his servants shall worship him," where "they shall see his face, and his name shall be on their foreheads," where "the Lord God will be their light, and they shall reign forever and ever" (vv. 3–5): then and there, communion will be complete; what is begun in this life will, at long last, be consummated. "And so we will be with the Lord forever" (1 Thess 4:17 NIV). Until that time, alongside the church's other devotional and liturgical practices, the book of the apostles and prophets draws us forward into that city, or rather, reaches back into our mundane affairs with its red-stained fruit and healing leaves, and offers us a taste of what is to come. These servants of God, now saints in glory, speak backwards and forwards in time at once, and their message is the same as it ever was. It is nothing less than the Spirit's standing invitation: "Oh, taste and see that the LORD is good!" (Ps 34:8 ESV; cf. 1 Pet 2:3).

32. Figured by Christ in Bethlehem, on whose flesh we feed as animals feed in a manger.

33. Continuing the figural reading, let us say that the river of life signifies Christ, watering each "side," or covenant, of the selfsame city of God; each side therefore figures a Testament of one and the same canonical scriptures. And just as the number of elders surrounding the throne is twenty-four, so here the twelve kinds of fruit are present on both sides of the messianic river. So that on one side it is the sons of Jacob and thus the tribes of Israel (or the Law and the Prophets and the Writings), whereas on the other it is the apostles of Jesus and thus the fruit of the mission to the nations (the Gospels and Epistles and Apocalypse)—all united in the person of the Son, himself the seed of Abraham, Isaac, and Jacob, of David and Solomon, of Ruth and Bathsheba, of Adam and finally of God.

5

Interpretation

There is no one right way to read the Bible. That is the first thing to say about
interpreting Scripture. There are as many fitting ways to read the Bible as
there are ends of the Bible; indeed, there are as many fitting ways to read
the Bible as there are occasions and persons to do such reading. That does
not mean there are no unfitting ways to read the Bible. It only means that to

exclude some does not mean to exclude all but one, or only a handful. That would presume a finite number of ways of reading the Bible. On the contrary, "we have no warrant for putting a limit to the sense of words which are not human but divine."[1] And if the sense is unlimited, then so are the ways by which to arrive at it. Like other complex activities—especially games: chess, basketball, tennis—there are rules, norms, and predictable patterns. But there is always development and innovation within the ongoing tradition of the practice.[2] We will never reach a time when the possibilities of chess are exhausted, or when a coach can no longer draw up a new out-of-bounds set play. So for interpreting Scripture: new ways of reading, new readings *of* Scripture, will continue so long as Scripture endures in the church. Which is to say, until the End.

The reason, then, that the church gives attention to strategies of scriptural interpretation is not because there is a very short list of "correct" strategies, possibly consisting of a single entry. It does not stem from an anxious need to specify in advance "the" "right" way to read the Bible. The reason, instead, is quite practical and straightforward. It is to help the church's members in their reading, whether they be teachers or laypersons, so that they might successfully accomplish their various goals in accordance with the multiple ends of Scripture. Theological hermeneutics, on this view, is less like a referee during game play (making its presence known only in moments of violation), and more like a combination of two roles: that of coach or manager, on the one hand, and that of a rules committee for a sports league, on the other. The former exists for the sake of the players and their several individual and common ends: to set this screen here, to trap that guard there, to coordinate a play to score within the shot clock. The coach does not control: she instructs, encourages, rebukes, guides, models, commands—from the sidelines, or before or after live play. If a player improvises within the scheme drawn up by the coach, or in the wake of a scheme's failed execution, the virtuous coach applauds rather than scolds: that is just what the player ought to do, *so long as* the improvisation serves the larger ends of the team. Which is to say, so long as the improvisation is wise. A coach exists to make her players wise; the supremely wise player renders her coach redundant,[3] because she has so internalized the coach's mind, in conjunction with her own skill and intelligence, that she knows the right thing to do

---

1. St. John Henry Newman, *Development*, 106.

2. See, e.g., MacIntyre, *After Virtue*; MacIntyre, *Three Rival Versions*.

3. In theory, not in practice, since all sports, even basketball, are postlapsarian. Though perhaps the ideal of the player-sage is found in the player-coach, à la Bill Russell, or a director directing himself as an actor, à la Clint Eastwood.

at the right time in the right way, in accordance with the ultimate aim of her team: winning the game.[4]

That is what the church's reflection on faithful exegesis of Scripture is like. Through instruction, encouragement, rebuke, guidance, example, and command, the church seeks to form wise readers of Scripture in accordance with the several ends of Scripture, in service to the final end of both Scripture and the church: the glorious felicity of God's triune life.

The church acts as more than coach, though. Whereas the referee calls the shots moment to moment during a game, the rules committee makes adjustments to the rulebook itself on an occasional, usually annual, basis. In the form of its teaching office and, closer to the ground, its ordained pastors, the church gathers the wisdom of all that it has observed across the centuries and identifies, sometimes sharply, those lines that must not be crossed. This is the negative function of a rule: to break it is to transgress, to have done something one ought not to do. There is, the church teaches, transgression in exegesis. But there is also a positive function of the church's hermeneutical rulebook. On the one hand, it presents plentiful examples of what counts as acceptable or good "play," and examples are just what is needed in order to know how to go on in any practice, including biblical interpretation.[5] On the other hand, much is left unspecified, precisely because, so long as one is playing within the rules, there is no violation and thus no transgression. Freedom is only freedom within limits, and like the rules committee for a sport—after all, there would be no sport were there no rules—the church provides the boundaries within which the liberty of the Christian reader of Scripture flourishes. Nor is the potential infinity of faithful readings and ways of reading hampered by such boundaries: their existence makes the reading determinate rather than formless, empty, and void.

This chapter is about hard-won wisdom and trustworthy rules for faithful Christian interpretation of Holy Scripture. Built on the theological foundation of chapters 1–3, it looks backward to chapter 4, which outlines the ends of Scripture, and forward to chapter 6, which treats the authority of Scripture in relation to the authority of the church as its interpreter. So the cumulative case is building, but will not be complete until the book's conclusion. As for what follows: The first section defines terms that are often used or understood in different ways in theological hermeneutics. The second section focuses on liturgy and devotion as the primary public and

---

4. For wisdom and improvisation in theological reasoning, see Treier, *Virtue*; Treier, *Theological Interpretation*; Vanhoozer, *Drama of Doctrine*; Vanhoozer, *Faith Speaking Understanding*; Ford, *Christian Wisdom*; Wells, *Improvisation*. Cf. Young, *Art of Performance*.

5. See further Wittgenstein, *Philosophical Investigations*.

private spheres of scriptural reading—lest we be inclined to think first of the study or the classroom.[6] Here I also discuss the character of the reader herself. The third section addresses hermeneutical principles for reading Scripture, including reasons why reconstruction of the original human authorial intention of the text need not control Christian interpretation. The fourth section continues this latter topic by discussing the goods and ends of historiographic investigation into the Bible while distinguishing it from the ideological shibboleths of modern historical criticism.

1. A Hermeneutical Lexicon

Much confusion attends discussion of biblical interpretation due to imprecision in the definition and use of terms. My own understanding of the terms that follow is largely traditional, but at times it is idiosyncratic. That cannot be helped, not least since some of the terms are so controverted. One can but stipulate and hope to be consistent.

"Reading," "interpretation," and "exegesis," whether in verbal or nominal form, are synonymous in my usage. They may seem more or less proper to a certain sentence given their resonance, but I do not mean them to denote different activities. To read, interpret, or exegete—or, importantly, to hear or hearken to—a text is to make sense of its signs in accordance with the hermeneutical conventions and aims of the community to which one belongs, the character of the text one is engaging, and the questions or interests one has brought to the encounter.

"The reader" denotes the individual engaging the text in whatever form or fashion—a person understood to be among the baptized, that is, a Christian. "Reading-as-activity" means the practice of reading; "reading-as-product" means the resulting proposal of one fitting way to understand or receive a text: the interpretation, not the deed of interpreting.

"History" is whatever happened in the past; "historical" refers that which it modifies to whatever happened in the past. "Historiography" is human or scholarly construction or reconstruction of whatever happened in the past.[7] "Historical criticism" is a contingent set of presuppositions and

---

6. Or, God forgive us, the university. In the opening sequence of *Indiana Jones and the Last Crusade*, a rain-drenched Harrison Ford growls at a villain regarding a treasured artifact, "It *belongs* in a *museum!*" (To which the villain duly replies: "So do you!") Think of this chapter as well as the book as a whole as one long gruff assertion of the same regarding Scripture: It *belongs* in the *church!*

7. It will be seen below that this term and its variants are cumbersome. That is part of the point: to undercut our too-easy recourse to what are finally, and frankly, equivocal uses of "history" and "historical" in biblical scholarship. For example, although N. T.

procedures for determining both the original historical meaning (or range of plausible such meanings) of an ancient text and, in relation to what the text depicts or narrates, what really happened then and there (or, by likelihood, the most probable plausible range of options). These presuppositions and procedures rose to prominence in the eighteenth and nineteenth centuries and were codified by the twentieth, though they continue to evolve and are always in dispute.[8] The "historical-critical sense" means the reading proposed by a practitioner from this methodological family. It does not mean the correct, true, or sole meaning of the text or account of the history "behind" the text's production or narration. Nor is it synonymous with "historical" reading considered generally, either premodern, modern, or postmodern. The attention given by, for example, Origen or St. Jerome to historical matters in interpretation is not what historical criticism names, nor is historical criticism merely a development of such attention (given wider scope, say, or greater depth of rigor). More on this in the last section.[9]

The "plain sense" names, not a neutral or a historical meaning, but the Christian interpretive practice of reading the way the canonical words run, that is, remaining at the surface of the text and attending to the letter. "The letter" refers to the lexical, grammatical, semantic, and other features of the passage's words just as they stand, in their ordinary signification.[10] Now, "ordinary signification" includes but is not limited to the historically or authorially plausible, for this hermeneutic is a Christian practice of reading the canon qua canon: it remains God's word, and the reader rightly expects God to speak in and through the plain sense, *in the context* of the larger whole of Scripture. A Christian reader reading for the plain sense of Genesis 3 or Genesis 12 or the Psalms will produce different readings than Jews or biblical scholars reading the same texts (in accordance with their own—rabbinic or historical-critical— conventions, commitments, and aims). A Christian reader who understands Genesis 3 to depict "the fall"

Wright spends a whole chapter in *History and Eschatology* stipulating his multiple but distinct intended meanings for "history" (73–127), in practice he wields the term in consistently confusing and unclear ways.

8. See now Legaspi, *Death of Scripture.*

9. See further my "Hermeneutics," as well as, e.g., Levering, *Biblical Exegesis*; Rae, *History and Hermeneutics*; Williams, "Historical Criticism"; Plantinga, "Scripture Scholarship"; van Inwagen, "Critical Studies." Against this paragraph, see Barton, *Biblical Criticism*; cf. Watson, "Historical Criticism." For nuanced treatment of historiography, theological interests in interpretation, and academic biblical scholarship, see Bockmuehl, *Seeing the Word*; Moberly, *Bible, Theology, and Faith*; Sarisky, *Reading the Bible.*

10. "The way the words run" is a translation of a phrase in St. Thomas Aquinas's *De Potentia* by David Yeago, quoted in Rogers, "Virtues," 74n.22, and popularized by its use in Ayres, *Nicaea*, 32.

is not (yet) reading spiritually or figurally; she need not name Christ, or find him in the seed of Eve who will trample the head of the serpent. She is merely reading canonically for the plain sense, in the same way that a reader of a novel, on a second reading, will see new things or understand characters more deeply in virtue of knowing the full story.[11] Such a reader is not engaging in allegory. The same goes for the Christian reader of the plain sense of Holy Scripture.[12]

The "spiritual sense" names the inner depths, the multitude of potential meanings, for which the church reads Scripture as God's word. These depths, in all their variety, derive from and are upheld by the singularity of Scripture's *res* and thus its ultimate referent: Jesus Christ, the incarnate Son and Word of God. Because the Spirit of Christ is the principal author of the canon, every jot and tittle therein bears witness to Christ and exists for his sake. To read the Bible spiritually is to read it with a view to its explicit or implicit attestation of the mystery of the gospel of the Word made flesh, intrinsic to which is the mystery of his mystical body, the church. All Scripture speaks of him, the Lord Jesus. It speaks *in* his person, it speaks *of* his person; it speaks *in* his body, it speaks *of* his body. Spiritual interpretation penetrates beneath the surface of the plain sense to dwell in the depths of this mysterious, life-giving speech.

Medieval hermeneutics disaggregated spiritual reading into three senses: the "allegorical," the "tropological," and the "anagogical."[13] Roughly speaking, these denote the way in which the spiritual sense of (a) an Old Testament text prefigures the advent of the New, (b) any canonical text (one that is not itself direct paraenesis) offers moral wisdom to the contemporary reader, and (c) any canonical text prefigures the life of the world to come. Call the second the moral sense and the third the eschatological.[14] The trouble comes with the first. "Allegory" has hit on hard times, and rightly so, construed in a certain way. If *Pilgrim's Progress* is an allegory, then Holy Scripture categorically is not, and should not be read as such.[15]

11. See Steinmetz, "Second Narrative."

12. Here and below, I am using "canonical" in a different way than the project advanced by Brevard Childs.

13. See, e.g., de Lubac, *Medieval Exegesis*; de Lubac, *History and Spirit*; Levy, *Medieval Biblical Interpretation*; Stanglin, *Letter and Spirit*.

14. Jenson makes the point this way in *Triune God*, 283. The typical example is that "Jerusalem" signifies at once the city of David (literal), the church (allegorical), the soul (tropological), and heaven (anagogical).

15. If, however, a genre calls for it (e.g., a parable, prophecy, or vision), then such a reading strategy would be appropriate to that particular pericope. See further Lewis, "Biblical Criticism." For a defense of the term, the concept, and the practice of allegory, see Wilken, "Allegory."

In both colloquial and technical usage, allegory often means a word's self-annihilating reference: it signifies that which it is not, and in conducting the reader to that unnamed but nevertheless symbolized reality, it is itself no longer needed; it has no significance in and for itself. The ladder is kicked away once one has climbed it. That, again, is not how any part of Scripture should be read. It is not what St. Paul means in Galatians 4:24 (*hatina estin allegoroumena*),[16] nor is it what St. Thomas Aquinas means by *allegoria*. For the best of the premodern tradition, the spiritual is contained in the literal: that is, the signification of Christ in, say, the Psalms of David does not obviate the plain sense of David's words, which speak of enemies and dangers and trials and sufferings and the Lord's temple and sacrifices offered there[17] and so forth: these signify just what they suggest on their face. Their significance is doubled, however, and in signifying the one they signify the other.

The term I will use for this more specific doubled signification is "figural" reading.[18] For example: Genesis 2 figures the birth of the church from the side of the second Adam, hanging "asleep" on a cross; Genesis 3 figures Mary the God-bearer whose seed would defeat that ancient liar, the devil, once for all; and so on. Figural reading includes and builds upon the plain sense of the text, but never erases or replaces it—though it may illumine or complicate it.

In avoiding allegory and its pitfalls as a term, then, I also avoid "literal," and for the same reasons. Properly understood, to read *ad litteram* is simply to read according to the letter, following what is written, neither more nor less. But not only is its usage hotly contested in both Protestant and Catholic hermeneutics, its connection to historical-critical reading renders it finally useless in a contemporary doctrine of Scripture.[19] Moreover, nothing turns on its recovery. Doubtless it may be used to good effect in certain discursive

16. One way of telling the story of theological hermeneutics for the past two millennia is simply studying the reception history of this single passage; the varying interpretations are fascinating in themselves.

17. The fathers would suggest that talk of temple sacrifice in the words of David (e.g., Ps 51:18–19) is a clue to their more-than-literal signification.

18. See further, e.g., Auerbach, *Mimesis*; Auerbach, "Figura"; Daniélou, SJ, *From Shadows to Reality*; Dawson, *Figural Reading*; Frei, *Biblical Narrative*; Young, *Biblical Exegesis*; Radner, *Time and the Word*; Griffiths, *Song of Songs*; Seitz, *Figured Out*; Collett, *Figural Reading*. I lack the space adequately to discuss typology in relation to figuralism, whether they are synonymous or refer to distinct hermeneutical practices. It seems to me that in practice they often are indistinguishable (*figura*, after all, is merely the Latin translation of the Greek *typos*), but that in some important respects, in the hands of certain interpreters and as developed in different exegetical-ecclesial traditions, they are not in fact identical.

19. For different perspectives, see Childs, "Sensus Literalis"; Frei, "Literal Reading"; Tanner, "Plain Sense"; Greene-McCreight, *Ad Litteram*.

contexts; and important terms always have a way of returning eventually, reclaimed for a new need or occasion. But for now, for my purposes, we can do without it.

Two final comments. First, part of the project of St. Thomas and others to root the spiritual sense in the literal entailed the claim that everything reported in Scripture as history, read *ad litteram*, happened, and happened exactly as reported. The spiritual sense is then not a feature of the text per se but of the historical realities thereby signified by the text: human beings communicate with signs; God communicates with both signs and things, as the Creator of both.[20] So that the *person* of David and the *events* of his life (themselves having been signified to non-contemporaries by the scriptural texts) may, by God's providential design, signify other things: in this case, the person of Jesus and the events of his life. What should we make of this? On the one hand, I think it important to maintain the theological claim here, that God so orders salvation history that the actual persons and events therein *are*, ontologically speaking, figures of Christ. On the other hand, we need not maintain, with St. Thomas, the strict correspondence of each and every detail of each and every historical reportage with historical happenings.[21] This opens up, moreover, the figural power not only of narrative texts that may not align with modern standards of historiography, but also of those parts of Scripture—by no means few in number—that belong to non-narrative genres. For example, there is a plain sense, but not necessarily a "historical" sense, to the wisdom literature; but the lack of a historical sense in no way precludes its having a spiritual sense. In other words, the Song need not be the *actual* epithalamium of the historical Solomon in order to figure Christ (that is, without resort to "bad" allegory). Without exception, therefore, Scripture's texts all have a plain sense, and thus they all have the power, by the Spirit, to figure that of which they do not explicitly speak, whether or not they refer to "things" in the world (things that, in turn, God might use to signify further things).

Second, I have spoken little in this book of "theological interpretation." For those unfamiliar with this phrase, it refers to a loose movement in the theological academy spanning the last two or three decades that seeks, on

---

20. St. Thomas takes this scheme (in *Summa Theologica* I Q1 A10) from St. Augustine, *De Doctrina*.

21. Incidentally, this makes for a better theory of both Scripture and language. The perennial temptation in theology of Scripture is to overcommit to a single, culturally or otherwise determined, theory of language that may or may not, as a matter of fact, be true. One of the many benefits of attending to scriptural exegesis from past eras of the church—with the presumption that they knew what they were doing and have something to teach us—is that we may be rescued from the parochialism of the present day.

the one hand, to move beyond strict adherence to historical-critical methods in biblical interpretation and, on the other hand, to recover premodern practices of reading Scripture.[22] This chapter may be read as an instance of or contribution to that endeavor. But I am not concerned with it as such, nor does much of importance ride on the quality, success, or inner workings of theological interpretation considered as an intra-academic phenomenon. I am concerned, instead, with a theological description of what it means for Christians to read the Bible as Holy Scripture within the life and worship of the church and under the guidance of its long-standing interpretive traditions. How the ongoing debates among scholars play out regarding the proper stance toward *that* is not germane to the point.

2. Liturgy, Devotion, and the Reader

The home of Holy Scripture is worship. It is the public, not the private, reading of Scripture that is definitive for Scripture's role in the life of the church. The assembly of the faithful gathered, in expectant silence, to hear the word of the Lord read aloud from the testimony of the apostles and prophets: that is both the initial and the enduring primary location—in reality and in doctrine—for encounter with and reception of the biblical text.[23]

We do not often associate "interpretation" with such a setting. The trope of public reading is not the assumed background for treatises in exegetical method. But to lose sight of it is to forget why we are reading Scripture in the first place, along with the ends that our reading ought to serve. "Private" interpretation of Scripture, that is to say, interpretation of the text that occurs elsewhere than in the liturgy, is nevertheless always dependent upon and symbiotic with it.[24] The further one moves away from the liturgy,

22. See, e.g., Fowl, *Engaging Scripture*; Fowl, *Theological Interpretation*; Treier, *Theological Interpretation*; Vanhoozer et al., *Dictionary*; Green, *Theological Interpretation*; Bartholomew and Thomas, *Manifesto*; Billings, *Word of God*; Hays, "Theological Exegesis"; Hays and Davis, *Art of Reading Scripture*.

23. Allow me to remind the reader that this is a diachronic snapshot. The very point of the foregoing chapters is that the church comes into being *in media res*, and accordingly, so does the existence, formation, and (at the tail end) doctrine of Scripture. The church began with "only" the prophets (that is, what we call the Old Testament) and slowly, bit by bit, added texts into the liturgical reading rotation from that assortment of apostolic texts we now call the New Testament. But we certainly do already find messianic assemblies in the first century that gather for (among other things) the reading of both Israel's scriptures and a document written by an apostle.

24. Another modifier presents itself, but since it has negative connotations, we should limit our use of it to describe academic interpretation of Scripture, which most certainly is *parasitic* upon ecclesial and liturgical usage.

the more one's reading of the text will become detached from the nature, uses, and ends that the church confesses, by God's gracious will, to be true of the text. Think of Scripture as a living thing: it requires its native habitat for deep roots, good light, and rich air. That habitat is the living people of God in convocation, eager to receive together the living word of God spoken aloud for all to hear. Removed from that habitat, text and reader alike grow malnourished, emaciated, desiccated. Neither can be transplanted to another environment without loss.

There is an important historical point here in addition to the theological. For most of the church's history, access to Scripture has been bound up with access to worship. Literacy rates combined with technologies of text production have meant at best a modicum of popular engagement with Scripture. Even today, with much higher literacy rates and universal free availability of the text in hundreds of translations online, most believers encounter God's written word principally when it is read aloud on Sunday morning. These facts should chasten our post-Gutenberg, post-Reformation, post-Enlightenment presumptions about the relationship between individual Christians and the Bible. Most Christians most of the time have not had—whether through inability, inaccessibility, or sheer lack of leisure (labor in the fields, labor in the home)—the kind of daily, immediate, intimate relationship with Scripture often presupposed today as either precondition or goal of the believer's proper relationship with God. Accordingly, we ought to reconsider this inherited picture of ordinary Christian life.[25]

25. I do not mean to suggest that individual reading of the Bible ought to be discouraged. Much less do I mean to imply that scriptural engagement was superior or to be preferred when literacy rates were far lower, or that efforts to translate the Bible into all the languages of the world are of secondary importance. On the contrary, few tasks are more pressing for the church's mission—or more heroic—than the extension of Scripture into each and every known human tongue. Rather, what I mean to emphasize here is fourfold. First, we ought not to paint an ahistorical picture of the Christian life that would exclude most believers, past and present. Second, it is not clear *from the Bible itself* that individual, personal reading of the text is either the *sine qua non* of faithful discipleship or the principal mode of hearing God's word. Third, given how minimal individual reading of the Bible is even within highly literate communities with readily available translations, we ought not to use an idealized portrait as the standard, but instead work the other way around. And fourth, if it therefore remains true that most Christians encounter Scripture primarily in the public liturgy, *and* that that is in fact the theologically primary site of such encounter, then we may take that as a useful convergence for both doctrine and practice. (It might even suggest a sort of middle ground between liturgy-centric and devotion-centric accounts of "reading" Scripture. As the rest of this chapter and the next insist, personal reading is not and should not be *for* "doctrinal" interpretation but rather for, or in accordance with, Scripture's sacramental mode. If accepted, this view would simultaneously coordinate devotional reading more closely with public worship and specify the types of reading practices, and texts, best

Furthermore, if "interpretation" still occurred across centuries, continents, and cultures whenever the baptized congregated to hear the scriptures read aloud, sometimes for long stretches of time, then we ought to expand our concept of when, where, and how interpretation happens, and by whom.[26]

Stated most broadly, the aim of Christian reading of Scripture is to hear the word of God. Hearing God speak, we may be—alternately or simultaneously—delighted, struck dumb, cut to the heart, edified, instructed, brought to our knees, filled with the Spirit, convicted of sin, equipped for some good work, or commissioned for a task. That is one of the many reasons why Scripture's reading is an essentially liturgical act: it occurs in that set-apart time when prayers and hymns and psalms and incense and confession and creed and Communion enwrap the self amid the body of believers and enfold the whole into the grace and mercy and love of God the blessed Trinity. *Then and there* the Lord speaks; *then and there* one hears his voice. Devotional reading of Scripture is a kind of extension of liturgical reading: a chapel branching off from the nave of the great hermeneutical cathedral.[27] On its own, it is nothing.[28] It relies upon and contributes to the central thing. It takes its cues from the weekly rhythm of the Prophets and Psalms, the Epistles and Gospels; it is a local practice contingent upon the global. (This is quite literally true, if the personal and ecclesial are both following the lectionary.) In both cases, the aim is the same, whatever the particular end of the individual reader: to hear God speak through the embassy of his servants.

Practices of preparation for hearing God speak cross both modes of reading. Liturgical convention varies by tradition. One may do any of the following: bow before the scriptures; kneel or stand when the words are read; kiss the page; cense it; move it from the altar to the center of the assembly; bless the text, oneself, the people; acclaim the holy gospel of the Lord, and give glory to God; cross one's mind, one's lips, one's heart; proclaim the word of the Lord, and give thanks to God. This is only a sample. But the practices are illustrative. They offer a pattern that ought to characterize the faithful throughout their daily lives whenever they engage the text. The

---

suited to the private Christian reader. There is a reason why the daily office always features a Psalm and not, say, a chapter from Ezekiel.) For a provocative proposal on these themes, see Hauerwas, *Unleashing the Scriptures*.

26. See now the samples from world Christianity in Gorman, *Scripture*.

27. I take this image from Smith, *Desiring the Kingdom*, 220, who uses it to describe Christian colleges as extensions of the church's life and work.

28. That is to say, it would be nothing were it not for the public liturgy of the church, just as individual Christian life would be nothing were it not for the community of the church. On its own *as* an extension of the church's life with Scripture, devotional reading is far from nothing; it is often the lifeblood of personal piety.

pandect Bible—not to mention Bible apps on smartphones and tablets—can deceive believers into treating it like any other book. But it is *not* like any other book, and should not be read as such. The church recognizes this in its scriptural choreography. And if devotional reading, which does not exclude the scholar in her study, is a chapel within the larger cathedral, then we should expect to find such choreography there, too.

The ensemble of embodied gestures before the book, however, is not for its own sake, much less an empty ceremony or a conjuring act. It is the outward expression of the set of spiritual dispositions proper to the believer who would dare to approach God's word expecting to hear him. The same fear and trembling that is fitting for the reception of the visible words of the holy sacrament is equally fitting for the reception of the audible words of Holy Scripture. St. Paul's admonition to discern the body, lest we eat and drink judgment on ourselves (1 Cor 11:29), applies no less to the Bible, lest seeing we do not see and hearing we do not hear (Matt 13:13), and walk away sad, without understanding (Mark 10:22). St. Gregory of Nazianzus writes that the work of theology is not for everyone, but only for those who "have undergone, or at the very least are undergoing, purification of body and soul."[29] All the more for the private reading of the sacred page.

What more might we say regarding the habits and virtues desirable in the Christian reader? The topic as a whole is well described as a kind of ascetics of reading, or hermeneutical ascesis.[30] Humility is chief here. The reader is not master of the text, but servant, both of the text and of the God who speaks therein. Nor is the reader judge: though she must make judgments, and we err if we avoid that fact (whether in rhetoric or in substance), those judgments ought to be a function of obedience rather than autonomy. We are not a law to ourselves; the Lord is our law, and the law he writes on our hearts he writes by the same Spirit who wrote the scriptures.

Next is expectation. We go to Scripture because we hope to find something there, or rather Someone. That need not mean we go expecting to find *answers*. Neither in prayer nor in reading does the Lord meet us on our own terms.[31] We meet him on his. But if he has directed us by his church to these writings, there to hear his voice, we are right to approach them with hope and eager anticipation. The word we hear may surprise us; and we may very well mishear. But to open the scriptures as if they were any other work, as if

---

29. St. Gregory of Nazianzus, *Theological Orations* 27.3.

30. John Webster is acute and unsparing on this point: see *Holy Scripture*, 68–106; *Domain*, 3–31; *Culture*, 63–80.

31. Henri Nouwen makes this point eloquently in *Way of the Heart*.

they comprised a vast overworked field, dead and uprooted, requiring our labor to replant and harvest: that is a grave mistake.

The humble, expectant reader should also be teachable. There is an element of docility here, but to the extent that that word implies passivity, teachableness is to be preferred. We are disciples and therefore students in the school of Christ. For disciples are *mathetai*, learners: what we learn is the way of Christ; where we learn is the body of Christ; how we learn is the Spirit of Christ; whence we learn is the saints of Christ. The saints teach by their example and by their words, but privileged among them are those who prefigured and those who first proclaimed the gospel of Christ. We find their lives and their speech inscribed in Holy Scripture. The faithful reader ought to desire with undimmed zeal to learn at their feet.

Because the reader is a believer, she is baptized, which is to say, the reader is a sinner reborn in Christ. As a sinner, she ought to approach Scripture penitently, chary of the flesh (cf. Mark 14:38; John 6:63; Rom 8:5; 13:14). She is herself in the midst of a lifelong process of mortification and revivification, which is the sanctifying work of the Holy Spirit (cf. Eph 4:20–24; Rom 8:3; Titus 3:5–6). Reading Scripture is not incidental but central to this process.[32] Penitent reading is not self-flagellating but, on the one hand, mindful of our proclivities to self-justification and self-deception: I want the text to confirm me in my wants and habits as they are, not to put the old self to death (Rom 6:6) or to take my thoughts captive for Christ (2 Cor 10:5). On the other hand, then, penitent reading is vigilant about resisting the temptation to use the text in harmful ways toward others: misusing or abusing it to serve my own interests or to elevate myself over against others. But Scripture is not *pro me* in either of those ways. It is for me as the sinner I am. Knowing this, penitent reading runs to Scripture in order to hear again the merciful word of the Lord Jesus: "My son, your sins are forgiven" (Mark 2:5).

Thus does Jesus speak to the reader through Scripture. But to encounter Jesus is to go on one's way rejoicing (cf. Luke 17:11–19; Acts 5:41; 8:39), so that Scripture becomes the site and occasion of joy.[33] Accordingly, the Christian reader considers the canon with affection. It is not finally an alien or intrusive word. It is not principally a word of judgment or of stern rebuke. It is the word of God, and therefore the word of love: "for God is love" (1 John 4:8). She errs not who returns to the word over and over again, looking for consolation and reassurance of the Lord's loving-kindness. Such a reader

32. See chapter 4 as well as the works by Webster cited above.

33. Though not always: the rich man "went away sorrowful; for he had great possessions" (Mark 10:22; cf. Matt 19:22). Scripture's hearers and readers may do the same, having not falsely but most truly encountered the person and word of Jesus in the text. My thanks to Justin Hawkins on this point and for his comments on this whole section.

approaches the text with the prayer of the psalmist on her lips: "Do not thou, O LORD, withhold thy mercy from me, let thy steadfast love and thy faithfulness ever preserve me!" (Ps 40:11). Humble, hopeful, and penitent, she is confident the Lord will reply resoundingly through his holy word.

Beyond the virtues to be sought and the gestures to be performed in one's encounter with the text, certain practices prepare the reader for the act of reading. These include but are not limited to: regular participation in eucharistic worship; disciplines of fasting, silence, and solitude; broad reading in the doctors and saints who succeeded the apostles; service to the least of these; and, over all and uniting them together, prayer. To read Scripture without prayer—to leave Scripture *unprayed*—is an exercise in missing the point. A contradiction in terms, it is as if one were to chew one's food without swallowing it, or to start one's car without putting it in drive. It involves a wholesale failure to see the thing for what it is, to engage it on its own terms, to put it to use for its own ends. The Bible is still a book, and those who seek to read the texts it contains unleavened by prayer may still come to understanding, even insight, regarding certain aspects of it. But they are rather like a reader of Shakespeare's plays who actively avoids seeing them performed; or an avid collector of recipes who resolutely refuses to cook them; or an enthusiast of film criticism who stays away from the theater. Or perhaps they are like an astronomer who in spite of her research believes in a geocentric universe, or a geologist who goes about her work convinced the earth is flat. Such things can be done, but they make very little sense. And they performatively contradict the very object of their work and affection. So for prayerless exegesis.[34]

Other practices and virtues recommend themselves for a full picture of the faithful reader, not least patience, perseverance, and the theological virtues of faith, hope, and love. Here is the crucial point, though. Because reading Scripture is not a natural or an autonomous act but a fundamentally spiritual and ecclesial act, the ascesis proper to Christian life as a whole is essential here as well. Reading is encompassed and enclosed within the reign of the risen Christ. His session at God's right hand presides over our reading as it does all else (*ta panta* brooks no exceptions). Hence, the economy of reading Scripture is nothing other than the economy of grace. To read the texts that bear to the church what it confesses to be the word of the Lord is to find oneself caught up in the saving movement of the gospel: reading here is a mode of discipleship, an occasion for taking up one's cross and following

---

34. One thinks of novels that depict the continuance of scriptural or liturgical rituals in the wake of a devastation so great it has rendered their meaning opaque, lost, or nonsensical: see Miller Jr., *Canticle for Leibowitz*; Moore, *Catholics*; McCarthy, *The Road*.

Jesus.[35] The baptized reader is filled with the selfsame Spirit who inspired the scriptures. To read them prayerfully means to beg the Spirit to shed his loving light upon them, that we might perceive the voice of the One whose Spirit he is. Divine illumination is thus the condition of the possibility of our hearing the Lord speak through the text. We do not read well apart from him; we cannot hear his voice apart from his help.

Baptized reading, in short, is a Spirit-enabled action of the body of Christ, as a whole and in each of its members, to the glory of God the Father. For reading to be baptized means for it to be drenched in the power of the Holy Spirit: washed clean, slain and made alive again, dead to sin but alive in the Lord. To read according to the flesh is to read as if the Bible were like any other book and the reader like any other person. "But you are not in the flesh," writes St. Paul, "you are in the Spirit, if in fact the Spirit of God dwells in you. Anyone who does not have the Spirit of Christ does not belong to him" (8:9), and those who do not belong to him do not hearken to his voice in Scripture. "But if Christ is in you, although your bodies are dead because of sin, your spirits are alive because of righteousness" (v. 10), for "all of us who have been baptized into Christ Jesus were baptized into his death" (5:3), and "he who has died is free from sin" (v. 3). Now "the death [Christ] died he died to sin, once for all, but the life he lives he lives to God" (v. 10), by the power of the Holy Spirit. And if "the Spirit of him who raised Jesus from the dead dwells in you, he who raised Christ Jesus from the dead will give life to your mortal bodies also through his Spirit which dwells in you" (8:11). This Spirit is the Spirit of Sonship, through whom believers are adopted as God's children (vv. 14–15): by this Spirit "we cry, 'Abba, father!'" (v. 15).

Following the divine apostle, we may say that the baptized reader reads Scripture in accordance not with the flesh but with the Spirit. Such reading is supernatural in source and scope: it is reading in the power of the resurrection. Above all, it is reading as a child of God. The voice one aches to hear in the text is therefore not that of a stranger, nor of a judge, nor of a distant imperious ruler. It is the voice of one's Father, "the Father [who] loves me" (John 10:17).[36]

---

35. See now Taylor, *Reading Scripture*.

36. As Jesus says elsewhere in the same gospel, "the Father loves the Son" (3:35; 5:20), the very One whose Sonship the Spirit of the Father confers upon those who believe that Jesus is the Messiah and Son of God come in the flesh, giving them eternal life as God's own children (20:31; 1 John 3:23; 4:2–3; 5:1).

3. The Hermeneutics of Holy Scripture

Although Scripture has many ends, one traditional way of gathering those ends together is by coordinating them with Scripture's authority. This authority is twofold. First, Scripture has authority to bear the living word of the gospel both to the church and to the world. In this word the living Christ speaks by his Spirit to convict, to convert, to mortify and revivify, to justify and sanctify—to effect salvation in and among sinners. This authority is less a matter of what we do with Scripture and more a matter of what the Holy Trinity does with it in and to us. The freedom of the Spirit to blow where he wills (John 3:8) means that his uses of Scripture—the texts he illuminates, the word that women and men receive from him—are unbound by either the letter or our construal of it. It means that we will be surprised, even shocked, by the conjunction of text, message, and hearer. And that is as it should be.

The second mode of Scripture's authority is its function as a norm or rule for Christian teaching. This is Scripture's statutory authority over the beliefs and behavior of Christian life. Here the range and import of Scripture's texts are circumscribed, inasmuch as their status precisely as texts, along with the proper modes of receiving them as such, calls for clarification. One needs guidelines for how to read different parts of Scripture in fitting ways as an authority for doctrine. The rule needs rules for reading it.[37] Leviticus and Ruth and Job and Daniel are just there, waiting in the canon. Doubtless God speaks through them in the first mode of Scripture's authority. But how are they, how can they be, authoritative in the second mode?

The next chapter will unpack this schema and the implications for scriptural authority within the church. For now I want to focus on the question of how to interpret Scripture from within, or according to, this latter function: for the sake of instruction; with a view to doctrine. Words are for communication, and reading is for understanding. How ought the Christian reader to read the words of the Bible for the sake of understanding what the text teaches?[38]

By way of an answer let me offer a series of theses or principles, more or less elaborated, each of which will build on the others. These will in turn raise the issue of reading scriptural texts to mean what they could not have

---

37. This will occupy us in the next chapter: how Scripture is unruled by other authorities, inasmuch as nothing may contradict what it teaches; yet its reading is and must be ruled *ab extra*, both because it does not provide the terms of its own interpretation and because, thus unruled, its reading will inevitably degenerate into false teaching (that is, reading Scripture to teach what it does not teach).

38. Remembering that "what the text teaches" is always convertible with, or glossed by, "what God wants to teach us by means of the text."

been intended or understood to mean in their original historical context. Accordingly, I will conclude the section by explaining why Christians may engage in such reading. But let me begin with the principles of interpretation.

First, Christian interpretation reads Holy Scripture as the inspired word of God. It does not bracket its knowledge of the ontology of the text, of its source and being and ends. It need not do so because nothing at all is gained from doing so.

Second, Christian interpretation reads Holy Scripture under the guidance of the Holy Spirit. This is a fact and an imperative. It is a fact because there is no avoiding the Spirit's reach: "Where shall I go from your Spirit? Or where shall I flee from your presence?" (Ps 139:7). It is an imperative because only in the Spirit, only by the Spirit's sovereign freedom, will the word of the Lord in the scriptures be unveiled as the testimony to Christ that it is (cf. 2 Cor 3:1–18).

Third, Christian interpretation reads Holy Scripture as a product of and gift to the church of Jesus Christ. Scripture is an ecclesial document from start to finish. That is to say, it comes from and exists in and for the covenant people of God, the seed of Abraham according to the flesh and according to the Spirit, Messiah's kin by birth and by baptism. The texts of Scripture may certainly be read otherwise, and the church may profit from such readings. But whether at interpretation's outset or at its conclusion, Scripture's status as the church's book ought to inform how it is read.

Fourth, Christian interpretation reads Holy Scripture canonically. That is, it reads the collection of sacred writings *as* a collection; it does not treat discrete texts as isolated from the others, much less alien to them. The Christian reader presumes that the church's decision to gather together these texts in a single volume was guided by the Holy Spirit. And if that is true, then the church's historic practice of reading each of the parts in light of the whole is more than justified. For example, St. Augustine suggests that unclear passages in Scripture be read in light of the clearer ones.[39] The Protestant reformers term this practice the analogy of faith, whereby readers interpret Scripture by Scripture: the first chapter of Genesis by the first chapter of St. John's Gospel, Leviticus by Hebrews, the Synoptics by the Psalms, the Epistle of St. James by the Epistle to the Galatians—and vice versa. Again, this practice is underwritten by theological claims: that the Spirit is the source of both (a) the texts themselves and (b) the specific selection of texts in the canon, and that (c) the same Spirit guides the church today. Absent that threefold pneumatological confession, canonical reading falls to the ground.[40]

39. See Books 2 and 3 of St. Augustine, *De Doctrina.*

40. Kelsey, *Eccentric Existence*, 132–56, makes the useful observation that there is a

Fifth, Christian interpretation reads Holy Scripture through the Rule of Faith. At a minimum, this means exegesis is normed by the gospel: Jesus of Nazareth, the crucified Messiah raised by Israel's God from the dead, is Lord and Savior of all peoples. More, it means that the baptismal summaries eventually codified in the Apostles' Creed and the Creeds of Nicaea and Constantinople function as rules of thumb, guiding Christian readers in their understanding of what the Bible says. The Rule of Faith is thus, as we saw in chapter 1, a kind of textual St. Philip to the Ethiopian eunuch of the ordinary reader. It rules out misreadings and guides the reader to fruitful exegetical paths. Better: it carves out the space in which the reader may explore and test the fruitfulness of a variety of readings, any one of which may prove edifying, wise, or true—even delectable. Most expansively, reading through the Rule of Faith means reading Scripture in light of and in accordance with the mind of the church as it has matured and developed in the intervening centuries between the apostles and the present time. Privileged here are the seven ecumenical councils; though far more ought to be included, that will depend on one's ecclesial membership.

The fact that the last millennium has seen the church in schism and then in ever-multiplying division means that interpretation of Scripture, like the truth of the gospel, is called into question.[41] Not even the canon is one. In light of the interpretive anarchy generated by this ecclesial chaos, the dominant academic response has been to forestall the hermeneutical task, by means of rigorously circumscribing its boundaries, conventions, and aims. This circumscription takes the form of heavily regulating those practices of interpretation previously universal in the church, and coordinating the reduced set of permissible procedures to a single end: "the" original historical "meaning" of the text as most plausibly intended by its author or understood by its first audience. I will say more about this hermeneutic below. For now let me underline its mistaken character as a response to church division and exegetical disagreement. On the one hand, we are no closer to "scientific" or scholarly consensus on "the" meaning of any text in the canon than we were one or two centuries ago. If consensus is the criterion of success, the endeavor has been a failure. (Fortunately, there are other criteria by which to measure it.) On the other hand, there is no reason to suppose either (a) that each biblical text (and how would we even specify where one pericope ends and another begins?) has a single meaning or (b) that the primary or controlling meaning of any text must be its original (intended or received) meaning.[42]

---

difference between a collection of authoritative texts and an authoritative collection of texts. The canon is the latter.

41. See Radner, *End of the Church*; Radner, *Hope Among the Fragments*.

42. Part of the challenge here is genre. It is manageable to ask (and to attempt to

Call this the Rahner's Rule of Scripture[43]—or rather, so as not to sully Rahner with a theory he did not propound, let us term it Jowett's Rule: the one true meaning of the text is the authorially intended meaning in its original historical context, and vice versa.[44] It is a pervasive, powerful, and compelling theory. And it offers much: an end to interpretive anarchy; resolution of exegetical argument; agreement in the essentials of the faith; perhaps even reunion of divided traditions.[45] But it delivers on none of these, because it is a bankrupt idea. Which is not to say that *historiographic investigation* into the texts' original contexts of production, revision, and reception is bankrupt: far from it. It is arguably the greatest gift, at least of an intellectual or theological sort, that the Western church has to offer the church catholic since the Enlightenment. But historiography is not historical criticism. Historical criticism is the ideological hegemon that arose in the wake of Jowett's Rule of Scripture assuming hermeneutical precedence in the church (or at least in those institutions where its scholars study, write, and train pastors).

---

answer) what St. Paul's argument or purpose is in his letter to St. Philemon; less so with the book of Jeremiah, the Psalms, Exodus, Revelation, or any of the Gospels. Poetry, prophecy, law, apocalypse, narrative, and other genres are the norm, not the exception, in the canon; to interpret them well is not to reduce them to discrete "meanings" but rather—the switch to metaphor is unavoidable—to inhabit the worlds of meaning they project. Such inhabiting is the task of commentarial reading, about which see below.

43. I owe this idea to Todd Hains. The so-called "Rahner's Rule" names the formulation of Karl Rahner, SJ, regarding the identity of the Trinity in his works *ad intra* and *ad extra*: "The economic Trinity is the immanent Trinity and *vice versa*" (*Trinity*, 36). On the topic at hand, see Rahner, *Inspiration*. In *Development*, 285–89, St. Newman suggests that this approach to Scripture's meaning is a heresy prefigured by certain teachers from the "Antiochene school" of exegesis.

44. After Benjamin Jowett, who in authoring "Interpretation" forever associated his name with the claim that the Bible should be read like any other book, that is, in accordance with its original historical and cultural context, absent any and all ecclesial or other tradition interposing itself between then and there and here and now; such interposition being by definition an imposition. See further Noble, "The 'Sensus Literalis,'" for a useful account of Jowett's hermeneutic in response to its contested reception in Brevard Childs and James Barr. Cf. Barr, "Jowett and the Reading of the Bible"; "Jowett and the 'Original Meaning.'"

45. In this respect, theological liberalism functions similarly to political liberalism, where the latter, understood to bracket "unanswerable" teleological questions about the good, is meant, as a theory and practice of politics, to be precisely an end to politics. The incommensurate desires of the public are safely retired to the private and the individual; the *agon* of deliberation is thus pacified via technique. Whereas theological liberalism posits an end to the *agon* of interpretation via *Wissenschaft*: if only we left behind who we are and why we care, we could reach consensus about the meaning of the text through recourse to a "neutral," "public" method.

Many of the reasons that explain why this Rule is bankrupt have been canvassed already, both in this chapter and in the preceding four. Supreme among them: Scripture's nature as God's inspired and sanctified word means that it is unlike any other book, for in and through its humanly authored words God speaks. That sacramental function will always outstrip attempts to straitjacket its potential to mean any number of things to any number of the faithful. But there are other reasons why Christian interpretation need not proceed along the lines set by Jowett's Rule.

First, the apostles did not do so. The church has long taken apostolic exegesis of Scripture—which is to say, interpretation of the Old found in the New—to be exemplary: both excellent and worthy of imitation. Shot through every book of the New Testament is the belief, operative hermeneutically, that the Law and the Prophets and the Writings are best read, which is to say, most truly understood, only *in light of the person and work of Jesus*. The light that shone through his flesh at Mount Tabor is the divine light of his glorious resurrection, and this same light now, through the Spirit, shines upon Israel's scriptures, transfiguring them before the unveiled minds of the baptized.[46] Thus radiant with the glory of the Lord's Messiah, the texts of Tanakh prefigure his coming, his identity, his destiny, and his saving mission in the Spirit. "And Paul went in [to the synagogue], as was his custom, and on three sabbath days argued with them from the scriptures, explaining and proving that it was necessary for the Messiah to suffer and to rise from the dead, and saying, 'This is the Messiah, Jesus whom I am proclaiming to you'" (Acts 17:2–3). The Gospels root this way of reading the scriptures in the teaching of Jesus, both before and after his death and resurrection. Upon his arrest, for example, regarding his ability to stop the soldiers with legions of angels, he asks rhetorically: "But how then should the scriptures be fulfilled, that it must be so?" (Matt 26:54). Likewise, after rising and appearing to his disciples, he "said to them, 'Thus it is written, that the Christ should suffer and on the third day rise from the dead,'" having "opened their minds to understand the scriptures" (Luke 24:46, 45).[47]

The upshot, in sum, is that "sacred scripture admits of several senses."[48] For what is spoken of in the Law and the Prophets may be read (a) according to the letter, that is, concerning the stories and deeds of Moses or Ruth or

46. Cf. Mark 9:2–8; Matt 28:1–4; Acts 9:1–9; 2 Pet 1:16–21; Rev 1:12–19; 2 Cor 3:1—4:18.

47. Happily, St. Luke's rendering of the words of the risen Jesus and of the apostle to the gentiles overlaps substantially: *houtos gegraptai pathein ton Christon kai anastenai ek nekron te trite hemera* (Luke 24:46); . . . *apo ton graphon . . . hoti ton Christon edei pathein kai anastenai ek nekron . . .* (Acts 17:2–3).

48. St. Thomas Aquinas, *Quodlibetal Questions* VII Q6 A1 resp.

Hannah or David or Israel as a whole or its imperial neighbors or the doings of the priests in the temple or what have you; and (b) according to the Spirit, that is, concerning the temporal missions of the Son and the Spirit of God the Father. St. Thomas Aquinas lays down the rule: "When it comes to the things said in the Old Testament, the first thing we have to maintain is their literal truth. But since the Old Testament is a figure of the New, many of the things set down in the Old Testament are said in a way that signifies something else figuratively."[49] Nor does this mean there is *one* plain meaning of a text and *one* spiritual meaning. St. Thomas elaborates:

> The principal author of sacred scripture is the Holy Spirit, who can have many more things in mind with one word of sacred scripture than the commentators on sacred scripture can even set out. Nor is there anything unacceptable about a person serving as an instrumental author of sacred scripture and having more than one thing in mind with one word of Scripture. As Jerome says in his comments on Hosea, the prophets spoke of present occurrences while also intending to signify future ones. Hence it is not impossible to think of more than one thing at a time when one of them stands for the other.[50]

If even a human speaker can intend more than one thing at once, how much more may the canonical texts of Scripture, inspired by the Spirit, contain more than one sense or meaning?

This principle guided the church in its reading from the time of the apostles up to the Protestant Reformation. And even though the reformers sought to constrict the range of meanings for the sake of doctrinal unity, repudiating the quadriga inherited from medieval hermeneutics, they and the traditions they birthed continued to read the Bible canonically as the instrument of God's word to God's people.[51] This entailed, willy-nilly, figural and other reading strategies, particularly for the Old Testament. How else could they make sense of the New Testament's reception—which is to say, recontextualization and thus reinterpretation—of the Old? Indeed, it is fair to say that the spiritual interpretation of Scripture continued apace

49. St. Thomas Aquinas, *Quodlibetal Questions* III Q14 A1 resp.

50. St. Thomas Aquinas, *Quodlibetal Questions* VII Q6 A1 ad5. The objection to which this is an answer reads: "Any sense drawn from the words of scripture that its author did not intend is not its own proper sense, but a foreign one. Yet the author of one part of scripture can only have had one thing in mind, since it is impossible to think of more than one thing at a time, as the Philosopher says. Therefore, sacred scripture cannot possibly have several proper senses of its own."

51. See, e.g., the subtle treatment of Scripture's multiple senses, allegory, and typology in Gerhard, *Interpreting Sacred Scripture* 7.131–8.146.

after the Reformation across the divisions in the church, albeit in different forms and governed by different magisteria.[52] Considered purely in terms of hermeneutics, one can imagine organizing the divergent ecclesial traditions as "schools" of a unified community of interpretation: one more aligned with St. John Chrysostom, another with St. Augustine, still another with St. Thomas, another with St. Gregory of Nyssa. In any case, it is important to see that, although spiritual—one is tempted simply to say "Christian"—interpretation waned in elite scholarly spheres as the centuries went on, it has never ceased, and surely remains the prevailing popular mode of reading Scripture common to all Christians.

This is the second reason why Jowett's Rule of Scripture is false. It is unknown to the church prior to the Enlightenment,[53] and, though regnant ever since in Western institutions of scholarly and pastoral training, it is still in the minority in terms of church practice and certainly among believers across the globe. And there is a third reason contained within the second. Not only is it implausible as a matter of ecclesiology to suggest that a theory of scriptural meaning developed only recently is the one true hermeneutic for Holy Scripture. It is impossible as a theological claim. For central to the doctrine of Scripture is that the Spirit has provided the canon for the sake of the church's life, worship, and mission. Yet the high claims of historical criticism suggest both (a) that the essential means of understanding Scripture have been unknown to the church heretofore and, therefore, (b) that the true meaning of Scripture's texts has been hidden from the church until now—when, fortunately enough, the methods of historical-critical study enable that meaning to be uncovered. For such a thing to be true, however, the gospel would have to be false.[54] The only alternative would be that the church wandered aimlessly for centuries, nay millennia, ignorant of Scripture's teaching, because misguided in its practices of interpretation. I know of no account of divine providence that could make sense of such a claim. Either the church has had tools adequate to its needs—in

52. Stanglin is excellent on this point: see *Letter and Spirit*, 77–152. Cf. Radner, *Time and the Word*, 44–82.

53. Not to say that, for example, the church fathers did not read for what the text's authors meant. They did. But in and through human authorial intention *and in addition to it* they read for what the Spirit meant. That is the difference.

54. "What likelihood is there that the Holy Spirit has hidden himself from all antiquity, and that after 1,500 years he has disclosed to certain private persons the [meaning] of the true Scriptures?" (St. Francis de Sales, *Catholic Controversy* 1.6; the original word replaced in brackets is "list," as the subject in context is the canon). Cf. St. Newman: "though allegory can be made an instrument for evading Scripture doctrine, criticism may more readily be turned to the destruction of doctrine and Scripture together" (*Development*, 288).

other words, the minimum ability to make sense of the basic truths of the Bible—or the Spirit provided the church with the canon in vain.[55] If we choose the latter option (and it is important to see that the methodological skepticism and vaunted claims of historical critics have often led many to do so), then we had better give up theology altogether, since we are only fooling ourselves, and of all persons most to be pitied. But if we choose the former option, then we may bid adieu to Jowett's Rule at once, and waste not one more minute on its vain assertions.

There are two more reasons worth mentioning for rejecting the historical-critical sense as either the only or the primary meaning of the text. Before turning to the positive role of historiographic inquiry in scriptural interpretation, let me touch on these briefly.

On the one hand (this is the fourth overall reason), those of us who are gentiles have a claim to the Jewish scriptures *if and only if* it is the case that Jesus, the Jewish Messiah, has through the cross made a way for the nations to be incorporated into the one covenant family of Abraham. If that is the case, then Moses and David and Solomon and Isaiah have a word from the Lord for me, too, and not only for the biological descendants of Abraham. If it is not the case, I am trespassing on others' ground, and unjustly—arguably violently—appropriating their texts for my own purposes. No gentile has a right to Israel's scriptures. They are the sacred writings of Abraham's children. Gentiles by birth may read and receive them as "theirs" only if "they" become part of the "we" of the Lord's people; and that only happens by conversion to Judaism, or baptism into the body of Christ. And through the latter, gentiles give glory to the God of Israel when they read the prophets as forewitnesses to the Israelite who sits at God's right hand: Jesus, the Lord.

On the other hand (this is the fifth and final reason), believers of all kinds read the scriptures in order to apply them in their lives. But most of the Bible has no obvious application ready to hand. Moreover, for many texts there is a doubled distance related to the point above. Not only are they not "practical" in genre; they concern persons, places, times, and activities that are either no longer with us or, by theological principle, ought *not* to be obeyed by believers today. Consider the dietary regulations of Torah. Gentile

---

55. The phrasing of this sentence may sound exaggerated; the reader may suppose I am not representing historical critics fairly. This is not the case. Speaking in general will always admit exceptions, to be sure, but within the guild, for the last two centuries, the disregard and even ridicule for premodern ecclesial exegesis *as* exegesis is rampant and explicit. It is as if the particular mode of reading coterminous with the rise of historical consciousness were itself the invention of reading as such, and therefore, as a simple matter of course, prior practices of reading were either nothing of the sort or failed attempts at the real thing, only lately extant. Sadly, this intellectual posture is equally present in Christian and in non-Christian scholarship.

Christians are commanded by St. Paul not to keep kosher precisely because they are meant to belong to God's new covenant *as gentiles*, not as Jews. How then are they supposed to read those regulations? Or commandments regarding burnt offerings and temple sacrifices, or the vestments and rituals of the Levitical priesthood? The church fathers repudiated one answer: to read them as nothing but history, or solely as prelude to Christ. Indeed they are history, and they are a prelude to Christ. But they are also Holy Scripture. And Scripture is *propter nos*, "for our sake" (1 Cor 9:10: Greek *di' hemas*). Are whole swaths of Scripture not subject to this principle? Are they "just there," to be avoided or at least digested as little more than theological vegetables, "deep background" to the real drama? No: the fathers developed a rich, sophisticated hermeneutic for reading the Old Testament—all of it—as *propter nos in Christo*. This hermeneutic is figural exegesis. It delights in discovering or proposing the unlimited ways in which each and every jot and tittle of the scriptures figures Christ and, in him, all that touches his person and work: his mother, his career, his Spirit, his sacramental body. Numbers and Joshua and Chronicles and Nahum are for us because they are for Christ; they are books of the Christ and of his coming; in and through them, he speaks, of himself and of us.[56] Find Christ there, and everywhere else in Scripture: for (to repurpose Terence) Christ is scriptural, and nothing scriptural is alien to him.[57]

4. Anachronism, History, and Scripture

It may appear, even to the patient and generous reader, that in the foregoing I have excluded scholarly historiographic study of the Bible while rubber stamping whatever the church has read the Bible to say across the centuries.

---

56. In the words of Karl Barth, the Bible is "the book of Christ" (*Church Dogmatics* I/1, 109; cf. I/2, 513). For contemporary theological interpretation of, e.g., Exodus, Leviticus, and Numbers as they bear on the Christian doctrine of God, see the first two volumes of Sonderegger, *Systematic Theology*.

57. In the words of Hugh of St. Victor: "All of Divine Scripture is one book, and that one book is Christ, because all of Divine Scripture speaks of Christ, and all of Divine Scripture is fulfilled in Christ" (*De arca Noe morali* 2.8). Cited in de Lubac, *Medieval Exegesis*, 237, who elaborates: "Jesus Christ brings about the unity of Scripture, because he is the endpoint and fullness of Scripture. Everything in it is related to him. In the end he is its sole object. Consequently, he is, so to speak, its whole exegesis. . . . Scripture leads us to him, and when we reach this end, we no longer have to look for anything beyond it. Cornerstone that he is, he joins together the two Testaments just as he joins together the two peoples. He is the Head of the body of the Scriptures, just as he is the Head of the body of His Church. He is the Head of all sacred understanding, just as he is the head of all the elect. He is the whole content of Scripture, just as he contains all of it in him."

Let me do my best to dispel that impression. In every age the church has misread Scripture. Nor has any age, even the wisest, come close to comprehending the mysteries of Scripture. There is always much to unlearn and much to learn anew. Study of the social, linguistic, cultural, and historical origins and conditions of the Bible's events, authors, and texts is a crucial feature of Christian interpretation of Scripture; in one form or another, it has always been present in the church's exegesis; and in recent centuries it has attained heights scarcely imaginable to previous generations of exegetes. What St. Peter says of the angels regarding the gospel may be said of all those forebears, like St. Jerome, who would have been delighted at the discoveries and learning of modern biblical scholarship: they "long[ed] to look into these things" (1 Pet 1:12).

I therefore have not sought to denigrate contemporary scholarly methods of investigating biblical texts in their historical or any other aspect. I have sought instead to do four things. First, to defend premodern Christian reading strategies and to justify theologically their past as well as their ongoing practice. Second, to reject both claims of the so-called Jowett's Rule of Scripture, namely that each biblical text contains a single meaning and that historical-critical methods (however construed) are the privileged means by which to arrive at that meaning. Third, to expand our notion of what Scripture is, what it is for, and therefore how it may be read well: since how we read depends entirely on who we are, where we are, and for what purpose we are reading. Reading Scripture to hear the Lord speak what he may, or to chew with pleasure on the cud of the text, or to find direction for how to resolve a moral dilemma, or to seek contemplative union with the undivided Trinity: none of these aims calls for methodologically agnostic inquiry into the mind, say, of the final Deuteronomistic redactor. That is one reading strategy, fitted to one particular hermeneutical goal. It is not a catchall for reading Scripture as such.

Fourth and finally, then, I have sought to clarify and elaborate upon the historic hermeneutical conviction of the church that Scripture has more than one sense, or phrased differently, that it admits of many—potentially infinite—readings. Nor is there any need to massage Jowett's Rule to allow something like this, so that, for example, we might say there are many, potentially infinite, perspectives on what is nevertheless a single meaning of any one biblical text.[58] It is true that any one text only *says* one thing, in the sense of its literal verbiage. As Jesus asks the lawyer, "What is written . . . ?"

---

58. At least in earlier moments in the still-unfolding project of Kevin Vanhoozer, this seemed to be a claim he would endorse. I think he continues to stand by a version of it, though I may be mistaken. See Vanhoozer, *Meaning*; Vanhoozer, "Ascending the Mountain."

What is written is one thing; how we understand it is another: "How do you read?" (Luke 10:26). The text calls for interpretation. And the text admits of many interpretations—not all, perhaps not even most of them, plausibly intended by the author.

What I have done, in other words, is presented an argument in favor of anachronism in Christian interpretation of the Bible. If Psalm 110 speaks of the son of Mary, but neither the author nor the first hearers of that psalm knew or could have known the name of Mary's son (since his birth was yet to come for some centuries), then plainly that is an instance of interpreting a text anachronistically. Yet it is a first principle of historiographic inquiry to avoid anachronism at all costs: anachronistic "history" is not history at all. A letter attributed to Abraham Lincoln that makes mention of wireless internet is, by definition, a forgery. So how can a theological hermeneutic that affirms anachronism also affirm the scholarly historiographic study of the Bible? Is it not to speak out of both sides of one's mouth?

It is not, so long as we have abolished Jowett's Rule. Because that Rule has been so entrenched for so long in the institutions, conventions, and standards of excellence of biblical scholarship, it is difficult to disentangle the one from the other. But absent the Rule, no problems are forthcoming. In *that* sense investigation of the historical and related features of the Bible is a continuous project stretching from the church fathers to the present. Beginning with Origen, it continues with St. Jerome and his heirs (not least St. Methodius and St. Cyril), finds renewal in humanists and reformers such as Erasmus, Luther, Calvin, and their epigones, and expands exponentially from the eighteenth century up to the present. Its subjects and tasks are innumerable. Philology, text criticism, redaction criticism, study of the histories "behind" and "within" the texts, investigation of the texts' authors and their influences and biographies, analysis of the sociopolitical milieu of the texts and their prescriptions for communal life: all this and more is entirely to the good. Nothing in this list or anything like it is at odds with the practices and presuppositions of Christian interpretation outlined above. That lack of conflict obtains for at least three reasons.

First, such study concerns the plain sense of the text, not the spiritual. The text's power, by God, to signify what its author could not imagine or to figure that which lay in the future is not a matter for the scholar's research. She can neither confirm nor disconfirm it, any more than a physicist can pronounce on the existence of God or an astronomer on the existence of angels. It does not belong to her expertise, nor is it an object of her study. What the biblical scholar studies is the text in its plain sense, and even then, a rather restricted component of the plain sense: its most probable original public meaning.

Second, such study requires neither naturalism nor agnosticism, whether of a methodological or any other kind. A Christian historian who believes the biblical text is the inspired word of God is perfectly capable of asking of the text questions proper to her academic discipline. Whether or not St. Paul's visit to Jerusalem narrated in Galatians 2 is the Jerusalem council of Acts 15 is such a question; so is whether he was Torah-observant throughout his career as a traveling teacher of the gospel; so is whether, when, and how the five books of Moses were revised, redacted, or expanded during and after the Babylonian exile. Nothing in the creeds or the catechism or elsewhere proscribes or qualifies the asking or answering of such questions. Nor are they rendered suspect by the presence of theological convictions, any more than they are rendered suspect by the absence of such convictions.[59]

Third, such study is proper to the texts, according to Christian teaching, because the doctrine of Scripture does not deny but upholds the historicity and humanity of the canon's documents and origins. When we interpret Christian Scripture, we are not divining runes carved by the finger of God but reading legible texts written by human beings. Biblical texts are texts just as water from the baptistry is water. Better: biblical texts remain texts just as the baptized individual is, empirically speaking, no different when she rises up from the water than when she went down into it. No measurable or phenomenal difference is effected in the baptizand. Rather, her soul has been marked.[60] She belongs to Christ. She is now a vessel of Christ's Spirit and a citizen of the kingdom of which he is king. So for the texts of Scripture: their historicity is not qualified, much less undone, by the Spirit's work, so much as suffused by it. It is their appointment for the heraldry of the gospel, their instrumentality as the sacrament of the divine word, that makes them

---

59. I should mention, though, a more thorough-going critique of historiography even as it is practiced by non-ideologues and those skeptical of historical criticism. This critique calls into question the notion of "history" as a wholly immanent or God-absent domain, which is therefore wholly susceptible to empiricist and historicist methods (thus rendering other methods unnecessary). The resulting analysis feigns neutrality, but according to this philosophical and theological critique, it is anything but neutral. Rather, it presumes, trades on, and inculcates a metaphysic that both predetermines and undermines the results of any and all investigation into "history," arbitrarily ruling out a range of options whose plausibility simply calls for an alternative metaphysics. But since the study of history is not itself adequate to the articulation of a metaphysic, or an adjudication between different metaphysical proposals, to accept one and reject another is capricious and prejudicial. See again the texts cited above by Rae, Levering, Plantinga, and van Inwagen, as well as Adams, *Historical Method*; Hahn and Wiker, *Politicizing the Bible*; Hahn and Morrow, *Modern Biblical Criticism*; Morrow, *Theology, Politics, and Exegesis*; Morrow, *Pretensions of Objectivity*.

60. Though cf. Griffiths, *Christian Flesh*.

unique among texts. Their textuality remains, along with everything that characterizes textuality in general. Careful, honest, rigorous examination of that textuality can only be welcomed by the church.[61]

Welcomed, I should say, with a caveat. We do well to remember, when undertaking this sort of study of the canon, that the results are neither "sure deliverances" nor more fundamental than the spiritual claims that the church confesses of necessity to be true of the canon. On the one hand, this means remembering that all scholarly proposals are just that: proposals, subject to further investigation and extensive cycles of confirmation, clarification, and disputation. They are hypotheses and speculations, sometimes well-reasoned and compelling, sometimes less so.[62] On the other hand, it also means that, even having put away Jowett's Rule, there still remains the temptation to make historiographic judgments a kind of sediment upon which all other exegetical judgments must be built. But this is to confuse the restricted scope of the former sort of inquiry with the totality of the plain sense. (Hence the confusion of the so-called literal sense with what I call the historical-critical sense.) Moreover, it is to forget that the figural signification of Scripture is not secondary to its meaning, though it is contained within the plain sense. That is to say, the Psalms' ability to speak of Christ is equiprimordial with their original historical sense (authorially intended or otherwise). The twofold testimony of Scripture is, in a word, irreducible. That the methods of historians are unable to inquire into one-half of Scripture's enduring communicative power is a function of the delimitation of that discipline, not of the restriction of Scripture's signification.[63]

The fullness of that signification can be a source at once of delight and of confusion. It invites the reader to drink deeply from the divine word, free from anxiety that the well might go dry. But it can also be difficult to understand how the senses of Scripture work in practice, not least in light

61. To instance one such recent examination, see Pierce, *Divine Discourse*. Cf. Hill, *Trinity*.

62. What is striking is how quick biblical scholars are to forget this basic point. Each generation of scholars writes as though it finds itself at the end of (scholarly) history, and that nothing is more to be trusted than those points of loose consensus most recently established. Yet nothing is more certain than that one of the most treasured assumptions taken for granted by virtually all biblical scholars today will be overturned by subsequent scholars sometime in the near future. We simply don't know which one it is. (Nor, I hasten to add, will such overturning mean that it was wrong! The epistemic status of this or that scholarly claim is unrelated to the percentage of scholars who at any one time believe it to be true.)

63. This is *inter alia* why historiographic probability is not the sole criterion for what a Christian may reasonably believe to be historical. The Christian has other reasons, other kinds of grounds, than the solely historiographic. See further chapter 6. Cf. Martin, *Single Savior*; Martin, *Pedagogy*; Martin, *Biblical Truths*.

of the "natural" differentiation internal to the canon. Let me therefore close with three comments along these lines, regarding the diversity of Scripture's meanings, the diversity of the texts that constitute Scripture, and the hermeneutical implications of both.

First, readers generally desire interpretive closure. We want the text before us, whatever it is, to mean one thing; we want that meaning to be graspable, we want to get our arms around it; we want the meaning we discern to correspond to "the" meaning "in" the text; and we want that to be the end of the story. Though common and perhaps universal,[64] this is a tendency to avoid, even with texts outside of the canon. For no text, however simple, is "closeable" in this way. The page can always be turned back, the cover always reopened. The desire to close the matter is the desire to be the last interpreter: but so long as we language animals endure, there will always be more interpreters on the scene, just as there will always be texts new and old to interpret. In a way, to want to be the final interpreter is simply a gloss on the offer of the serpent to Eve: "your eyes will be opened, and you will be like God, knowing . . ." (Gen 3:5). Simply fill the ellipsis with the hermeneutical task. Interpretive closure is thus knowing as a settled fact, not a discursive journey; knowledge *that* the text means *such-and-such* and nothing else: no more to be said. Because it is the end of interpretation, such closure is the end of speech.[65]

The problem is even more acute with Scripture, however. There it is more than a tendency or inclination. It is a temptation, a spiritual trial even. To which, accordingly, the faithful response is principled resistance. Interpretive closure is figured by Potiphar's wife: though it beckons, the Christian reader trained in the ascetics of Scripture will, like Joseph, flee. To resist closure is not to say that Scripture is indeterminate.[66] Nor is it to say that certain texts, topics, questions, or doctrines remain perpetually unanswered or (what's worse) perpetually revisable.[67] What it means is that the depths of Scripture are never finally plumbed. The same texts that teach us the truth of the triune God and the preexistent Christ and the incarnation and the God-bearer always have more to teach us, and not just more of the same. Of the writing of commentaries there shall be no end—and that is a very good thing. It is not a redundancy owing to generational turnover, much less an ongoing accumulation that, like an asymptote, draws ever nearer its terminus. Commentarial reading, rather,

---

64. Though I doubt that.

65. For discussion, see Smith, *Fall of Interpretation*.

66. See Fowl, *Engaging Scripture*, 32–61.

67. For productive dialogue on this point, see Williams, *On Christian Theology*, and Jenson's review of the book in *Pro Ecclesia*.

is the *sine qua non* of Christian engagement with Scripture, the preeminent sign of a healthy ecclesial culture of interpretation.[68]

Commentary, in short, will never cease because interpretation will never cease. And the latter is true of the Bible not only because it is a text but also because it is Scripture, and Scripture contains multiple senses, which generate many readings. This diversity of readings, in turn, is closely related to the diversity of the canonical texts. How to read these texts as contents of a single canon? Consider the story of the exodus, which takes on quite a different shape depending on how wide one stretches the narrative-canonical frame. Does it encompass the book of Exodus as a whole? The entire Torah? Does it continue through Joshua, Judges, and the establishment of the monarchy? Does it stretch to and through the exile, so that the former anticipates the latter and the latter recapitulates the former? Does it include the death and resurrection of Jesus, whose final supper with his disciples is a Passover Meal remembering the exodus and establishing a new covenant in his blood? What of the celebration of the Eucharist in the early messianic communities, celebrations that, in the words of St. Paul, proclaimed "Christ our Passover is sacrificed for us: therefore let us keep the feast" (1 Cor 5:7–8 AKJV)? Each stage in the ever-expanding hermeneutical context makes a significant difference for how the "original" story is understood.[69] And this raises the question of whether biblical texts may or ought to be read "on their own" (seemingly meaningful but ultimately vacuous variations abound here: "on their own terms," "in their own voice," "with their own integrity," etc.), as opposed to reading them in light of the rest of the canonical witness.

The short answer is yes, but much hangs on what one means by that affirmation. It does not mean "to the permanent exclusion of" or "refusing the imposition of" or "keeping the text pure from the influence of" or "avoiding the eisegetical intrusion of" the rest of the canonical witness—whether that be from the same Testament as the text in question or from the other. The saying is sure: *It is never improper to read a biblical text in light of the whole of Scripture.* But depending on the genre of the text, the purpose for which one is reading, the context of one's reading, and the use to which one seeks to put the reading, it may be fitting to limit one's focus to a particular passage and

68. See, e.g., Griffiths, *Religious Reading*; Henderson, *Commentary*.

69. For rich discussion, see Roberts and Wilson, *Echoes of Exodus*. Let me also reiterate the central contention of the previous chapters, namely, that "the ever-expanding hermeneutical context" to which I refer in the passage above is not only scriptural (the canon) or literary (the conciliar and dogmatic tradition). It is ecclesial. That, too, makes a difference for interpretation. For a recent work that proposes how the history of the church and the lived experience of believers makes a difference for understanding the Bible, see McCaulley, *Reading While Black*.

to refrain from recourse to any others. It is worth knowing, for example, the message of Qoheleth "on its own." The same goes for the poetic cycles of Job, for St. Paul's appeal to St. Philemon, for the Seer's visions in the Apocalypse. The church's book is composed of smaller books, and each book is worth knowing in and for itself. But this ought never to become a fetishization of the ostensible integrity, inviolate and inviolable, of each discrete text cordoned off from the others.[70] The texts are part of a collection, and that fact is hermeneutically foundational. It cannot but inform how we read, because the status of being canonical materially changes both the genre and the meaning of a text. Had the Song of Songs not been included in the canon, it would not have meant what it now means as a canonical book.[71] Pretending it is not in the canon serves no one and nothing. At best, it constitutes a baseless act of willful denial.

To read a text "on its own," in sum, may contingently be a worthy endeavor, but the Christian reader need not bracket her convictions in doing so. One is still reading for the plain sense of the text, which is a function of its status as canonical; one simply desists from drawing on the resources of the wider canon to illuminate the text. Even here, though, things are not as tidy as we might prefer. Think of the Creator's use of the first-person plural in Genesis 1, or the thrice-holy confession in Isaiah 6, or the likeness of a human form seated above the likeness of a throne in Ezekiel 1. The church's premodern exegesis read for the plain sense in these passages and discerned, respectively, the singular voice of Father, Son, and Holy Spirit; the vision of the triune God of Israel; and the prefigural appearance of Christ enthroned as Lord. The boundaries, in other words, between plain and figural readings are porous and imprecise. They cannot be delineated neatly in advance. Think of still other texts: Psalm 8 and Isaiah 53 may indeed be read "on their own terms" without reference to Christ.[72] But can any

70. Much less hypothetical Ur-texts reconstructed from the final form of the text as we have it.

71. See Davis, *Song of Songs*, 231–37; Jenson, *Song of Songs*, 1–15.

72. R. W. L. Moberly does this in *God of the Old Testament*, which is typical of Moberly's work in being circumspect, scholarly, irenic, and theological all at once. Consider his reading of Psalm 82, about which he writes that "I do not propose to discuss NT and patristic interpretations of Ps. 82 in which . . . v. 6 plays an important role because of its citation in John 10:33–36" (104). He goes on: "The issues raised by the citation lead into fascinating areas that are *nonetheless distinct from the psalm's own concerns*. The psalm's content is open to a different use and construal when thus recontextualized; but that is not my present concern" (emphasis mine). This is a characteristically generous interpretive posture: Moberly neither repudiates nor sidelines patristic readings of the text rooted in the Johannine gloss, but acknowledges them while stating simply that they are not what concern him. My only query is the suggestion that "the psalm" possesses "concerns" of its "own," apparently apart from or prior to its various contextualizations

honest Christian reader avoid the reference? Best to be explicit about the intrinsic and unavoidable figural reach of these texts, *and thereupon* remark on the plain sense of the passages, understood according to the letter: genre, socioreligious context, location in Israel's history, theological evocation, and so on. For the figural preserves and elucidates the plain sense, just as the plain sense grounds and signifies the figural. Neither is complete without the other, and both call for patient exegetical care.

Finally, the diversity of the canon's texts has given rise in the late modern period to consideration of Scripture's pluralism.[73] Sometimes this is a matter of anxiety, sometimes a matter of celebration, sometimes a cudgel used to beat back traditional claims in the doctrine of Scripture.[74] I have very little to say about the Bible's so-called pluralism. Not because it is unimportant: it is important, and it is a testament to the Spirit's beautiful creativity in drawing together such profoundly different voices to join one another in a single chorus or polyphony *ad maiorem Dei gloriam*. Scripture is in this way a kind of mirror of the church's unity in diversity, itself rooted in the unity of the Trinity. No, I have little to say because one's assessment of the canon's internal pluralism is largely a matter of aesthetic, not doctrinal, judgment. In a catholic theological approach, one does not ask, "Where are the logical (or historical, or theological, or moral) contradictions?" One asks, "How does the whole thing hang together—if it does?" Christians are those who suppose, or at least confess, that it does. This is an aesthetic judgment, at the hermeneutical level, rooted in a spiritual judgment. For if the canon is one then it is one because God the Father, Son, and Holy Spirit is one. And like the truth of the triune God, the unity of canonical Holy Scripture will not be fully or finally revealed in this life. It follows that, in the course of the mission of the church (the unity of which is also a matter of trust, not sight), the oneness of the canon functions as a kind of promise, the fulfillment of which will only be disclosed at the End, on the day of Christ. That it *does* all hold together, that it really bears reliable witness to the one true and living God, and how: on that day this, too, will be made manifest. Until then, we walk by faith.

(in the Jewish or Christian canon, in the synagogue or church, etc.). To paraphrase Stephen Fowl, *texts do not have concerns; readers do*. To claim otherwise implies a certain kind of hermeneutical bedrock, presumably understood to be essential or foundational to the text in a manner antecedent to actual readers (whoever they may be) engaging the text (in whatever way) in a concrete context (whenever and wherever that may be). Such a bedrock, however, is the text alone, just as it stands; to suppose anything further is either question-begging or already constituent in the hermeneutical act.

73. See chapter 2 for brief discussion of the significance of "scriptures" in the plural.

74. See, e.g., Collins, *Bible After Babel*.

6

Authority

And Jesus came and said to them, "All authority in heaven and on earth has been given to me. Go therefore and make disciples of all nations, baptizing them in the name of the Father and of the Son and of the Holy Spirit, teaching them to observe all that I have commanded you; and lo, I am with you always, to the close of the age."
—Matthew 28:18–20

Then it seemed good to the apostles and the elders, with the whole church, to choose men from among them and send them to Antioch with Paul and Barnabas. They sent Judas called Barsabbas, and Silas, leading men among the brethren, with the following letter: "The brethren, both the apostles and the elders, to the brethren who are of the Gentiles in Antioch and Syria and Cilicia, greeting. Since we have heard that some persons from us have troubled you with words, unsettling your minds, although we gave them no instructions, it has seemed good to us, having come to one accord, to choose men and send them to you with our beloved Barnabas and Paul, men who have risked their lives for the sake of our Lord Jesus Christ. We have therefore sent Judas and Silas, who themselves will tell you the same things by word of mouth. For it has seemed good to the Holy Spirit and to us . . . ."
—Acts 15:22–28

It is the church's confession that Holy Scripture is the word of the Lord. This word is not episodic, but reliable; not aimless, but purposive; not immediate, but mediated. The congregation approaches the scriptures with fear and trembling, not because the Lord might not speak, but because he surely will. Since God's word is for God's people—for their edification, encouragement, and sanctification—their fear and trembling is interwoven with joyful expectation. That happy anticipation, however, is eschatologically qualified: what will be heard when the text is read aloud is a human voice speaking human words, *through which* the divine word will resound. That is a gift and a blessing to the faithful, but it is also a down payment for the future. Though the church honors and loves the apostles and prophets, their writings arouse as much as they sate the soul's hunger to hear the Lord without interposition. The Lord's word spoken through his servants is thus a double sign: of provision as well as need, grace as well as lack, presence as well as absence. It stokes the flames of desire in the process of quenching them. As R. S. Thomas writes of preaching,

> When I speak,
> Though it be you who speak
> Through me, something is lost.[1]

Though we might want to substitute another word for "lost," the sentiment Thomas captures is true, too, of hearing Scripture. To hear the text of Scripture read is to hear the Lord speak, yes, but to hear him speak "through." The thanksgiving we offer in response is sincere, but it is simultaneously a petition: *Here below, here and now, speak to us "through"; but promise, in the hereafter, to speak to us unmediated, with that "through" struck through. No more servants, heralds, ambassadors. Give us yourself alone.*[2]

The gospel announces just that: the immediate presence of God's own self, in Christ and in the world to come. Until then, the Lord's presence is mediated to us by Christ's body: the company of the baptized; the divine liturgy; the sacraments; the Holy Eucharist; and the word of the Lord in Scripture. Because it is mediated by the apostles and prophets, this word is not naked but clothed: enfolded in the covenant, transmitted by apostolic succession, wrapped in the swaddling bands of sacred tradition.[3] This en-

1. Thomas, "Kneeling," in *Collected Poems*, 199. He concludes the poem: "The meaning is in the waiting."

2. Ps 62:1–2, 5, 8: "For God alone my souls waits in silence; from him comes my salvation. He only is my rock and my salvation. . . . For God alone my soul waits in silence, for my hope is from him. He only is my rock and my salvation."

3. I have in mind the metaphor of Martin Luther: Israel's scriptures are "the swaddling cloths and the manger in which Christ lies. . . . Plain and lowly are these swaddling

velopment—at once a robe, a shroud, a veil, and a sheath—is what calls for a doctrine of Scripture in Christian theology. If reading Scripture amounted to inquiring of the Lord, say by means of the urim and thummim, we would have little need for theological reflection, much less hermeneutics.[4] Divinization is cut and dry; interpretation is an art—which is to say, it is a wooly and unpredictable affair.

All that is by way of prelude to thinking about the authority of Scripture. Nothing would be simpler than if consulting Scripture's authority as God's word consisted in rolling the holy dice and receiving a yes or no answer to a concrete question. But as we have seen in the previous five chapters, Scripture comprises dozens of books spanning hundreds of years in a diversity of genres bound, not in a simple collection, but in two distinct Testaments. What does it mean for such a complex volume to exercise ongoing authority in a community across time? This is the purpose of Scripture we left unaddressed in chapter 4: that the canon is the unruled rule, the norm nonpareil, for the life, worship, mission, and faith of Christ's church—in perpetuity. We take it up last because we needed theological scaffolding to make sense of the intricate relationship between the authority of God, the authority of the canon, the authority of tradition, and the authority of the church. After all, the church is in one sense the author of the canon, and the canon is itself an item of the church's tradition. How to maintain the preeminence of Scripture while granting those historical and theological realities? At a minimum, it involves affirming the unruled character of Scripture as the rule *for* faith, while acknowledging on the one hand that, historically speaking, Scripture's organizing principle was the Rule *of* Faith; and on the other hand that, theologically speaking, though it admits of many readings, Scripture ought to be read by the church in accordance with that Rule.

Thus the question: Does the historical and theological priority of the Rule of Faith thereby undermine the primacy of Scripture as the rule for faith? The short answer: no, it does not. The long answer is found in the rest of this chapter.

The chapter has three sections. The first considers the concept of authority itself and how the authority of both God and Scripture modifies or extends that concept. The second discusses the nature, scope, and exercise of Scripture's authority in the church. The third turns to the church as a living community; it seeks to clarify the church's twofold relationship to Scripture, standing beneath its authority *as* its authoritative interpreter. Throughout these sections, it should be kept in mind that whether or not a particular

---

cloths, but precious is the treasure, Christ, who lies wrapped in them" ("Preface," 48).

4. See Exod 28:30; Lev 8:8; Num 27:21; Deut 33:8; 1 Sam 14:41; 28:6.

community maintains and respects the authority of Scripture is finally an empirical question, answerable less by recourse to its doctrinal statements and more by attention to its common life. Authority is *lived* as much as it is acknowledged. No account of Scripture's authority will be adequate that forgets that simple truth.

1. Divine Authority

In a recent essay, philosopher Michael Rea offers a useful framework for understanding what it means to say that a text is authoritative. Both the framework and the terminology he employs will help our theological depiction of the authority of God as that is exercised through the canon of Holy Scripture.[5]

First, Rea distinguishes between authority and truth.[6] Although Christians, especially evangelical Christians, often use these terms regarding Scripture in synonymous or coterminous ways, they are distinct. A parent's authority over her child speaks to a role, not to her propensity for being wise or correct. In the case of instructions for a board game, though they are certainly authoritative for players, the concept of truth is not even applicable. The rules are "true" in the sense that they establish and govern game play; they are not "true" in the wider sense of describing a state of affairs, prescribing proper conduct, or being falsifiable.

Second, Rea observes that authority is always circumscribed: it belongs to a particular domain.[7] A parent lacks authority over another person's child (under ordinary circumstances); the rules for Spades do not obtain for chess; a doctor of philosophy does not qualify one for the activities and prerogatives of a doctor of medicine. To speak of an authoritative text, one must specify the realm in which that text bears authority, under what conditions, and with respect to what objects: persons or things, beliefs or behavior, and so on.

Third, Rea divides the kinds of authority into two groups: theoretical, or belief-guiding, and practical, or action-guiding.[8] A chemistry textbook

---

5. Rea, "Authority and Truth." For a clarifying disagreement over the issues raised by framing Scripture's authority in terms of its own, deputized authority or in terms of God's authority exercised through it, see Wright, *The Last Word*, 21–32; and the comments of O'Donovan, *Church in Crisis*, 54–55. I owe this connection to Swain, *Trinity, Revelation, and Reading*, 72n.21.

6. Rea, "Authority and Truth," 872–73.

7. Rea, "Authority and Truth," 873–74.

8. Rea, "Authority and Truth," 874–76.

might be authoritative with respect to the truths of chemistry and thus what one ought to believe. But it lacks authority over how one ought to live. Conversely, a university code of conduct is authoritative over the actions of those students enrolled in the university (perhaps only when they are on campus, or during the school year); but such students may believe what they please—including that the code of conduct is in error in some of its behavioral requirements.

Fourth, Rea elaborates upon the relationship between diverse authorities.[9] The presence of a defeater, for example, might mean that an otherwise decisive authority need not be obeyed: a teacher commands a student to eat pork, unaware that she is Jewish; the student does not comply, obedient to a prior authority. Conflicting authorities call for discernment: which is more authoritative than the other, and which, if any, constitutes a foundational authority. A foundational authority is one that, for particular persons within particular domains, brooks no defeaters, since nothing else is more authoritative than it. Now there can be more than one foundational authority, since they may apply to different persons and/or within different domains. But there can also be more than one foundational authority for the same person within the same domain, since in that case none would be *more* authoritative than the other(s).[10] Finally, though by definition at any one time no defeaters are known to exist for a foundational authority, if one learned of reasons to doubt or to qualify the authority of the latter, then that would provide sufficient evidence for it no longer to function as a foundational authority. Far from being inert, enervating, or immutable, therefore, the presence and operation of such authorities is a dynamic, empowering, and essential process in the life of individuals, communities, and institutions.

Rea sums up his account with a definition:

> To call a text (genuinely, *de jure*) authoritative is to say that, within some domain and for some individual or individuals, the text supplies reasons for belief or action (or both) that are, absent defeaters, decisive. Again, it doesn't follow from this that the supplied reasons motivate the relevant beliefs or actions. Nor does it even follow that the individual or group in question will recognize them as decisive. (*De jure* authorities might fail to be *de facto* authorities—as often happens, we might think, when people casually and habitually act contrary to state laws

---

9. Rea, "Authority and Truth," 876–84.

10. Thus equal but perhaps incommensurate foundational authorities.

or common moral intuitions.) But they will, nonetheless, decisively justify the relevant beliefs or actions.[11]

In light of this definition, consider the claim of Johann Gerhard: "The
divine authority of Scripture rises from and depends on the efficient principal cause of Holy Scripture, which is God. Because Holy Scripture has God
as its author, by whose immediate inspiration the prophets, evangelists, and
apostles wrote, it obtains its divine authority therefrom and therefore."[12] If
we would consider Scripture as an authority, but Scripture's authority derives from God's, then we ought first to consider the authority of God.

Divine authority, unlike all other authorities, is absolutely indefeasible
and universal in scope. There is no domain in which divine authority is not
operative and sovereign. To be created—and all that is not God is created
from nothing—just *is* to be subject to this authority; there is no escaping or
mitigating it. Divine authority is not, however, alien to the creature, in the
sense of being an extrinsic force on a continuum with the powers and identity of the creature, and thus in competition with them. Divine authority is
positively rather than inversely related to the freedom of the creature. The
creature flourishes within and beneath it. For the authority of God is one
with his rule, and his rule is one with his gracious will to create and redeem.
God rules for our benefit, to his glory.[13] His authority establishes, upholds,
and perfects our life in relation to him. He alone knows what we need and
what we are for, for he alone is our Maker, Sustainer, and Savior. Our good
as creatures lies in alignment with—ultimately in union with—the good
itself, God the Trinity, who is our source and end. When he commands, it
is to draw us toward what is good; when he rebukes, it is to cut us off from
what is bad (in itself and for us). There is no authority except that which he
ordains and serves his will; all true authority that is not God's own comes
from him, and all false or corrupted authority stands in opposition to him.[14]
No other authority, however foundational or wide in scope, stands to creatures in the same way as God himself. To him alone do we owe unqualified
submission.[15] Such submission is the secret wellspring of the deepest joy
and highest freedom possible for human life.

11. Rea, "Authority and Truth," 883.

12. Gerhard, *Nature of Holy Scripture* 3.33.

13. Westminster Shorter Catechism, Question 1: "What is the chief end of man? A:
Man's chief end is to glory God, and to enjoy him forever."

14. This is merely a gloss on passages such as Rom 13:1–7; Rev 13:1—14:20; John
18:33—19:11.

15. Even John Calvin, whose teaching on submission to rulers and on their divinely
given authority is uncompromising, makes allowance for when obedience to God must
trump such submission; see the discussion in Calvin, *Institutes* 4.20.17–32.

Scripture, as Gerhard writes, partakes of this divine authority, because it derives from it. But it is not synonymous with it. Why? Principally because the scope of Scripture's authority is not universal in the same way. Though Scripture applies to the life of believers in every facet of their lives, it does not speak *to* every such facet. There is no such thing as "biblical" cooking, dieting, exercise, hygiene, dating, voting, clothing, sleeping, or any number of other common activities. Moreover, there is no such thing as "biblical" astronomy, physics, chemistry, math, sociology, geology, or architecture. The Bible may be authoritative *in* such endeavors, but it is not an authority *for* them, except in quite indirect ways. Both its theoretical and its practical authority is therefore heavily circumscribed.[16]

Furthermore, the domain of Scripture's authority is not universal in the way that God's is. True, there is a sense in which Scripture is authoritative for all humanity, inasmuch as the gospel is for all the nations, and thus each and every human being is invited to be baptized into Christ's body and consequently to submit to his authority in Scripture. But that is only another way to say that the domain of Scripture's authority is the Christian church. Missionaries are not shocked or bemused by nonbelievers' ignorance or repudiation of Scripture; they do not seek conversions the way a police officer might instruct the uninformed about laws that apply to them whether they know it or not. They proclaim the gospel and, *following* the profession of faith at baptism, instruct neophytes in the scriptural rule to which they now will be expected to conform their lives.

The relative domain of Scripture's authority is evident as well in those institutions and spheres of society in which other norms have pride of place. These include hospitals, schools, courts, and markets, not to mention those bodies that enact and execute the law (in the U.S., the Congress and the White House). Again, the Bible may inform any of these, even explicitly; but at the level of daily practice it functions at best as a kind of unseen infrastructure, offering principles or basic guidelines that call for extension, elaboration, and application—as well as additional materials.

Finally, because Scripture is a fixed canon, even where it does speak directly it does not always do so in an exhaustive manner. The most acute examples of this kind are moral questions. Does the Bible speak authoritatively regarding, for example, artificial contraception? What of in vitro fertilization? What of abortion? Or embryonic stem-cell research? What of the justifiable reasons for engaging in warfare, or justifiable modes of prosecuting it? Or to limit the topics to theological practice, what of the writing

16. See Smith, *Bible Made Impossible*, but also Leithart's review, "Biblicism," and Smith, "Reply."

and veneration of icons? What of asking the saints in heaven to pray for the living on earth? What of the adoration of the eucharistic host? Scripture manifestly does not answer these questions. In that sense, too, the range of its authority is far from universal. Doubtless some questions unaddressed by Scripture may be deduced from principles enunciated in the text or by a kind of accumulation of arguments following the mind of Scripture; such reasoning is usually a matter of *convenientia*. But not all of them may be so deduced. And few of them with definitiveness.[17]

If no dispositive answer is forthcoming from Scripture on any number of questions that the church might have in the course of its mission, then we are presented with one of three options. Either (a) all such questions, from the least to the greatest, if truly *unanswerable* by recourse to Scripture, are adiaphora in the Christian life; or (b) such questions, though not adiaphora, call for *provisional* discernment of the Spirit's guidance, such that believers must act in accordance with their conscience while respecting the differing answers of fellow believers; or (c) such questions, when bearing on matters of great import, are an occasion for the church's leaders to discern the Spirit's guidance in a *conclusive* way, in order to teach the faithful, by the authority of the Spirit, what to do or believe (or, as the case may be, how rightly to understand Scripture in light of the question at hand).

This book presumes the third option. The next two sections unpack why, and how it works in practice.

2. Scriptural Authority

It would seem that I have eliminated a good deal of the potential authority of Scripture. Whereas God's authority extends over all, in all, and to all—no nook or cranny being excluded from its reach—Scripture's authority belongs

---

17. Recall the hermeneutical rule of the Westminster Confession of Faith: "The whole counsel of God concerning all things necessary for his own glory, man's salvation, faith and life, is either expressly set down in Scripture, *or by good and necessary consequence may be deduced from Scripture*" (1.6, my emphasis). By way of example, see Calvin's repudiation of eucharistic adoration in the *Institutes* 4.17.35–36; or Article 26 of the Belgic Confession on "The Intercession of Christ," which rejects the practice of the intercession of the saints on the grounds that Christ alone is believers' true and perfect mediator. But the logic of the latter argument implies that Christians on earth need not offer intercessory prayers on others' behalf. The disagreement is therefore not one of theological principle—surely the Reformed may allow the *possibility* that the souls of the saints in heaven pray for those of us on earth (cf. Rev 6:9–11)—but one of Scripture's silence: lacking canonical mandate for the practice, we ought to forbear. By comparison, see the "Confession of Dositheus" (Chapter 6 of *The Acts and Decrees of the Synod of Jerusalem*), Decree 8.

primarily in the domain of the church, and within the church, it covers only certain aspects of believers' lives in a direct way.

Now, this description calls for clarification. The Decalogue is delimited, being only ten commandments, but it encompasses the whole of one's life. If God through Scripture mandates that I tell the truth, I must do so in every area of my life. The same goes for Scripture's theoretical authority: if Christ calls me to confess his name before others—which is to say, to put faith in him alone as Lord and Savior—I am not permitted to do so selectively. The authority of Scripture in this way pervades and implicates every one of my beliefs, words, deeds, and desires. It does not leave any untouched; what is untouched is unbaptized: but baptism touches the whole person, soul and body.[18] All belongs to Christ in the life of faith. Nothing may be kept from him.

Having said that, we have not thereby obviated the need for interpretation. Even those express commands found in Scripture whose meaning and authority no one disputes must be interpreted. Is it ever, under any circumstances, permissible to lie? If the answer is yes, or if one allows that reasonable Christians may disagree in their answer, then it is not so much Scripture as such whose authority is in view but Scripture *rightly interpreted*. That is to say, Scripture may be taken to mean all kinds of things—some of which may be plausibly drawn from the plain sense of the text—but that does not mean per se that the authority of Scripture endorses it. Scripture must be understood correctly, which is another way of saying that it must be read faithfully, for its authority to be exercised properly.

Before addressing the question of how Scripture may be interpreted in a trustworthy manner, and by whom, let us return to a distinction we have had occasion to mention already in the preceding chapters. This distinction comes from the Lutheran scholastics in their reflections on how Scripture exercises authority in the church.[19]

The distinction is twofold. The primary authority of Scripture is its capacity, by the Spirit of Christ, to bear the living word of God to sinners.

---

18. Rooted in the christological dogma that what is unassumed is unhealed. See St. Gregory of Nazianzus, *First Letter to Cledonius*, Letter 101.5 (in *Theological Orations*, 155–65, at 158).

19. See Johann König, *Theologia Positiva Acroamatica* §83. Johannes Musäus uses the terminology "inciting [or] productive authority" and "canonical or normative authority" to designate what I below call Scripture's sacramental and doctrinal authority, respectively; see *Introductio in theologiam* 2.3. Cited and discussed in Jenson, *Triune God*, 28–29; *Triune Story*, 146–54. Michael Horton terms the two roles "sacramental" (Scripture as means of grace) and "regulative" (Scripture as canonical rule for faith and practice); see Horton, *Christian Faith*, 152–55. I owe this reference to Taylor, *Reading Scripture*, 112; I had not read Horton prior to drafting this chapter.

As God's living word it has the power to do what God does in the gospel: to convict of sin; to call to repentance; to convert to Christ; to elicit faith; to heal the sick; to forgive the transgressor; to build up the frail; to comfort the downtrodden; to expel the devil; to rebuke the wicked; to instruct the faithful; to sanctify the elect; to equip the saints; and much more. This is the effectual spiritual power of Holy Scripture, or what we have called its sacramental character. Its home is the liturgy, which in turn sends believers out into the world to encounter God's word in their daily lives, whether by recitation, prayer, song, or devotional reading. It is in service to this power—the divine authority of God's word in Scripture—that preaching exists. The sermon points to what is indicated in the text and seeks, in ordinary words, to draw the church's attention to it in awe, wonder, and praise. It proclaims the gospel out of the text, reiterating in one's own words the *res* attested in the inspired words of the apostles and prophets. The faithful sermon is one that seeks to perform that reiteration, in all of one's frailty, petitioning God's help at every turn. The successful sermon is one that the Spirit, in sovereign freedom, elects to use as a vehicle through which to speak again—as a kind of echo of Holy Scripture—the selfsame word of the Lord. And like the word written in Scripture, the word spoken from the pulpit may, by God's grace, be a means of the saving power of Christ.[20]

The secondary authority of Scripture is its role as supreme rule for Christian doctrine regarding faith and morals. In this it is the *norma normans non normata*, that which judges but is not itself judged. Call this Scripture's doctrinal authority. It names Scripture's statutory role, precisely as a fixed canon of texts, to teach the church's members what to believe and how to behave. There is a sense in which the primary, sacramental authority of Scripture is in principle as unlimited as God's own authority, since God may use a text that concerns X to speak to person Y about matter Z, and that in the most concrete yet unverifiable manner. ("I heard the Lord say to me . . .")[21] Howsoever that may be, the doctrinal authority of Scripture is

20. Is there a kind of *ex opera operato* in preaching, by analogy to the efficacy of the sacraments? One wants to say yes, but a sermon can fail in a way that baptism cannot. See again the relevant sections in chapters 1 and 2, as well as my "Theses on Preaching."

21. Consider the following anecdote from Jenson: "In the summer of 1963, I and some other then 'younger' theologians were variously occupied in Harvard's libraries, while Cambridge's NAACP was recruiting for what turned out to be the 'I have a dream' march in Washington. We dithered. On the Sunday before the march, at the service most of us attended, the lectionary Gospel was the parable about the son who said, 'I go' and went not, and the son who said, 'I go not' and went. The preacher then mounted the pulpit and simply repeated the address of the sign-up center. That afternoon we marched straight there. This too was scriptural authority in action, to mandate and liberate, or in the Lutheran phrase, to be 'law and gospel'" (*Triune Story*, 152).

significantly delimited by comparison, exactly in the ways canvassed above (toward the end of the previous section). It is this exercise of authority that we are concerned with here and in the rest of the chapter.

In point of fact, there is very little to say regarding Christians' relationship to Scripture's doctrinal authority. For it is simply stated: the relationship is properly one of *submission*, that is, of faith and obedience to the text as God's written word to his people. Regarding what to believe, for example, Scripture teaches that God is one; that he alone created all that exists; that he chose the people Israel and covenanted with them; that he drew near in the person of Mary's son, Jesus; that Jesus is the Son and Word of God incarnate; that he suffered and died on a cross; that he rose on the third day; that through his life, death, and resurrection, God accomplished salvation for sinners; that this salvation is available to all people, Jew and gentile alike; that Jesus poured out the Spirit of God from heaven, a gift for all who by faith are baptized into his body; that he shall return in glory to judge the living and the dead. This is little more than a paraphrase of the Creed, and thus only a sampling of Scripture's theoretical authority—that is, its doctrinal authority with respect to belief.

With respect to behavior, its practical authority[22] likewise calls for an incomplete list: Scripture teaches God's people to worship God alone; to put faith in Christ alone; to invoke the Holy Spirit alone; to serve those in need; to forgive those who harm us; to avoid all hypocrisy and vengeance; not to steal, murder, or commit adultery; and much more. These commands are binding on the church, precisely because Scripture commands them. That is not to resolve their relationship to our salvation (i.e., whether our failing to keep them might endanger it). Only to say that, given the relationship between Christians and the Bible and the practical authority of the latter over the former, it is axiomatic that this and other moral teaching applies to Christians' lives as a matter of course, and without exception.

The pressing theological question is therefore not the nature of either the theoretical or the practical authority of Scripture in the church. That is, or should be, a given. The question, or rather questions, are found elsewhere. Indeed, they are multifaceted and rather extensive. I have grouped them into the following sets, which together ought to give a sense of the complexity of the matter.

---

22. So that there are two sets of distinctions operating here: that between belief-guiding and action-guiding (or theoretical and practical) authority, on the one hand, and that between Scripture's sacramental and doctrinal authority, on the other. The former is inherited from Rea, and applies to any kind of authority. The latter applies only to Scripture, and is my own appropriation of an earlier Lutheran distinction. Here, I am distinguishing Scripture's doctrinal authority with respect first to belief then to action.

1. To whom falls the obligation to discern what Scripture teaches Christians to believe and to do? Is it the church as a whole (that is, in the form of its representative leaders), the local congregation, or the individual Christian?

2. How are the express teachings of Scripture regarding faith or morals to be interpreted? If casuistry in either doctrine or ethics is called for, how should it be undertaken, and by whom?

3. How should the Old Testament be read as authoritative for gentile believers?[23] Which parts of it continue to command assent on the church's part, whether theoretically or practically, and which do not? How may we know, and who decides?

4. How is the teaching of Scripture authoritative in different ways for different groups of people? Beyond the unique example of Jews and gentiles and the developmental case of children and adults, the church has long read certain teachings as applying to men but not to women, and vice versa. Or what of rulers versus subjects: is scriptural regulation of beliefs or morals somehow qualified in the former case?[24] Or consider the historic distinction between commands common to all believers and evangelical counsels, or counsels of perfection. The celibate poverty of Jesus and St. Paul was taken in the early church as a sign of the advent of the new age; through the Spirit's power, the baptized could now begin to live into the perfection of the kingdom here and now, bearing witness in the present to its future consummation. But these and other examples would suggest that Scripture's authority is not "flat" but highly differentiated, even within the New Testament, even focusing solely on the teachings of Jesus himself.

5. How do different genres of Scripture "teach" in an authoritative way? Consider sapiential aphorisms, or poetry, or prophecy fulfilled, or apocalyptic literature, or simple historical narrative. In what way are such texts authoritative for believers, and how is that authority exercised?[25]

23. The same question applies in a different way to the numerically smaller portion of believers who are Jewish. See, e.g., Nanos and Zetterholm, *Paul within Judaism*; Kinzer, *Messianic Judaism*; Fredriksen, *Paul*; Rudolph, *A Jew to the Jews*.

24. That is, may rulers "sin boldly," in the way rulers do? May they lie? May they take life in ways or for reasons that the church repudiates? May they make promises they know they cannot keep?

25. Here, as in previous chapters, is where both a distinction in the modes of Scripture's authority and the hermeneutical procedures fitting to them show their necessity. Otherwise whole blocks of the Bible would simply be lost to the contemporary gentile reader.

6. What of those parts of Scripture that appear to presume or to oblige beliefs, practices, or institutions that, in retrospect, believers may reasonably understand to be products of the sociocultural contexts of the canon's human authors? Topics arranged by category might include cosmology, chronology, monarchy, marriage, warfare, medicine, slavery, even something as simple as women's head-coverings (1 Cor 11:2–16) or greeting one another with a holy kiss (Rom 16:16; 1 Cor 16:20; 2 Cor 13:12; 1 Thess 5:26).

7. What is the "style" of Scripture's authority? Is it regulative, excluding anything and everything—in the domain, let us stipulate, of worship, doctrine, and morals—that it does not plainly command or allow? Is it permissive, excluding nothing at all that it does not thus command or allow? Or is it authorizing, that is, does it deputize individual believers, local congregations, and/or ordained leaders to make such judgments on a case-by-case basis?[26]

8. More broadly, in what way, if at all, is Scripture authoritative in the domain of what Christians are to believe and to do regarding those beliefs and deeds about which the text is utterly silent?[27]

9. Under what conditions and for what sorts of reasons may the church, in the form of either its leaders or its members, question what was once (or what was for long stretches of time) taken to be the express teaching of Scripture on a particular matter about which the text does not keep silent but speaks plainly? When does such questioning constitute a doubting of the authority of Scripture itself, and when does it constitute a reconsideration of how rightly to interpret the teaching of Scripture's (unquestioned) authority? How are believers to tell the difference between the two?

26. See again O'Donovan, *Church in Crisis*, 54–55; O'Donovan, "Moral Authority"; O'Donovan, *Resurrection*, 121–62; Jenson, *Triune Story*, 183–86; Johnson, *Scripture and Discernment*, 40–44.

27. Technology is the fly in the ointment here. Consider works of science fiction, such as Lewis's *Space Trilogy*, Herbert's *Dune*, Le Guin's *Hainish Cycle*, Wolfe's *Book of the New Sun*, Robinson's *Mars Trilogy*, Corey's *Expanse* series, Faber's *Book of Strange New Things*, Russell's *The Sparrow* and *Children of God*, or Garland's *Ex Machina*. These and others are useful prompts for the church to imagine the shape of its faithfulness in the face of almost unimaginably new forms of life in what is no longer the distant future. And given the combined power of capitalist modernity and technological development to undercut and transform long-established forms of life, including the church's, it is unthinkable for Christians to rely on nothing but their own well-meant and ever-provisional inferences from the canon. Whether as charter, challenge, or critique, such inferences will only fall like so many dominoes before the "progress" of transhumanism, CRISPR, cloning, and the rest.

10. Applying the same set of questions to the doctrine of Scripture, when and why might it be proper, given new evidence or knowledge, to reconsider the church's theological understanding of Scripture's authority? Is it appropriate for, say, the works of Copernicus and Galileo and Darwin and Einstein to prompt a revision in the doctrine of Scripture, such that, for example, the church modifies its expectations of what Scripture teaches authoritatively? In Rea's terms, this would mean redrawing the boundaries of Scripture's domain. If the answer is yes, that it is potentially appropriate, it follows that the church needs criteria and procedures by which to ascertain the fittingness of such cases. These would stand in contradistinction to those misbegotten attempts, all too frequent, to correlate doctrine by cultural and intellectual trends, the latter serving as judge over the former. As the saying has it, when the church marries the spirit of the age, she finds herself a widow in the next.[28] So the revisability of the domain of Scripture's authority cannot mean a naïve chasing after the winds of cultural change, nor a perpetual narrowing until there is no more domain to speak of.[29]

Thus the questions posed by the authority of Scripture. I cannot hope to answer them in adequate fashion in this space. But I list them out in detail in order to demonstrate the complexity contained within the simplicity of Scripture's doctrinal authority. The simplicity is that Scripture teaches what the church is to believe and do; to what it says, believers ought to submit. The complexity is in how that submission plays out in the subtleties and unruliness of interpretation. The text must be read, by different people in various places across the arc of time. That is the great challenge of Scripture's authority in action. Try as we might, it is not a challenge we can resolve in advance. The freedom of life in the Spirit means daily discernment of the will of God for one's life, discernment that ought never to stray far from Holy Scripture. Because God is living, he continues to lead his people through all the helps provided in the church: not only the Bible, but liturgy, sacrament, prayer, intercession, icons, saints, pastors, fellow believers, and more. We theologians do our best to systematize, leaving no stone unturned, no question unanswered. But the life of faith is far too untidy for that.

28. William Inge is generally credited with the line.

29. See now Legaspi, *Death of Scripture*; Reventlow, *Authority of the Bible*; Sheehan, *Enlightenment Bible*.

For now, let me close this section by heading off two understandable but misguided responses to the complications outlined above. The first was popularized a few decades ago by the scientist Stephen Jay Gould. Occasioned by apparent conflicts between faith and reason—or "religion" and "science"[30]—he proposed what he called "non-overlapping magisteria," or NOMA for short.[31] Scientific inquiry is distinct from religious or theological inquiry, and the authorities proper to each are similarly distinct. Therefore, scientific authority is foundational, or magisterial, for all inquiry in the realm of science, just as religious authority is foundational, or magisterial, for all inquiry in the realm of religion. Thus demarcated, each authority may be respected and acknowledged as truly authoritative within its own domain. And so long as each authority remains within its proper domain, no conflict should arise between the two: for science has nothing to say about God's existence or the Lordship of Jesus, just as religion has nothing to say about subatomic particles or special relativity. Any perceived conflict is, within this framework, a category mistake, like saying the Mona Lisa ran a fast mile or the moon failed an exam. Such crossover is merely metaphorical. Or, to the extent that one side accepts the other's teaching—which, on this view, religion is required to do and science is permitted to do—it may at most have the potential to be mutually illuminating.[32]

This is a worthy proposal, and to an extent it succeeds. Certainly the Bible, as we have already discussed, touches directly or in detail on very little that scientific inquiry takes as its subject matter. Moreover, it is salutary for scientists to recognize that their expertise prepares them not at all to speak with authority on theological, philosophical, metaphysical, or moral matters. That does not mean they may not or should not thus speak. It means that the authority rightly due them in their domain of expertise does not extend past that domain into others. Much nonsense could be avoided if Gould were heeded here.[33]

The church cannot accept the total proposal, however. This is for at least two reasons. First, however qualified the character of scriptural and thus Christian claims regarding empirical realities, they are not finally negligible.

30. See Harrison, *Science and Religion*.

31. See Gould, *Rocks of Ages*.

32. Note that the normativity of the magisteria is asymmetrical—science authoritatively describes the world as such and should be accepted by all persons, including the religious, whereas religion authoritatively describes the same world *for adherents of said religion* and none others—and thus a particular metaphysics is already baked in to NOMA.

33. Such nonsense as that outlined and criticized in Hart, *Atheist Delusions*; Hart, *Experience of God*; Hart, "Gods and Gopniks"; and elsewhere.

They cannot be erased without lethal consequences for the faith. Consider simple examples. Jesus was a Galilean Jew who lived and taught in Palestine in the early first century and was crucified under the Roman governor Pontius Pilate. This is a falsifiable claim, but it is also nonnegotiable. If it were falsified, the gospel would be falsified along with it. The bare historicity of other persons and events are crucial to the faith as well, and thus to the testimony of Scripture. One need not be an inerrantist to draw lines around certain individuals and happenings as essential, apart from which the Christian confession would not be true.[34] Miracles are another example. Whether or not they could be falsified in principle, whether or not they could have been falsified at the time but can be no longer, the church has taught without ceasing from the beginning that signs and wonders have attended the life of God's covenant people, above all in the coming of Christ and the Spirit. Was Mary a virgin? Did Jesus heal the sick? Did he rise from the dead? Did his apostles speak in tongues? To be sure, Protestant liberalism has at times bid adieu to these claims as either adiaphora or prescientific superstitions and thus outmoded legends.[35] But this is a fraction of the church catholic, unrepresentative of believers past or present, and theologically erroneous in any case.[36] In short, the magisterium of at least the *Christian* religion overlaps at certain points with the magisterium of the empirical sciences.

The second reason why NOMA cannot be fully accepted follows from the first. It is that Christians may be obliged by their magisterium—in Scripture or the church—to believe certain things about empirical realities that the sciences either cannot certify or positively contest. That is to say, Christians are not limited to empirical reasoning when making judgments about empirical matters. If, for example, historiographic inquiry suggests that it is less rather than more likely that X historical person existed or Y historical event happened as narrated in the Bible, that does not settle the matter for believers. For however reliable the historiographic inquiry in question, believers may have other reasons to suppose that their belief in X or Y is justified. Historiographic (not to mention literary or archeological) judgments of probability are almost always underdetermined. Rarely do they rule out the possibility of X or Y, only the relative likelihood of its occurrence. In

34. In this I disagree with the proposal of Martin, *Biblical Truths*.

35. For a sample, see Dorrien's *The Making of American Liberal Theology* trilogy, esp. ch. 5 in the third volume.

36. There are many reasons why it is erroneous, but one feature of this move is illuminating: namely, the way in which, far from being motivated by philosophical, theological, or scientific argument, it is funded instead by the ostensibly self-evident epistemic—read: socio-rhetorical—implausibility of accepting miracles "in a modern age" or "by modern man."

this way, too, the Christian magisterium intrudes upon the empirical, *not* because it has methods or deliverances to offer to scientific practitioners, but because it has other sources of knowledge, and furthermore possesses a domain of authority that, in some respects, extends to the world as such.[37]

NOMA, then, is a well-intended but inadequate response to the nuances of Scripture's doctrinal authority. The second such response comes not from without the church but from within. This is the doctrine of *sola scriptura*. The reader by now knows that this book does not affirm the Reformation principle of "Scripture alone." Both the presuppositions laid out in the opening chapters and the proposals offered since should together make clear why. But before turning to the next section, which will unpack the nature of the church's authority as Scripture's interpreter, let me say a bit more on this topic.

Consider again the list of questions above regarding Scripture's authority. In a way it doubles as an implicit argument against *sola scriptura*, and this in two respects. First, Scripture does not provide the terms of its own interpretation, much less a doctrine that defines its source, scope, and meaning. Scripture, we recall, is a document of the church's inner life. It arises within the church and is composed, collected, and published by the church. Humanly speaking, the question of the canon's provenance and significance—what it means, why it exists, what it is for—admits of a concrete answer: one simply points to the church. Nor are there "gaps" in the canon's ecclesial character, gaps we might be tempted to fill with divine activity. It is human and ecclesial from start to finish. Now, it is *also and simultaneously* divine and spiritual. But that fact does not mitigate the former claim. Furthermore, it is known as such only by means of an ecclesial confession posterior to the creation of the canon. The church is inextricably involved, therefore, with not only the conception but also the reception of Scripture. And if Scripture does not specify its import in advance, then it must be discerned by the church, in accordance with rules established and honed over time by the tradition of the church.

Second, Scripture's silence about so much cannot mean the church's silence or timidity on pressing matters of the day. Theologically construed, such matters are not free-floating "issues." They are questions and obstacles in the *missio Dei* to which the church's life is committed. The church must

---

37. There is more to be said here, not least about the hard sciences compared to historiographic disciplines. One example of ongoing negotiation of the "overlap" between magisteria would be reformulations of classic doctrines such as original sin in light of scientific learning. See, e.g., McFarland, "Original Sin"; McFarland, *In Adam's Fall*. See also Griffiths's searching reflections on magisterial error in matters of fact in "Under Pressure."

be able to speak in the present and not only in the past tense. It must have a living teaching office. But this office is a function of the church's authority more broadly, an authority that at once stands beneath the authority of Scripture and serves as its authoritative interpreter. For the church's magisterium is an outgrowth of Scripture's teaching, not a second or independent tradition alongside it. The tradition of the church is one, within which the authority of Scripture is preeminent: nothing the church says or does may undermine, diminish, or contradict Scripture's teaching.[38] Phrased positively, the church's teaching ought to stand as the supreme fitting interpretation and extension of Scripture's teaching. Where Scripture is ambiguous, underdetermined, or silent, the church speaks in accordance with the mind of Scripture, expanding the reach of the text through its own living voice, under the guiding hand of the Holy Spirit. So that, to appropriate the language of the parable, the seed of the gospel grows together with the church to make the greatest of trees, so that all the nations, from the least to the greatest, come and find rest beneath its branches.[39]

3. Ecclesial Authority

The authority of Scripture generates and requires the interpretive authority of the church. *Sola scriptura* is ultimately inadequate, therefore, because it fails to recognize the authority bestowed upon the church by God.[40] This came by the gift of the Holy Spirit upon the apostles. The divine authority of the risen Christ commissions the church to go into all the world, making disciples of all the nations (Matt 28:18–19). His promise to be with them until the end of the age (v. 20) is fulfilled at Pentecost (Acts 2:1–42), for the ascended Christ is present to the baptized through the indwelling of his Spirit (cf. Rom 5:1–5; 6:1–14; 8:1–27; 1 Cor 2:6–16; 3:16–17; 6:15–20; 2 Cor 3:14–18; 1 John 3:24). This dominical promise forms the second of a pair in the Gospel of St. Matthew. The first is Jesus's response to St. Peter's confession of his identity as "the Messiah, the Son of the living God" (Matt 16:16 NRSV): "Blessed are you, Simon son of Jonah! For flesh and blood has not revealed this to you, but my Father in heaven. And I tell you, you

38. This is a characteristically Orthodox point, but it is notable that none other than Karl Barth echoes it in *Church Dogmatics* I/1, 102.

39. Cf. Matt 13:31–32; Rev 22:2.

40. This chapter was drafted before reading a similar scriptural account of the church's deputized interpretive authority in Levering, *Mary's Bodily Assumption*, 111–46, esp. 119–24: "To rely on the Bible . . . is to recognize the teaching authority of the Church. Jesus Christ's living authority is present and active in both. The question then is why Jesus willed this ecclesial mediation of his authority" (123–24).

are Peter, and on this rock I will build my church, and the gates of Hades will not prevail against it. I will give you the keys of the kingdom of heaven, and whatever you bind on earth will be bound in heaven, and whatever you loose on earth will be loosed in heaven" (vv. 17–19 NRSV).[41] The gifting of the keys reappears two chapters later (18:18–20), now addressed to the church as a whole.

When we turn to the Fourth Gospel, we find all these themes—the resurrection, an appearance of the Lord to the disciples, the commissioning of the Twelve, the bestowal of authority, and the gift of the Spirit—combined in a single scene. In the upper room,

> Jesus came and stood among them and said to them, "Peace be with you." When he had said this, he showed them his hands and his side. Then the disciples were glad when they saw the Lord. Jesus said to them again, "Peace be with you. As the Father has sent me, even so I send you." And when he had said this, he breathed on them, and said to them, "Receive the Holy Spirit. If you forgive the sins of any, they are forgiven; if you retain the sins of any, they are retained." (20:20–23)[42]

In this way the risen Christ deputizes his apostles. The clearest example of this deputized authority is found in Acts 15. There we find a condensed report of a council of "the apostles and the elders"[43] meeting in Jerusalem to decide the fate of gentiles in the church. Should they keep Torah like their Jewish sisters and brothers, or should they remain gentiles, subject to Messiah's Law but not to Moses's? After verbal testimony, prayer, contemplation, and consultation of the scriptures, St. James the Just delivers a verdict (vv. 19–21), with which the other assembled leaders agree. The narration of the decision thrice repeats a notable phrase: "it seemed good." It "seemed good to the apostles and the elders, with the whole church" (*edoxe tois apostolois kai tois presbyterois syn hole te ekklesia*; v. 22); it "seemed good

---

41. It is no coincidence that these paired promises connect, on the one hand, the church's indefectibility with Christ's unceasing presence to it, and on the other hand, the church's authority with that of the apostles, as represented in the person of St. Peter.

42. Note well that the Johannine fusion of themes does not depart from the Matthean emphasis on Petrine priority, but goes on, in the Epilogue (21:1–25), not only to restore St. Peter to fellowship with Christ but also to highlight his role as shepherd of Christ's flock. Indeed, Jesus's final command, "Follow me!" is one that this wayward but headstrong disciple will heed, through "the kind of death by which he would glorify God" (v. 19 NRSV).

43. A phrase repeated six times between 15:2 and 16:4, and found nowhere else in Acts. After 16:4, moreover, the very word "apostle" drops from the text; only "elders" are referenced (whether in Ephesus, Jerusalem, or elsewhere).

to us, having come to one accord" (*edoxen hemin genomenois homothy-madon*; v. 25); it "seemed good to the Holy Spirit and to us" (*edoxen gar to pneumatic to hagio kai hemin*; v. 28). By this subtle narrative phrasing, St. Luke leads the reader to a particular conclusion about the relationship between the will of the council and the will of God. What we might call this conciliar "seeming" (from *dokeo*),[44] which names the common good pleasure of the apostles and elders gathered together, *just is* the will of the Holy Spirit mediated through the church's leadership. It is nothing less than the magisterium of the church speaking with authority. And it turns not only on a matter of practical authority (ought gentile believers to be circumcised?) but also on a question of biblical interpretation. Does Moses not say that circumcision is the sign of the covenant, and that all sons of Abraham ought to be circumcised (cf. Gen 17:9–14)? The question could not be left alone; it had to be decided. The practice of the church, indeed the fate of the gospel, turned on this question: one either unanswered by Scripture or, if answered, apparently in the opposite manner of St. James and the rest of the council.

It is worth noting as well that the teaching of Jesus during his ministry did not anticipate this challenge. But he did not leave his followers unequipped. As he says just before his arrest:

> I have said these things to you, that when their hour comes you may remember that I told you of them. I did not say these things to you from the beginning, because I was with you. But now I am going to him who sent me; yet none of you asks me, "Where are you going?" But because I have said these things to you, sorrow has filled your hearts. Nevertheless I tell you the truth· it is to your advantage that I go away, for if I do not go away, the Counselor will not come to you; but if I go, I will send him to you. . . . I have yet many things to say to you, but you cannot bear them now. When the Spirit of truth comes, he will guide you into all the truth; for he will not speak on his own authority, but whatever he hears he will speak, and he will declare to you the things that are to come. He will glorify me, for he will take what is mine and declare it to you. All that the Father has is mine; therefore I said that he will take what is mine and declare it to you. (John 16:4–7, 12–15)

What is of the Father belongs to the Son, and what is of the Son belongs to the Spirit; hearing what the Father says and receiving what is the Son's, the Spirit thereupon speaks to the church, leading it into all truth by declaring with divine authority the truth of the triune God. This work happens in

---

44. An ecclesial docetism of a different sort!

countless small ways in the daily endeavors and common life of the faithful. But in moments of great controversy or severe trial, the Jerusalem council stands as the enduring archetype for appealing to the Spirit for help while exercising authoritative judgment on behalf of the church catholic.[45]

The question that divides Christians on this matter may be separated into four components. First, is it licit for the post-apostolic church to gather in council and issue teaching in the form of canons, creeds, and confessions? Though some in recent centuries have said no, most of the church, past and present, answers in the affirmative. Second, may conciliar teaching be promulgated or received as dogma—that is, as irrevocable teaching binding on all the faithful? For the most part, the Protestant answer is negative and the catholic answer (East and West) is affirmative. Functionally, though, many Protestants (especially Anglicans, but some Lutherans and Reformed as well) offer a qualified affirmative. For they operate as though, or explicitly teach that, the teaching of the initial (two? four? six?) ecumenical councils is irreversible.[46] The doctrine of the Trinity, for example, is no more up for grabs in such traditions than is the resurrection of Jesus from the dead. But it is important to see that, though it is true that the Trinity is biblical teaching, the doctrine of the Trinity is one among many possible interpretations of the Bible's total witness to the identity of God. It is not explicit in the way the resurrection is.[47] As I observed in earlier chapters, an instability obtains in those Protestant traditions that implicitly treat some ecumenical councils as infallible interpretations of Scripture's teaching—and thus as interpretations whose authority is logically equivalent to Scripture's own, for the former is the sole proper lens for understanding the latter—given those traditions' stated commitment to *sola scriptura*. It seems to me that honesty requires letting go of one or the other. Between biblicism and dogma there is finally no third way.[48]

The third component is whether the church's conciliar or magisterial authority extends beyond the plain teaching of Scripture. May the church speak decisively regarding matters about which Scripture speaks neither

---

45. As indeed it was in fact the model for later synods and ecumenical councils, a point emphasized in the opening pages of von Hefele, *Council of Nicea*, 1–2.

46. Charles Hodge, in his letter declining to attend Vatican I, claims all but Nicaea II, for obvious reasons.

47. See the nuanced discussion in Sanders, *Triune God*.

48. The analogy to jurisprudence again presents itself. Precedent in interpretation of the Constitution attains a measure of authority that, subsequent to the Constitution, becomes equal to it *as* its decisive interpretation. In other words, there is precedent the rejection of which would bring the whole constitutional edifice tumbling down. Such constitutional primitivism (originalism radicalized) would simply restart the nation from scratch.

directly nor (with sufficient clarity) indirectly? Here Protestants part ways definitively with Rome and Constantinople[49]—at least in terms of logical consistency. At both the popular and the official level, Protestant bodies regularly issue teaching that cannot be derived from or proved by reference to the Bible. But neither a radical *nuda scriptura* nor a confessional *sola scriptura* position is capable of speaking with confidence, much less authority, to issues as varied as cloning, genome editing, IVF, the pill, the age of the universe, evolution, the validity of miracles performed by believers today[50]—even, I would argue, devotional practices like asking the saints for intercession, venerating their relics, or adoring the host. It is true that these latter, ecclesial examples are not found authorized in Scripture. But that is a minor premise. The major premise required to rule them out is a doctrine of Scripture that understands its authority in highly limited, or regulative, fashion: what it does not explicitly permit or command is just thereby prohibited.[51] This principle is not itself found in Scripture, nor does it belong to a catholic hermeneutic of Scripture. It is an innovation datable to the sixteenth century, with a few antecedents scattered in the church's prior history. If it is true, there is no way to demonstrate its truth from Scripture, for by definition there is no canonical book written after the formation of the canon that can speak with Scripture's authority about Scripture's interpretation—unless, that is, one admits the church's authority so to speak.

Last, then, the fourth component, which underlies the three so far discussed, is the nature of apostolic authority. Does the authority of the

49. And, it is worth adding, with Alexandria, Antioch, Addis Ababa, Asmara, Etchmiadzin, Kerala, and other patriachates of the Oriental Orthodox and Church of the East. (Perhaps also with Canterbury, though that is more contested.)

50. To be clear, this is a diverse list, not all of whose items call for definitive decision. But even that question of discrimination—which requires authoritative response and which does not—is itself not given in advance, and thus is a function of authoritative judgment. It is notable that ecclesial bodies lacking magisterial organs nonetheless feel compelled to promulgate dogma-like pronouncements on these questions, such as evolution or the earth's age, when by the nature of the case the canonical texts are silent or underdetermined on the matter.

51. There is a rare but venerable middle ground: one that would permit beliefs or practices not proscribed by Scripture without "binding the conscience of the faithful," that is, without requiring the assent or participation of believers whose judgments about the matters in question differ from those who recommend them. It seems to me that the reason this position is a minority one is that it is both impracticable and question-begging. It is not as though Reformed pastors permit, without mandating, veneration of icons and petitions of the saints for their intercession; they discourage and forbid them. And understandably so, since the interpretation of multiple significant biblical passages is at stake. Moreover, such practices, and the beliefs they embody, require significant institutional support, instruction, and transmission for their flourishing. To commit them to individual consciences is a recipe at once for confusion and for their cessation.

apostles continue into the life of the church in the form of its leaders and pastors—properly speaking, its bishops, who trace their office back to the apostles—or does it cease with their death? The Protestant Reformation mounted a forceful assertion of the latter. That is the principle *sola scriptura* seeks to uphold: namely, the authority of the apostles continues in the church *solely by means of their writings*. In the wake of their death and ever thereafter, the church's leaders, along with the church as a whole, are in the very same position as those believers who were not apostles when the apostles still lived. The church is led no longer by living deputies of Christ. Its leaders now lack the authority to speak anew in his name, that is, to speak what seems good to the Holy Spirit in response to some unforeseen challenge. It follows that the apostolicity of the church is wholly material: the church is apostolic just to the extent that its life, worship, mission, and faith—in short, the gospel it proclaims and embodies—are normed by and thus in accordance with the apostles' teaching (as committed to writing in the texts contained in the New Testament). Scripture norms the church to this end: to keep it in step with the apostles.[52]

Now, the pre-Reformation church did not, and today's catholic communions do not, maintain the perpetual role of apostle. There are no apostles after their passing. Nor may the church teach anything contrary to the deposit of faith taught by the apostles, much less claim as revealed that which is not rooted in and an outgrowth of original revelation. Rather, just as *trinitas* and *homoousios* and *theotokos* are not found in the canon, but are terms that the church's leaders created or deployed in the service of understanding canonical teaching, so magisterial teaching on new topics, moral or theological, is likewise a terminological or conceptual innovation in the service of continued fidelity to the gospel handed on by the apostles and

---

52. For the best examples of this perspective, see Calvin, *Institutes* 1.6–9; 4.1–3, 8–9; Gerhard, *Nature of Holy Scripture* 17.362–23.493; Turretin, *Institutes* 2.20–21; Bavinck, *Reformed Dogmatics*, 455–74; Barth, *Church Dogmatics* IV/1, 712–25; Webster, *Holy Scripture*, 44–57. See also Flett, *Apostolicity*. In *Christian Imagination* Willie James Jennings offers a crucial cautionary note regarding the ambiguity of the apostolic mandate to make disciples (through baptism and instruction, i.e., word and sacrament; cf. Matt 28:18–20): Does discipleship follow teaching, or does teaching follow discipleship? Which precedes the other, or phrased differently, which contains the other? Jennings argues that when, in the early modern period, "discipleship was envisioned inside teaching" instead of the other way around (106), it was both a product of and contributed to ruinous colonialist practice that in turn corrupted Christian thought—a corruption that continues into the present (see 65–116). Such "pedagogical imperialism" (114) is a temptation for any Christian tradition that (rightly, in Jennings's view) prioritizes sound doctrine. The question is how that priority manifests on the ground, and how it is ordered to discipleship to Christ.

taught by Holy Scripture.[53] The authority deputed to the apostles was noth-ing other than the person of the Holy Spirit. Because the presence of this divine person continues in the church unabated, the authority conferred upon the apostles continues as well, only now in the episcopacy. It is in this sense that the West speaks of the apostolic office, and the East speaks of the church's tradition as but another name for the Spirit. For the tradition is the life of the church, and the life of the church is the Spirit, "the Lord and giver of life." Apart from the breath of the Spirit active in the tradition of the church, the body of Christ would be dead. But filled with the Spirit's life, its tradition is sacred, trustworthy, and true. No tradition, no Spirit; no Spirit, no church. Hence: no tradition, no church.

How does the church's authority operate in relation to Scripture's authority? Consider the promise of the convert to Orthodoxy: "I will ac-cept and understand Holy Scripture in accordance with the interpretation which was and is held by the Holy Orthodox Catholic Church of the East, our Mother."[54] It is, as I noted above, *Scripture rightly interpreted* that is su-premely authoritative for Christian faith and doctrine. How do we know Scripture's right interpretation? Not by ourselves, left to our own devices. And not provisionally, with local hypotheses indefinitely open to revision. No, the answer—the catholic answer—is that the church authoritatively teaches how Scripture's authoritative teaching ought to be understood and received by the faithful.[55]

St. Francis de Sales poses the problem and the solution with elegance: "I am not in doubt as to whether we must give belief to the holy Word; who knows not that it is in the supreme degree of certitude? What exercises me

---

53. In the words of the recently canonized John Henry Newman, "No doctrine is defined till it is violated" (*Development*, 151). See also the work of Rowan Williams, esp. *Arius*; *Why Study the Past?*; and *On Christian Theology*.

54. Quoted in Ware, *Orthodox Church*, 194.

55. Recall the very beginning of this book: an ecumenical catholic venture in the spirit of Robert Jenson's theology, with one foot planted in the present and one a mil-lennium ago, prior to the Great Schism and the Reformation both. I have sought to articulate what is the common heritage of the one church with respect to the doctrine and interpretation of its sacred scriptures—a heritage more or less universal for the first 1,000 to 1,500 years of the church. There are, naturally, additional questions to ask in the midst of a church as divided as it is today; certain questions would remain even if all Christian traditions agreed in principle on the issues discussed in this section regarding the relationship between the church's authority and Scripture's authority. Those ques-tions currently block full communion between Roman and Orthodox Christians, and most (not all) of the questions center on papal authority. I have bracketed that issue, primarily because it would take us too far afield, but also because it is not decisive for the account of ecclesial authority just offered, which long predated Western develop-ments in the last millennium regarding the singular authority of the bishop of Rome.

is the understanding of this Scripture—the consequences and conclusions drawn from it, which being different beyond number and very often contradictory on the same point, so that each one chooses his own, one here the other there—who shall make me see truth through so many vanities?" Regarding the Protestant proposal of the analogy of faith, he allows that "what all these reformers want" is "to take Scripture as judge. And to this we answer *Amen*." But that is not the end of the matter. For "our difference is not there; it is here, that in the disagreements we shall have over the interpretation, and which will occur at every two words, we shall need a judge. They answer that we must decide the interpretation of Scripture by collating passage with passage and the whole with the Symbol of faith. *Amen, Amen*, we say, but we do not ask how we ought to interpret the Scripture, but—who shall be the judge?" After all, the infallibility of Scripture's teaching is a moot point if one misunderstands Scripture. "There must be doctrine and there must be someone to propose it. The doctrine is in the Holy Word, but who shall propose it?" Moreover, "If he who has authority to propose can err in his proposition all has to be done over again."[56] The same *level* of authority—not the same in kind, or in honor, or in antiquity—must characterize both the text interpreted and the interpretation itself, at least with respect to those matters that pertain to salvation, that is, to the heart of the gospel itself.[57] In fullest formulation:

> Now as God revealed his Word and spoke, or preached, by the mouth of the fathers and Prophets, and at last by his own Son, then by the Apostles and evangelists, whose tongues were but as the pens of scribes writing rapidly, God thus employing men to speak to men; so to propose, apply, and declare this his Word, he employs his visible spouse as his mouthpiece and the interpreter of his intentions. It is God then who rules over Christian belief, but with two instruments, in a double way: (1) by his Word as by a formal rule and (2) by his Church as by the hand of the measurer and rule-user. Let us put it thus: God is the painter, our faith the picture, the colors are the Word of God, the brush is the Church. Here then are two ordinary and infallible rules of our belief: the Word of God, which is the fundamental and

---

56. St. Francis de Sales, *Catholic Controversy* 2.3.1.

57. Note well: This is not because the text, in its primary sacramental authority, "needs" the help of interpretation; much less that *God* needs such help, any more than God needs angels or prayers or pastors or creatures of any kind. Rather, the claim is that this is simply how God has willed to order and govern his people. He could have done otherwise, perhaps by avoiding the complications of hermeneutics altogether. But he did not, and so here we are.

formal rule; the Church of God, which is the rule of application and explanation.[58]

Transposing the metaphor, we might say that believers are a letter of which Christ is the author, his word (the canon) is the script, and his body (the church) is the pen.[59]

Turning to *Dei Verbum*, we find an equally concise and lovely expression of this relationship:

> there exists a close connection and communication between sacred tradition and Sacred Scripture. For both of them, flowing from the same divine wellspring, in a certain way merge into a unity and tend toward the same end. For Sacred Scripture is the word of God inasmuch as it is consigned to writing under the inspiration of the divine Spirit, while sacred tradition takes the word of God entrusted by Christ the Lord and the Holy Spirit to the Apostles, and hands it on to their successors in its full purity, so that led by the light of the Spirit of truth, they may in proclaiming it preserve this word of God faithfully, explain it, and make it more widely known. Consequently it is not from Sacred Scripture alone that the Church draws her certainty about everything which has been revealed. Therefore both sacred tradition and Sacred Scripture are to be accepted and venerated with the same sense of loyalty and reverence. Sacred tradition and Sacred Scripture [thus] form one sacred deposit of the word of God, committed to the Church. Holding fast to this deposit the entire holy people united with their shepherds remain always steadfast in the teaching of the Apostles . . . .[60]

In short, far from being a threat to the authority of the apostles, the interpretive authority of the church confirms the church in its apostolic character.[61] For, in the words of Matthew Levering, "the Church, as Christ's

58. St. Francis de Sales, *Catholic Controversy* Part 2, Introduction.

59. These metaphors might make for fruitful conversation with Vanhoozer, *Drama of Doctrine*. Cf. Vanhoozer's "Mere Protestant Response" found in Levering, *Was the Reformation a Mistake?* 191–231.

60. *Dei Verbum* 2.9–10. See also, from the East, the "Confession of Dositheus," Decree 2 (and throughout).

61. Consider two consecutive affirmations of the *Longer Catechism* of St. Philaret of Moscow: "We must follow that tradition which agrees with the divine revelation and with holy Scripture" (23); "[Tradition is necessary as] a guide to the right understanding of holy Scripture" (24). These follow prior teachings: namely, that "holy tradition [comprises] the doctrine of the faith, the law of God, the sacraments, and the ritual as handed down by the true believers and worshipers of God by word and example from one to another, and from generation to generation" (17); that the church "is the sure

Bride, receives interpretive authority by sharing in Christ's Spirit," the same Spirit poured out in the beginning on the apostles.[62] The Pentecostal character of Christ's body and bride means the Spirit infuses the whole of the church's life, making it a living sign and instrument—a sacrament—of God's kingdom. "Both the Church and divinely inspired Scripture in the Church are thus 'sacramental' realities whose purpose is the salvation of the human race. In the Holy Spirit, Christ the Teacher gives his authority to the mediations—the interrelated offices, charisms, and vocations that form his visible Body—in and through which he is efficaciously embodied and proclaimed in the world."[63] The freedom that results is not the freedom to do as we please or to read the text how we wish. It is, rather, the freedom of the cross: "the freedom of self-dispossession, the confidence that the grace of the Holy Spirit is in charge of the exegesis of the Son."[64] Because the Spirit is Lord of exegesis, believers will be surprised and awed by what he illuminates in the text, making Christ to shine forth in places where we might least expect to see him. But the rule of the Spirit in interpretation entails more than that. It means that the church is not alone in its reading. It means that ordinary believers may place their trust in the church's reading in the Spirit. And it means that in its reading the church may say with the apostles, "it seemed good to the Holy Spirit and to us."

That is the church's authority in action, and Scripture's authority, too.

---

repository of holy tradition" (18); and that, compared to the writings of Holy Scripture, "[t]he most ancient and original instrument for spreading divine revelation is holy tradition"—indeed, "[t]he necessity of tradition is . . . evident from this, that books can be available only to a small part of mankind, but tradition to all" (21). The venture of historic catholic Christianity is that each of these claims reinforces rather than excludes the others; that the hermeneutical circle thereby posited is virtuous, not vicious; that it not only makes theoretical sense but accounts for the living practice of the church; and ultimately that it reflects the will of the Holy Spirit.

62. Levering, *Participatory Biblical Exegesis*, 139.

63. Levering, *Participatory Biblical Exegesis*, 139–40.

64. Levering, *Participatory Biblical Exegesis*, 140.

In Place of a Conclusion

St. John Chrysostom
First Homily on the Gospel According to St. John[1]

They that are spectators of the heathen games, when they have learned that a distinguished athlete and winner of crowns has come from any quarter, run all together to view his wrestling, and all his skill and strength; and you may see the whole theater of many ten thousands, all there straining their eyes both of body and mind, that nothing of what is done may escape them. So again these same persons, if any admirable musician come among them, leave all that they had in hand, which often is necessary and pressing business, and mount the steps, and sit listening very attentively to the words and the accompaniments, and criticizing the agreement of the two. This is what the many do.

Again; those who are skilled in rhetoric do just the same with respect to the sophists, for they too have their theaters, and their audience, and clappings of hands, and noise, and closest criticism of what is said.

And if in the case of rhetoricians, musicians, and athletes, people sit in the one case to look on, in the other to see at once and to listen with such earnest attention; what zeal, what earnestness ought you in reason to display, when it is no musician or debater who now comes forward to a trial of skill, but when a man is speaking from heaven, and utters a voice plainer than thunder? For he has pervaded the whole earth with the sound;

---

1. John Chrysostom, *Homilies on the Gospel of Saint John and the Epistle to the Hebrews*, in vol. 14 of The Nicene and Post-Nicene Fathers, Series 1, ed. Philip Schaff (1889; repr., Peabody, MA: Hendrickson, 2012), 1–4 (Homily 1). Minor changes have been made to some of the capitalization in this homily to bring it into conformity with the rest of the book.

169

and occupied and filled it, not by the loudness of the cry, but by moving his tongue with the grace of God.

And what is wonderful, this sound, great as it is, is neither a harsh nor an unpleasant one, but sweeter and more delightful than all harmony of music, and with more skill to soothe; and besides all this, most holy, and most awful, and full of mysteries so great, and bringing with it goods so great, that if men were exactly and with ready mind to receive and keep them, they could no longer be mere men nor remain upon the earth, but would take their stand above all the things of this life, and having adapted themselves to the condition of angels, would dwell on earth just as if it were heaven.

For the son of thunder, the beloved of Christ, the pillar of the churches throughout the world, who holds the keys of heaven, who drank the cup of Christ, and was baptized with his baptism, who lay upon his Master's bosom with much confidence, this man comes forward to us now; not as an actor of a play, not hiding his head with a mask (for he has another sort of words to speak), nor mounting a platform, nor striking the stage with his foot, nor dressed out with apparel of gold, but he enters wearing a robe of inconceivable beauty. For he will appear before us having "put on Christ" (Rom 13:14; Gal 3:27), having his beautiful "feet shod with the preparation of the gospel of peace" (Eph 6:15); wearing a girdle not about his waist, but about his loins, not made of scarlet leather nor daubed outside with gold, but woven and composed of truth itself. Now will he appear before us, not acting a part (for with him there is nothing counterfeit, nor fiction, nor fable), but with unmasked head he proclaims to us the truth unmasked; not making the audience believe him other than he is by carriage, by look, by voice, needing for the delivery of his message no instruments of music, as harp, lyre, or any other the like, for he effects all with his tongue, uttering a voice which is sweeter and more profitable than that of any harper or any music. All heaven is his stage; his theater, the habitable world; his audience, all angels; and of men as many as are angels already, or desire to become so, for none but these can hear that harmony aright, and show it forth by their works; all the rest, like little children who hear, but what they hear understand not, from their anxiety about sweetmeats and childish playthings; so they too, being in mirth and luxury, and living only for wealth and power and sensuality, hear sometimes what is said, it is true, but show forth nothing great or noble in their actions through fastening themselves for good to the clay of the brickmaking. By this apostle stand the powers from above, marveling at the beauty of his soul, and his understanding, and the bloom of that virtue by which he drew unto him Christ himself, and obtained the grace of the Spirit. For he has made ready his soul, as some well-fashioned and jeweled lyre with strings of gold, and yielded it for the utterance of something great and sublime to the Spirit.

Seeing then it is no longer the fisherman the son of Zebedee, but he who knows "the deep things of God" (1 Cor 2:10), the Holy Spirit I mean, that strikes this lyre, let us hearken accordingly. For he will say nothing to us as a man, but what he says, he will say from the depths of the Spirit, from those secret things which before they came to pass the very angels knew not; since they too have learned by the voice of John with us, and by us, the things which we know. And this has another apostle declared, saying, "To the intent that unto the principalities and powers might be known by the church the manifold wisdom of God" (Eph 3:10). If then principalities, and powers, and cherubim, and seraphim, learned these things by the church, it is very clear that they were exceedingly earnest in listening to this teaching; and even in this we have been not a little honored, that the angels learned things which before they knew not with us; I do not at present speak of their learning by us also. Let us then show much silence and orderly behavior; not today only, nor during the day on which we are hearers, but during all our life, since it is at all times good to hear him. For if we long to know what is going on in the palace, what, for instance, the king has said, what he has done, what counsel he is taking concerning his subjects, though in truth these things are for the most part nothing to us; much more is it desirable to hear what God has said, especially when all concerns us. And all this will this man tell us exactly, as being a friend of the King himself, or rather, as having him speaking within himself, and from him hearing all things which he hears from the Father. "I have called you friends," he says, "for all things that I have heard of my Father, I have made known unto you" (John 15:15).

As then we should all run together if we saw one from above bend down "on a sudden" from the height of heaven, promising to describe exactly all things there, even so let us be disposed now. It is from thence that this man speaks to us; he is not of this world, as Christ himself declares, "You are not of the world" (John 15:19), and he has speaking within him the Comforter, the Omnipresent, who knows the things of God as exactly as the soul of man knows what belongs to herself, the Spirit of holiness, the righteous Spirit, the guiding Spirit, which leads men by the hand to heaven, which gives them other eyes, fitting them to see things to come as though present, and giving them even in the flesh to look into things heavenly. To him then let us yield ourselves during all our life in much tranquility. Let none dull, none sleepy, none sordid, enter here and tarry; but let us remove ourselves to heaven, for there he speaks these things to those who are citizens there. And if we tarry on earth, we shall gain nothing great from thence. For the words of John are nothing to those who do not desire to be freed from this swinish life, just as the things of this world to him are nothing. The thunder amazes our souls, having sound without significance; but this man's voice troubles none of the faithful, yea, rather releases them from trouble and confusion; it amazes the devils only, and those who are their slaves. Therefore, that we may know how it amazes them, let us preserve deep silence, both external and mental, but especially the latter; for what advantage is it that the mouth be hushed, if the soul is disturbed and full of tossing? I look for that calm which is of the mind, of the soul, since it is the hearing of the soul which I require. Let then no desire of riches trouble us, no lust of glory, no tyranny of anger, nor the crowd of other passions besides these; for it is not possible for the ear, except it be cleansed, to perceive as it ought the sublimity of the things spoken; nor rightly to understand the awful and unutterable nature of these mysteries, and all other virtue which is in these divine oracles. If a man cannot learn well a melody on pipe or harp, unless he in every way strain his attention; how shall one, who sits as a listener to sounds mystical, be able to hear with a careless soul?

Wherefore Christ himself exhorted, saying, "Give not that which is holy unto the dogs, neither cast your pearls before swine" (Matt 7:6). He called these words "pearls," though in truth they be much more precious than they, because we have no substance more precious than that. For this reason too he is wont often to compare their sweetness to honey, not that so much only is the measure of their sweetness, but because among us there is nothing sweeter. Now, to show that they very exceedingly surpass the nature of precious stones, and the sweetness of any honey, hear the prophet speaking concerning them, and declaring this superiority; "More to be desired are they," he says "than gold and much precious stone; sweeter are they also than honey and the honeycomb" (Ps 19:10). But to those (only) who are in health; wherefore he has added, "For your servant keeps them." And again in another place calling them sweet he has added, "to my throat." For he says, "How sweet are your words unto my throat" (Ps 119:103). And again he insists on the superiority, saying, "Above honey and the honeycomb to my mouth." For he was in very sound health. And let not us either come near to these while we are sick, but when we have healed our soul, so receive the food that is offered us.

It is for this reason that, after so long a preface, I have not yet attempted to fathom these expressions (of St. John), in order that everyone having laid aside all manner of infirmity, as though he were entering into heaven itself, so may enter here pure, and freed from wrath and carefulness and anxiety of this life, of all other passions. For it is not otherwise possible for a man to gain from hence anything great, except he have first so cleansed anew his soul. And let no one say that the time to the coming communion is short, for it is possible, not only in five days, but in one moment, to change the whole course of life. Tell me what is worse than a robber and a murderer, is not this the extremest kind of wickedness? Yet such an one arrived straight at the summit of excellence, and passed into paradise itself, not needing days, nor half a day, but one little moment. So that a man may change suddenly, and become gold instead of clay. For since what belongs to virtue and to vice is not by nature, the change is easy, as being independent of any necessity. "If you be willing and obedient," he says, "you shall eat the good of the land" (Isa 1:19). Do you see that there needs the will only? will—not the common wishing of the multitude—but earnest will. For I know that all are wishing to fly up to heaven even now; but it is necessary to show forth the wish by works. The merchant too wishes to get rich; but he does not allow his wish to stop with the thought of it; no, he fits out a ship, and gets together sailors, and engages a pilot, and furnishes the vessel with all other stores, and borrows money, and crosses the sea, and goes away into a strange land, and endures many dangers, and all the rest which they know who sail the sea. So too must we show our will; for we also sail a voyage, not from land to land, but from earth to heaven. Let us then so order our reason, that it be serviceable to steer our upward course, and our sailors that they be obedient to it, and let our vessel be stout, that it be not swamped amidst the reverses and despondencies of this life, nor be lifted up by the blasts of vainglory, but be a fast and easy vessel. If so we order our ship, and so our pilot and our crew, we shall sail with a fair wind, and we shall draw down to ourselves the Son of God, the true Pilot, who will not leave our bark to be engulfed, but, though ten thousand winds may blow, will rebuke the winds and the sea, and instead of raging waves, make a great calm.

Having therefore ordered yourselves, so come to our next assembly, if at least it be at all an object of desire to you to hear somewhat to your advantage, and lay up what is said in your souls. But let not one of you be the "wayside," none the "stony ground," none the "full of thorns" (Matt 13:4–7). Let us make ourselves fallow lands. For so shall we (the preachers) put in the seed with gladness, when we see the land clean, but if stony or rough, pardon us if we like not to labor in vain. For if we shall leave off sowing and begin to cut up thorns, surely to cast seed into ground unwrought were extreme folly.

It is not meet that he who has the advantage of such hearing be partaker of the table of devils. "For what fellowship has righteousness with unrighteousness?" (2 Cor 6:14). You stand listening to John, and learning the things of the Spirit by him; and do you after this depart to listen to harlots speaking vile things, and acting viler, and to effeminates cuffing one another? How will you be able to be fairly cleansed, if you wallow in such mire? Why need I reckon in detail all the indecency that is there? All there is laughter, all is shame, all disgrace, revilings and mockings, all abandonment, all destruction. See, I forewarn and charge you all. Let none of those who enjoy the blessings of this table destroy his own soul by those pernicious spectacles. All that is said and done there is a pageant of Satan. But you who have been initiated know what manner of covenants you made with us, or rather you made with Christ when he guided you into his mysteries, what you spoke to him, what speech you had with him concerning Satan's pageant; how with Satan and his angels you renounced this also, and promised that you would not so much as cast a glance that way. There is then no slight ground for fear, lest, by becoming careless of such promises, one should render himself unworthy of these mysteries.

Do you see not how in king's palaces it is not those who have offended, but those who have been honorably distinguished, that are called to share special favor, and are numbered among the king's friends. A messenger has come to us from heaven, sent by God himself, to speak with us on certain necessary matters, and you leave hearing his will, and the message he sends to you, and sit listening to stage-players. What thunderings, what bolts from heaven, does not this conduct deserve! For as it is not meet to partake of the table of devils, so neither is it of the listening to devils; nor to be present with filthy raiment at that glorious Table, loaded with so many good things, which God himself has provided. Such is its power, that it can raise us at once to heaven, if only we approach it with a sober mind. For it is not possible that he who is continually under the influence of the words of God, can remain in this present low condition, but he needs must presently take wing, and fly away to the land which is above, and light on the infinite treasures of good things; which may it be that we all attain to, through the grace and lovingkindness of our Lord Jesus Christ, through whom and with whom be glory to the Father and the All-holy Spirit, now and ever, and world without end. Amen.

Bibliography

Abraham, William J. *Canon and Criterion in Christian Theology: From the Fathers to Feminism*. New York: Oxford University Press, 1998.

―――. *Divine Agency and Divine Action, Vol. 3. Systematic Theology*. New York: Oxford University Press, 2019.

Adams, Samuel V. *The Reality of God and Historical Method: Apocalyptic Theology in Conversation with N. T. Wright*. Downers Grove, IL: IVP Academic, 2015.

Allen, Michael. "Reformed Retrieval." In *Theologies of Retrieval: An Exploration and Appraisal*, edited by Darren Sarisky, 67–79. London: T. & T. Clark, 2017.

Allen, Michael, and Scott R. Swain, eds. *Christian Dogmatics: Reformed Theology for the Church Catholic*. Grand Rapids: Baker Academic, 2016.

―――. *Reformed Catholicity: The Promise of Retrieval for Theology and Biblical Interpretation*. Grand Rapids: Baker Academic, 2015.

Anselm of Canterbury. *The Major Works: Including Monologion, Proslogion, and Why God Became Man*. Oxford World's Classics. Edited by Brian Davies and G. R. Evans. Oxford: Oxford University Press, 1998.

Aquino, Frederick D. *Communities of Informed Judgment: Newman's Illative Sense and Accounts of Rationality*. Washington, DC: Catholic University of America Press, 2004.

Auerbach, Erich. "Figura." In *Scenes from the Drama of European Literature: Six Essays*, 11–76, 229–37. 1959. Reprint, Gloucester, MA: Smith, 1973.

―――. *Mimesis: The Representation of Reality in Western Literature*. Princeton: Princeton University Press, 2003.

Augustine of Hippo. *Answer to Faustus, a Manichean (Contra Faustum Manichaeum)*. The Works of Saint Augustine: A Translation for the 21st Century, Part 1, Vol. 20. Translated by Roland Teske, SJ. Edited by Boniface Ramsey. Hyde Park, NY: New City, 2007.

―――. *The City of God*. Translated by Marcus Dodds. New York: The Modern Library, 1993.

―――. *Confessions*. Translated by Henry Chadwick. New York: Oxford University Press, 1991.

―――. *Expositions on the Psalms 1–32*. The Works of Saint Augustine: A Translation for the 21st Century, Part 3, Vol. 15. Translated by Maria Boulding, OSB. Edited by John E. Rotelle, OSA. Hyde Park, NY: New City, 2000.

————. *Letters 1–99.* The Works of Saint Augustine: A Translation for the 21st Century, Part 2, Vol. 1. Translated by Roland Teske, SJ. Edited by John E. Rotelle, OSA. Hyde Park, NY: New City, 2001.

————. *Teaching Christianity (De Doctrina Christiana).* The Works of Saint Augustine: A Translation for the 21st Century, Part 1, Vol. 11. Translated by Edmund Hill. Edited by John E. Rotelle, OSA. Hyde Park, NY: New City, 1996.

————. *The Trinity (De Trinitate).* 2nd ed. The Works of Saint Augustine: A Translation for the 21st Century, Part 1, Vol. 5. Translated by Edmund Hill. Edited by John E. Rotelle, OSA. Hyde Park, NY: New City, 1991.

Ayres, Lewis. *Nicaea and Its Legacy: An Approach to Fourth-Century Trinitarian Theology.* New York: Oxford University Press, 2004.

Balthasar, Hans Urs von. *Explorations in Theology, Vol. 2. Spouse of the Word.* Translated by A. V. Littledale, Alexandre Dru, and John Saward. San Francisco: Ignatius, 1991.

Barr, James. "Jowett and the 'Original Meaning' of Scripture." *Religious Studies* 18.4 (1982) 433–37.

————. "Jowett and the Reading of the Bible 'Like Any Other Book.'" *Horizons in Biblical Theology* 4.1 (1985) 1–44.

Barrett, Matthew. *God's Word Alone: The Authority of Scripture: What the Reformers Taught . . . and Why It Still Matters.* Grand Rapids: Zondervan, 2016.

Barth, Karl. *Church Dogmatics I/1: The Doctrine of the Word of God.* 2nd ed. Translated by G. W. Bromiley. 1975. Reprint, Peabody, MA: Hendrickson, 2010.

————. *Church Dogmatics I/2: The Doctrine of the Word of God.* Translated by G. T. Thomson and Harold Knight. 1956. Reprint, Peabody, MA: Hendrickson, 2010.

————. *Church Dogmatics IV/1: The Doctrine of Reconciliation.* Translated by G. W. Bromiley. 1956. Reprint, Peabody, MA: Hendrickson, 2010.

————. *Church Dogmatics IV/3.1: The Doctrine of Reconciliation.* Translated by G. W. Bromiley. 1961. Reprint, Peabody, MA: Hendrickson, 2010.

Bartholomew, Craig G., and Heath A. Thomas, eds. *A Manifesto for Theological Interpretation.* Grand Rapids: Baker Academic, 2016.

Barton, John. *Holy Writings, Sacred Text: The Canon in Early Christianity.* Louisville, KY: Westminster John Knox, 1998.

————. *The Nature of Biblical Criticism.* Louisville, KY: Westminster John Knox, 2007.

Basil the Great. *On the Holy Spirit.* Popular Patristics Series. Translated by Stephen Hildebrand. Yonkers, NY: St. Vladimir's Seminary Press, 2011.

Bavinck, Herman. *Reformed Dogmatics, Vol. 1. Prolegomena.* Translated by John Vriend. Edited by John Bolt. Grand Rapids: Baker Academic, 2003.

Beeley, Christopher A. *The Unity of Christ: Continuity and Conflict in Patristic Tradition.* New Haven, CT: Yale University Press, 2012.

Behr, John. *Irenaeus of Lyons: Identifying Christianity.* Christian Theology in Context. New York: Oxford University Press, 2013.

————. *John the Theologian and his Paschal Gospel: A Prologue to Theology.* New York: Oxford University Press, 2019.

————. *The Mystery of Christ: Life in Death.* Crestwood, NY: St. Vladimir's Seminary Press, 2006.

Belgic Confession of Faith. https://www.rca.org/about/theology/creeds-and-confessions/the-belgic-confession/.

Billings, J. Todd. *The Word of God for the People of God: An Entryway to the Theological Interpretation of Scripture.* Grand Rapids: Eerdmans, 2010.

Bockmuehl, Markus. *Seeing the Word: Refocusing New Testament Study.* Grand Rapids: Baker Academic, 2006.

Boersma, Hans. *Scripture as Real Presence: Sacramental Exegesis in the Early Church.* Grand Rapids: Baker Academic, 2017.

Boyd, Gregory A. *Inspired Imperfection: How the Bible's Problems Enhance Its Divine Authority.* Minneapolis: Fortress, 2020.

Braaten, Carl E., and Robert W. Jenson, eds. *Jews and Christians: People of God.* Grand Rapids: Eerdmans, 2003.

Brueggemann, Walter. "Foreword." In Tyler D. Mayfield, *Unto Us a Child Is Born: Isaiah, Advent, and Our Jewish Neighbors,* xi–xiii. Grand Rapids: Eerdmans, 2020.

Bryan, Christopher. *And God Spoke: The Authority of the Bible for the Church Today.* Lanham, MD: Cowley, 2002.

———. *Listening to the Bible: The Art of Faithful Biblical Interpretation.* New York: Oxford University Press, 2014.

Bultmann, Rudolf. "The Significance of the Old Testament for the Christian Faith." In *The Old Testament and the Christian Faith,* edited by Bernhard W. Anderson, 8–35. New York: Harper and Row, 1963.

Burtchaell, James Tunstead, CSC. *Catholic Theories of Biblical Inspiration Since 1810: A Review and Critique.* New York: Cambridge University Press, 1969.

Byassee, Jason. *Praise Seeking Understanding: Reading the Psalms with Augustine.* Grand Rapids: Eerdmans, 2007.

Callahan, James. *The Clarity of Scripture: History, Theology, and Contemporary Literary Studies.* Downers Grove, IL: InterVarsity, 2001.

Calvin, John. *Institutes of the Christian Religion.* Translated by Henry Beveridge. 1845. Reprint, Peabody, MA: Hendrickson, 2008.

Campbell, Alexander. "Reply." *Christian Baptist* 5 (1827) 208–11.

Carson, D. A., ed. *The Enduring Authority of the Christian Scriptures.* Grand Rapids: Eerdmans, 2016.

Castelo, Daniel, and Robert W. Wall. *The Marks of Scripture: Rethinking the Nature of the Bible.* Grand Rapids: Baker Academic, 2019.

Catherine of Siena. *The Dialogue.* The Classics of Western Spirituality. Mahwah, NJ: Paulist, 1980.

Cavanaugh, William T. *Migrations of the Holy: God, State, and the Political Meaning of the Church.* Grand Rapids: Eerdmans, 2011.

Charry, Ellen T. *By the Renewing of Your Minds: The Pastoral Function of Christian Doctrine.* New York: Oxford University Press, 1997.

Chesterton, G. K. *The Penguin Complete Father Brown.* 1929. Reprint, New York: Penguin, 1981.

The Chicago Statement on Biblical Inerrancy. https://www.etsjets.org/files/documents/ Chicago_Statement.pdf.

Childs, Brevard S. "The *Sensus Literalis* of Scripture: An Ancient and Modern Problem." In *Beiträge zur Alttestamentliche Theologie: Festschrift für Walther Zimmerli zum 70. Geburtstag,* edited by Herbert Donner, Robert Hanhart, and Rudolf Smend, 80–93. Göttingen: Vandenhoeck and Ruprecht, 1977.

Collett, Don C. *Figural Reading and the Old Testament: Theology and Practice.* Grand Rapids: Baker Academic, 2020.

Collins, John J. *The Bible after Babel: Historical Criticism in a Postmodern Age.* Grand Rapids: Eerdmans, 2005.

Collins, Kenneth J., and Jerry L. Walls. *Roman but Not Catholic: What Remains at Stake 500 Years after the Reformation*. Grand Rapids: Baker Academic, 2017.

Congar, Yves, OP. *The Meaning of Tradition*. Translated by A. N. Woodrow. San Francisco: Ignatius, 2004.

Corey, James S. A. *Leviathan Wakes*. The Expanse, Book 1. New York: Orbit, 2011.

D'Costa, Gavin. *Catholic Doctrines on the Jewish People after Vatican II*. New York: Oxford University Press, 2019.

Daniélou, Jean, SJ. *From Shadows to Reality: Studies in the Biblical Typology of the Fathers*. Translated by Dom Wulstan Hibberd. London: Burns and Oates, 1960.

Dante. *Paradiso. The Divine Comedy*, Vol. 3. Translated by Robin Kirkpatrick. New York: Penguin, 2007.

Davis, Ellen F. *Opening Israel's Scriptures*. New York: Oxford University Press, 2019.

———. *Proverbs, Ecclesiastes, Song of Songs*. Westminster Bible Companion. Louisville, KY: Westminster John Knox, 2000.

Davis, Ellen F., and Richard B. Hays, eds. *The Art of Reading Scripture*. Grand Rapids: Eerdmans, 2003.

Davis, Stephen T. *The Debate about the Bible: Inerrancy versus Infallibility*. Philadelphia: Westminster, 1977.

Davison, Andrew. *Why Sacraments?* Eugene, OR: Cascade, 2013.

Dawson, John David. *Christian Figural Reading and the Fashioning of Identity*. Berkeley: University of California Press, 2001.

de Lubac, Henri, SJ. *Catholicism: Christ and the Common Destiny of Man*. Translated by Lancelot C. Sheppard and Sister Elizabeth Englund, OCD. San Francisco: Ignatius, 1988.

———. *History and Spirit: The Understanding of Scripture According to Origen*. Translated by Anne Englund Nash. San Francisco: Ignatius, 2007.

———. *Medieval Exegesis, Vol. 1. The Four Senses of Scripture*. Ressourcement: Retrieval and Renewal in Catholic Thought. Translated by Mark Sebanc. Grand Rapids: Eerdmans, 1998.

Dei Verbum. Dogmatic Constitution on Divine Revelation Solemnly Promulgated by His Holiness Pope Paul VI, November 18, 1965. https://www.vatican.va/archive/ hist_councils/ii_vatican_council/documents/vat-ii_const_19651118_dei-verbum _en.html.

Dorrien, Gary. *Crisis, Irony, and Postmodernity: 1950–2005*. The Making of American Liberal Theology, Vol. 3. Louisville, KY: Westminster John Knox, 2006.

Dositheus. "Confession of Dositheus." In *The Acts and Decrees of the Synod of Jerusalem Sometimes Called the Council of Bethlehem Holden under Dositheus, Patriarch of Jerusalem in 1672*, translated by J. N. W. B. Robertson, 109–74. London: Thomas Baker, 1899.

Dupré, Louis. *The Enlightenment and the Intellectual Foundations of Modern Culture*. New Haven, CT: Yale University Press, 2004.

———. *Religion and the Rise of Modern Culture*. Notre Dame, IN: University of Notre Dame Press, 2008.

East, Brad. *The Church's Book: Theology of Scripture in Ecclesial Context*. Grand Rapids: Eerdmans, 2022.

———. "Five Theses on Preaching." *Mere Orthodoxy*. June 3, 2019. https://mere orthodoxy.com/five-theses-preaching/.

————. "The Hermeneutics of Theological Interpretation: Holy Scripture, Biblical Scholarship, and Historical Criticism." *International Journal of Systematic Theology* 19.1 (2017) 30–52.

————. "Reading the Trinity in the Bible: Assumptions, Warrants, Ends." *Pro Ecclesia* 25.4 (2016) 459–74.

————. "The Spector of Marcion." *Commonweal* 146.4 (2019) 12–13.

————. "What Are the Standards of Excellence for Theological Interpretation of Scripture?" *Journal of Theological Interpretation* 14.2 (2020) 149–79.

Ehrman, Bart D. *Jesus, Interrupted: Revealing the Hidden Contradictions in the Bible (And Why We Don't Know about Them)*. New York: HarperOne, 2009.

Enns, Peter. *The Bible Tells Me So: Why Defending Scripture Has Made Us Unable to Read it*. New York: HarperOne, 2014.

————. *Inspiration and Incarnation: Evangelicals and the Problem of the Old Testament*. Grand Rapids: Baker Academic, 2005.

Eusebius. *The History of the Church from Christ to Constantine*. Translated by G. A. Williamson. Revised and edited by Andrew Louth. New York: Penguin, 1989.

Evans, Rachel Held. *Searching for Sunday: Loving, Leaving, and Finding the Church*. Nashville: Nelson, 2015.

Ex Machina. Written and directed by Alex Garland. Produced by Film4 and DNA Films. Distributed by A24 and Universal Pictures. 2014.

Faber, Michel. *The Book of Strange New Things*. New York: Hogarth, 2015.

Farkasfalvy, Denis, O Cist. *A Theology of the Christian Bible: Revelation, Inspiration, Canon*. Washington, DC: Catholic University of America Press, 2018.

Farrow, Douglas. *Ascension and Ecclesia: On the Significance of the Doctrine of the Ascension for Ecclesiology and Christian Cosmology*. Grand Rapids: Eerdmans, 1999.

Ferguson, Everett. *The Rule of Faith: A Guide*. Cascade Companions. Eugene, OR: Cascade, 2015.

Feser, Edward, *The Last Superstition: A Refutation of the New Atheism*. South Bend, IN: St. Augustine's, 2008.

Flett, John G. *Apostolicity: The Ecumenical Question in World Christian Perspective*. Downers Grove, IL: IVP Academic, 2016.

Florovsky, Georges. *Bible, Church, Tradition: An Eastern Orthodox View*. The Collected Works of Georges Florovsky, Vol. 1. Belmont, MA: Nordland, 1972.

Ford, David F. *Christian Wisdom: Desiring God and Learning in Love*. Cambridge: Cambridge University Press, 2007.

Fowl, Stephen E. *Engaging Scripture: A Model for Theological Interpretation*. Malden, MA: Blackwell, 1998.

————, ed. *The Theological Interpretation of Scripture: Classic and Contemporary Readings*. Malden, MA: Blackwell, 1997.

Fredriksen, Paula. *Augustine and the Jews: A Christian Defense of Jews and Judaism*. New Haven, CT: Yale University Press, 2010.

————. *Paul: The Pagans' Apostle*. New Haven, CT: Yale University Press, 2017.

Frei, Hans. *The Eclipse of Biblical Narrative: A Study in Eighteenth and Nineteenth Century Hermeneutics*. New Haven, CT: Yale University Press, 1974.

Fujimura, Makoto. *Art and Faith: A Theology of Making*. New Haven, CT: Yale University Press, 2020.

Gerhard, Johann. *On the Nature of Theology and Scripture*. Theological Commonplaces. Translated by Richard J. Dinda. St. Louis: Concordia, 2006.

———. *On Sacred Scripture, On Interpreting Sacred Scripture, Method of Theological Study*. Theological Commonplaces. Translated by Joshua J. Hayes. Edited by Benjamin T. G. Mayes. St. Louis: Concordia, 2017.

Goldingay, John. *Do We Need the New Testament? Letting the Old Testament Speak for Itself*. Downers Grove, IL: IVP Academic, 2015.

———. *The First Testament: A New Translation*. Downers Grove, IL: IVP Academic, 2018.

Gordon, Joseph K. *Divine Scripture in Human Understanding: A Systematic Theology of the Christian Bible*. Notre Dame, IN: University of Notre Dame Press, 2019.

Gorman, Michael J., ed. *Scripture and Its Interpretation: A Global, Ecumenical Introduction to the Bible*. Grand Rapids: Baker Academic, 2017.

Gould, Stephen J. *Rocks of Ages: Science and Religion in the Fullness of Life*. New York: Ballantine, 1999.

Green, Joel B. *Practicing Theological Interpretation: Engaging Biblical Texts for Faith and Formation*. Grand Rapids: Baker Academic, 2011.

Green-McCreight, Kathryn. *Ad Litteram: How Augustine, Calvin and Barth Read the "Plain Sense" of Genesis 1–3*. Issues in Systematic Theology 5. New York: Lang, 1999.

Gregory of Narek. *The Festal Works of St. Gregory of Narek: Annotated Translation of the Odes, Litanies, and Encomia*. Translated by Abraham Terian. Collegeville, MN: Liturgical, 2016.

Gregory of Nazianzus. *On God and Christ: The Five Theological Orations and Two Letters to Cledonius*. Popular Patristics Series. Translated by Frederick Williams and Lionel Wickham. Crestwood, NY: St. Vladimir's Seminary Press, 2002.

Gregory of Nyssa. *Homilies on the Song of Songs*. Writings from the Greco-Roman World 13. Translated by Richard A. Norris Jr. Atlanta: Society of Biblical Literature, 2012.

———. *Life of Moses*. The Classics of Western Spirituality. Translated by Abraham J. Malherbe and Everett Ferguson. Mahwah, NJ: Paulist, 1978.

Griffiths, Paul J. *Christian Flesh*. Encountering Traditions. Stanford: Stanford University Press, 2018.

———. *Decreation: The Last Things of All Creatures*. Waco, TX: Baylor University Press, 2014.

———. "On Radner's *Time and the Word*." *Pro Ecclesia* 27.3 (2018) 300–306.

———. *The Practice of Catholic Theology: A Modest Proposal*. Washington, DC: Catholic University of America Press, 2016.

———. *Religious Reading: The Place of Reading in the Practice of Religion*. New York: Oxford University Press, 1999.

———. *Song of Songs*. Brazos Theological Commentary on the Bible. Grand Rapids: Brazos, 2011.

———. "Under Pressure." *Commonweal* 146.5 (2020) 30–37.

———. "Which Are the Words of Scripture?" *Theological Studies* 72 (2011) 703–22.

Gundry, Robert H. *Peter: False Disciple and Apostate According to Saint Matthew*. Grand Rapids: Eerdmans, 2015.

Frei, Hans. "The 'Literal Reading' of Biblical Narrative in the Christian Tradition: Does It Stretch or Will It Break?" In *The Bible and the Narrative Tradition*, edited by Frank McConnell, 36–77. New York: Oxford University Press, 1986.

Hahn, Scott W., and Jeffrey L. Morrow. *Modern Biblical Criticism as a Tool of Statecraft (1700–1900)*. Steubenville, OH: Emmaus, 2020.

Hahn, Scott W., and Benjamin Wiker, *Politicizing the Bible: The Roots of Historical Criticism and the Secularization of Scripture 1300–1700*. New York: Herder and Herder, 2013.

Harnack, Adolf von. *Marcion: The Gospel of the Alien God*. Translated by John E. Steely and Lyle D. Bierma. Reprint, Eugene, OR: Wipf and Stock, 2007.

Harrison, Peter. *The Territories of Science and Religion*. Chicago: University of Chicago Press, 2015.

Hart, David Bentley. *Atheist Delusions: The Christian Revolution and Its Fashionable Enemies*. New Haven, CT: Yale University Press, 2009.

———. *The Experience of God: Being, Consciousness, Bliss*. New Haven, CT: Yale University Press, 2013.

———. "Gods and Gopniks." *First Things*. May 2014. https://www.firstthings.com/article/2014/05/gods-and-gopniks.

Hatch, Nathan O. "The Christian Movement and the Demand for a Theology of the People." *The Journal of American History* 67.3 (1980) 545–67.

———. *The Democratization of American Christianity*. New Haven, CT: Yale University Press, 1989.

Hauerwas, Stanley. *Unleashing the Scripture: Freeing the Bible from Captivity to America*. Nashville: Abingdon, 1993.

Hays, Richard B. *Echoes of Scripture in the Gospels*. Waco, TX: Baylor University Press, 2016.

———. *Echoes of Scripture in the Letters of Paul*. New Haven, CT: Yale University Press, 1989.

———. "Reading the Bible with Eyes of Faith: The Practice of Theological Exegesis." *Journal of Theological Interpretation* 1 (2007) 5–21.

Hefele, Karl J. von. *A History of the Christian Councils, From the Original Documents, to the Close of Nicaea, A.D. 325*. Translated and edited by William R. Clark. Edinburgh: T. & T. Clark, 1871.

Henderson, John B. *Scripture, Canon, and Commentary: A Comparison of Confucian and Western Exegesis*. Princeton: Princeton University Press, 1991.

Henry, Carl F. H. *God, Revelation, and Authority*. 6 vols. Reprint, Wheaton, IL: Crossway, 1999.

Herbert, Frank. *Dune*. Boston: Chilton, 1965.

Herbert, George. *The English Poems of George Herbert*. Edited by C. A. Patrides. Rutland, VT: Charles E. Tuttle, 1991.

Hildegard of Bingen. *Scivias*. The Classics of Western Spirituality. Translated by Columba Hart and Jane Bishop. Mahwah, NJ: Paulist, 1990.

Hill, Wesley. "Death at the Tree of Life." *Commonweal*, October 30, 2018. https://www.commonwealmagazine.org/death-tree-life.

———. *Paul and the Trinity: Persons, Relations, and the Pauline Letters*. Grand Rapids: Eerdmans, 2015.

Hodge, Charles. "Letter to Pope Pius IX." *The Banner of Truth* 415 (April 1998) 22–25.

Holmes, Stephen R. "Calvin on Scripture." In *Calvin, Barth, and Reformed Theology*, edited by Neil B. MacDonald and Carl Trueman, 149–62. Eugene, OR: Wipf and Stock, 2008.

Horton, Michael. *The Christian Faith: A Systematic Theology for Pilgrims on the Way.* Grand Rapids: Zondervan, 2011.

Ignatius of Antioch. *Epistles.* In *The Apostolic Fathers in English,* translated and edited by Michael W. Holmes, 87–129. 3rd ed. Grand Rapids: Baker Academic, 2006.

Irenaeus of Lyons. *Against Heresies.* Vol. 1 of *Ante-Nicene Fathers.* Translated and edited by Alexander Roberts and James Donaldson. 1885. Reprint, Peabody, MA: Hendrickson, 2012.

———. *On the Apostolic Preaching.* Popular Patristics Series. Translated by John Behr. Crestwood, NY: St. Vladimir's Seminary Press, 1997.

Jennings, Willie James. *The Christian Imagination: Theology and the Origins of Race.* New Haven, CT: Yale University Press, 2010.

Jensen, Robin M. *Baptismal Imagery in Early Christianity: Ritual, Visual, and Theological Dimensions.* Grand Rapids: Baker Academic, 2012.

Jenson, Robert W. *Canon and Creed.* Interpretation: Resources for the Use of Scripture in the Church. Louisville, KY: Westminster John Knox, 2010.

———. *A Large Catechism.* 2nd ed. Delhi, NY: American Lutheran Publicity Bureau, 1999.

———. Review of *On Christian Theology,* by Rowan Williams. *Pro Ecclesia* 11.3 (2002) 367–69.

———. *Song of Songs.* Interpretation: A Bible Commentary for Teaching and Preaching. Louisville, KY: Westminster John Knox, 2005.

———. *Systematic Theology, Vol. 1. The Triune God.* New York: Oxford University Press, 1997.

———. *Systematic Theology, Vol. 2. The Works of God.* New York: Oxford University Press, 1999.

———. *The Triune Story: Collected Essays on Scripture.* Edited by Brad East. New York: Oxford University Press, 2019.

———. *Unbaptized God: The Basic Flaw in Ecumenical Theology.* Minneapolis: Fortress, 1992.

———. *Visible Words: The Interpretation and Practice of Christian Sacraments.* Philadelphia: Fortress, 1978.

Jenson, Robert W., and Eugene B Korn, eds. *Covenant and Hope: Christian and Jewish Reflections.* Grand Rapids: Eerdmans, 2012.

John of Damascus. *Exposition of the Orthodox Faith.* In The Nicene and Post-Nicene Fathers, Series 2, Vol. 9, edited by Philip Schaff and Henry Wace. 1899. Reprint, Peabody, MA: Hendrickson, 2012.

Johnson, Dru. *Knowledge by Ritual: A Biblical Prolegomenon to Sacramental Theology.* Journal of Theological Interpretation Supplement 13. Winona Lake, IN: Eisenbrauns, 2016.

———. *Scripture's Knowing: A Companion to Biblical Epistemology.* Cascade Companions. Eugene, OR: Cascade, 2015.

Johnson, Luke Timothy. *Scripture and Discernment: Decision Making in the Church.* Nashville: Abingdon, 1996.

Jowett, Benjamin. "On the Interpretation of Scripture." In *Essays and Reviews,* 330–433. London: Parker, 1860.

Julian of Norwich. *Revelations of Divine Love (Short Text and Long Text).* Translated by Elizabeth Spearing. New York: Penguin, 1998.

Justin Martyr. *The First and Second Apologies*. Ancient Christian Writers. Translated and edited by Leslie William Barnard. Mahwah, NJ: Paulist, 1997.

Kelly, J. N. D. *Early Christian Doctrines*. Rev. ed. New York: Harper and Row, 1978.

Kelsey, David H. *Eccentric Existence: A Theological Anthropology*. 2 vols. Louisville, KY: Westminster John Knox, 2009.

Kilby, Karen. *God, Evil, and the Limits of Theology*. London: T. & T. Clark, 2020.

Kinzer, Mark S. *Israel's Messiah and the People of God: A Vision for Messianic Jewish Covenant Fidelity*. Eugene, OR: Cascade, 2011.

———. *Postmissionary Messianic Judaism: Redefining Christian Engagement with the Jewish People*. Grand Rapids: Brazos, 2005.

König, Johann Friedrich. *Theologia Positiva Acroamatica (Rostock 1664)*. Translated and edited by Andreas Stegmann. Tübingen: Mohr Siebeck, 2006.

Law, Timothy Michael. *When God Spoke Greek: The Septuagint and the Making of the Christian Bible*. Oxford: Oxford University Press, 2013.

Lawson, Stephen D. "The Apostasy of the Church and the Cross of Christ: Hans Urs von Balthasar on the Mystery of the Church as *Casta Meretrix*." *Modern Theology* 36.2 (2010) 259–80.

Le Guin, Ursula K. *The Hainish Novels and Stories*. 2 vols. Edited by Brian Attebery. New York: Library of America, 2017.

Legaspi, Michael C. *The Death of Scripture and the Rise of Biblical Studies*. Oxford Studies in Historical Theology. New York: Oxford University Press, 2010.

Leithart, Peter J. "A Cheer and a Half for Biblicism." *First Things*, August 26, 2011. https://www.firstthings.com/web-exclusives/2011/08/a-cheer-and-a-half-for-biblicism.

———. *Deep Exegesis: The Mystery of Reading Scripture*. Waco, TX: Baylor University Press, 2009.

Levering, Matthew. "Aquinas and Supersessionism One More Time: A Response to Matthew A. Tapie's *Aquinas on Israel and the Church*." *Pro Ecclesia* 25.4 (2016) 395–412.

———. *Christ's Fulfillment of Torah and Temple: Salvation According to Thomas Aquinas*. Notre Dame, IN: Notre Dame University Press, 2002.

———. *Mary's Bodily Assumption*. Notre Dame, IN: Notre Dame University Press, 2015.

———. *Participatory Biblical Exegesis: A Theology of Biblical Interpretation*. Notre Dame, IN: University of Notre Dame Press, 2008.

———. *Was the Reformation a Mistake? Why Catholic Doctrine Is Not Unbiblical*. Grand Rapids: Zondervan, 2017.

Levy, Ian Christopher. *Introducing Medieval Biblical Interpretation: The Senses of Scripture in Premodern Exegesis*. Grand Rapids: Baker Academic, 2018.

Lewis, C. S. "Modern Theology and Biblical Criticism." In *Christian Reflections*, edited by Walter Hooper, 152–66. 1967. Reprint, Grand Rapids: Eerdmans, 1994.

———. *The Great Divorce: A Dream*. 1946. Reprint, San Francisco: HarperSanFrancisco, 2001.

———. *The Space Trilogy*. New York: Simon and Schuster, 2011.

Longenecker, Richard N. *Biblical Exegesis in the Apostolic Period*. 2nd ed. Grand Rapids: Eerdmans, 1999.

Louth, Andrew. *Discerning the Mystery: An Essay on the Nature of Theology*. New York: Oxford University Press, 1983.

Luther, Martin. *Luther's Large Catechism*. St. Louis: Concordia, 2010.

———. "Preface to the Old Testament, 1545 (1523)." In *The Annotated Luther, Vol. 6, The Interpretation of Scripture*, edited by Euan K. Cameron, 41–66. Minneapolis: Fortress, 2017.

MacIntyre, Alasdair. *After Virtue: A Study in Moral Theory*. 3rd ed. Notre Dame, IN: University of Notre Dame Press, 2007.

———. *Three Rival Versions of Moral Enquiry: Encyclopaedia, Genealogy, and Tradition*. Notre Dame, IN: University of Notre Dame Press, 1990.

Marshall, Bruce D. "Christ and Israel: An Unsolved Problem in Catholic Theology." In *The Call of Abraham: Essays on the Election of Israel in Honor of Jon D. Levenson*, edited by Gary A. Anderson and Joel S. Kaminsky, 330–50. Notre Dame, IN: University of Notre Dame Press, 2013.

———. "*Quasi in Figura*: A Brief Reflection on Jewish Election, after Thomas Aquinas." *Nova et Vetera* 7 (2009) 477–84.

———. "Religion and Election: Aquinas on Natural Law, Judaism, and Salvation in Christ." *Nova et Vetera* 14 (2016) 61–125.

Martin, Dale B. *Biblical Truths: The Meaning of Scripture in the Twenty-First Century*. New Haven, CT: Yale University Press, 2017.

———. *Pedagogy of the Bible: An Analysis and Proposal*. Louisville, KY: Westminster John Knox, 2008.

———. *Sex and the Single Savior: Gender and Sexuality in Biblical Interpretation*. Louisville, KY: Westminster John Knox, 2006.

McCarthy, Cormac. *The Road*. New York: Vintage, 2006.

McCaulley, Esau. *Reading While Black: African American Biblical Interpretation as an Exercise in Hope*. Downers Grove: IVP, 2020.

McDermott, Gerald R., ed. *The New Christian Zionism: Fresh Perspectives on Israel and the Land*. Downers Grove, IL: IVP Academic, 2016.

McDonald, Lee Martin. *The Biblical Canon: Its Origin, Transmission, and Authority*. Rev. and exp. ed. Peabody, MA: Hendrickson, 2007.

McFarland, Ian A. *From Nothing: A Theology of Creation*. Louisville, KY: Westminster John Knox, 2014.

———. *In Adam's Fall: A Meditation on the Christian Doctrine of Original Sin*. Malden, MA: Blackwell, 2010.

———. *The Word Made Flesh: A Theology of the Incarnation*. Louisville, KY: Westminster John Knox, 2019.

McGowan, Andrew T. B. *The Divine Spiration of Scripture: Challenging Evangelical Perspectives*. Leicester, UK: Apollos, 2007.

McKim, Donald K., ed. *Calvin and the Bible*. Cambridge: Cambridge University Press, 2006.

Metzger, Bruce M. *The Canon of the New Testament: Its Origin, Development, and Significance*. New York: Oxford University Press, 1997.

Miller, Walter M., Jr. *Canticle for Leibowitz*. Philadelphia: Lippincott, 1959.

Moberly, R. W. L. *The Bible in a Disenchanted Age: The Enduring Possibility of Christian Faith*. Theological Explorations for the Church Catholic. Grand Rapids: Baker Academic, 2018.

———. *The Bible, Theology, and Faith: A Study of Abraham and Jesus*. Cambridge Studies in Christian Doctrine. Cambridge: Cambridge University Press, 2000.

———. *The God of the Old Testament: Encountering the Divine in Christian Scripture.* Grand Rapids: Baker Academic, 2020.

Moore, Brian. *Catholics.* London: Penguin, 2006.

Morrow, Jeffrey L. *Pretensions of Objectivity: Toward a Criticism of Biblical Criticism.* Eugene, OR: Pickwick, 2019.

———. *Theology, Politics, and Exegesis: Essays on the History of Modern Biblical Criticism.* Eugene, OR: Pickwick, 2017.

Muller, Richard A. *Post-Reformation Reformed Dogmatics, Vol. 2. Holy Scripture: The Cognitive Foundation of Theology.* Grand Rapids: Baker, 1993.

Musäus, Johannes. *Introductio in theologiam, qua de natura theologiae, naturalis, et revelatae, itemque de theologiae revelatae principio cognoscendi primo, scriptura sacra, agitur.* Jena: Bielcke, 1679.

Nanos, Mark D. *Reading Paul within Judaism.* Collected Essays of Mark D. Nanos, Vol. 1. Eugene, OR: Cascade, 2017.

Nanos, Mark D., and Magnus Zetterholm, eds. *Paul within Judaism: Restoring the First-Century Context to the Apostle.* Minneapolis: Fortress, 2015.

Newman, John Henry. *An Essay on the Development of Christian Doctrine.* 6th ed. 1888. Reprint, Notre Dame, IN: University of Notre Dame Press, 1994.

Noble, Paul. "The *Sensus Literalis*: Jowett, Childs, and Barr." *The Journal of Theological Studies* 44.1 (1993) 1–23.

Noll, Mark. "A Brief History of Inerrancy, Mostly in America." In *The Proceedings of the Conference on Biblical Inerrancy 1987*, 9–25. Nashville: Broadman, 1987.

Novak, David. "Supersessionism Hard and Soft." *First Things* 290, February 2019, 27–31.

———. *Talking with Christians: Musings of a Jewish Theologian.* Radical Traditions. Grand Rapids: Eerdmans, 2005.

Nouwen, Henri M. *The Way of the Heart: Connecting with God through Prayer, Wisdom, and Silence.* New York: Ballantine, 1981.

O'Donovan, Oliver. *Church in Crisis: The Gay Controversy and the Anglican Communion.* Eugene, OR: Cascade, 2008.

———. "The Moral Authority of Scripture." In *Scripture's Doctrine and Theology's Bible: How the New Testament Shapes Christian Dogmatics*, edited by Markus Bockmuehl and Alan J. Torrance, 165–75. Grand Rapids: Baker Academic, 2008.

———. *Resurrection and Moral Order: An Outline for Evangelical Ethics.* Grand Rapids: Eerdmans, 1994.

Ochs, Peter. *Another Reformation: Postliberal Christianity and the Jews.* Grand Rapids: Baker Academic, 2011.

Origen. *The Commentary of Origen on the Gospel of St. Matthew.* 2 vols. Oxford Early Christian Texts. Translated and edited by Ronald E. Heine. New York: Oxford University Press, 2018.

———. *On First Principles.* 2 vols. Oxford Early Christian Texts. Translated and edited by John Behr. New York: Oxford University Press, 2017.

———. *The Song of Songs, Commentary and Homilies.* Ancient Christian Writers. Translated by R. P. Lawson. New York: Newman, 1957.

Ortlund, Gavin. *Theological Retrieval for Evangelicals: Why We Need Our Past to Have a Future.* Wheaton, IL: Crossway, 2019.

Orwell, George. *1984.* New York: Signet Classic, 1950.

Paddison, Angus. *Scripture: A Very Theological Proposal.* London: T. & T. Clark, 2009.

Pelikan, Jaroslav. *Interpreting the Bible and the Constitution*. New Haven, CT: Yale University Press, 2004.

Philaret of Moscow. *The Creeds of Christendom, Vol. 2. The Longer Catechism*. Translated by R. W. Blackmore and edited by Philip Schaff, 445–542. New York: Harper, 1877.

Pierce, Madison N. *Divine Discourse in the Epistle to the Hebrews: The Recontextualization of Spoken Quotations of Scripture*. Society for New Testament Studies Monograph Series 178. New York: Cambridge University Press, 2020.

Pinnock, Clark H., with Barry L Callen. *The Scripture Principle: Reclaiming the Full Authority of the Bible*. 2nd ed. Grand Rapids: Baker Academic, 2006.

Pitre, Brant. *Jesus and the Jewish Roots of Mary: Unveiling the Mother of the Messiah*. New York: Image, 2018.

Plantinga, Alvin. "Two (or More) Kinds of Scripture Scholarship." *Modern Theology* 14.2 (1998) 243–78.

Preus, Robert. *The Inspiration of Scripture: A Study of the Theology of the 17th-Century Lutheran Dogmaticians*. 2nd ed. St. Louis: Concordia, 1957.

Puckett, David L. *John Calvin's Exegesis of the Old Testament*. Columbia Series in Reformed Theology. Louisville, KY: Westminster John Knox, 1995.

Radner, Ephraim. *The End of the Church: A Pneumatology of Christian Division in the West*. Grand Rapids: Eerdmans, 1998.

———. *Hope among the Fragments: The Broken Church and Its Engagement of Scripture*. Grand Rapids: Brazos, 2004.

———. *Time and the Word: Figural Reading of the Christian Scriptures*. Grand Rapids: Eerdmans, 2016.

Rae, Murray A. *History and Hermeneutics*. Edinburgh: T. & T. Clark, 2006.

Rea, Michael C. "Authority and Truth." In *The Enduring Authority of the Christian Scriptures*, edited by D. A. Carson, 872–98. Grand Rapids: Eerdmans, 2016.

Rahner, Karl, SJ. *Inspiration in the Bible*. Quaestiones Disputatae. Translated by Charles H. Henkey, SJ. Revised by Martin Palmer, SJ. New York: Herder and Herder, 1964.

———. *The Trinity*. Milestones in Catholic Theology. Translated by Joseph Donceel. 1970. Reprint, New York: Crossroad, 1997.

Ratzinger, Joseph (Benedict XVI). *Church, Ecumenism, and Politics: New Endeavors in Ecclesiology*. Translated by Michael J. Miller et al. San Francisco: Ignatius, 2008.

———. *The Word of the Lord: Verbum Domini*. Post-Synodal Apostolic Exhortation. Washington, DC: United States Conference of Catholic Bishops, 2010.

Reventlow, Henning Graf. *The Authority of the Bible and the Rise of Modern World*. Translated by John Bowden. Minneapolis: Fortress, 1985.

Roberts, Alastair. "Rethinking Israel: A Response from Alastair Roberts." *Theopolis Institute*. October 17, 2019. https://theopolisinstitute.com/conversations/rethinking-israel-a-response-from-alastair-roberts/.

———. "The Rite of Circumcision: A Response to Dru Johnson." *Theopolis Institute*, April 18, 2019. https://theopolisinstitute.com/conversations/the-rite-of-circumcision-a-response-to-dru-johnson/.

Roberts, Alastair, and Gerald McDermott. *Via Media* Podcast, Episode 21. September 26, 2019. https://www.beesondivinity.com/the-institute-of-anglican-studies/podcast/2019/transcripts/Via-Media-Episode-21-Roberts.txt.

Roberts, Alistair, and Andrew Wilson. *Echoes of Exodus: Tracing Themes of Redemption through Scripture*. Wheaton, IL: Crossway, 2018.

Robinson, Kim Stanley. *Red Mars*. The Mars Trilogy, Book 1. New York: Bantam, 1993.

Rogers, Eugene F. "How the Virtues of an Interpreter Presuppose and Perfect Hermeneutics: The Case of Thomas Aquinas." *The Journal of Religion* 76 (1996) 64–81.

Rogers, Jack, and Donald K. McKim. *The Authority and Interpretation of the Bible: An Historical Approach.* 1979. Reprint, Eugene, OR: Wipf and Stock, 1999.

Rudolph, David J. *A Jew to the Jews: Jewish Contours of Pauline Flexibility in 1 Corinthians 9:19–23.* 2nd ed. Eugene, OR: Pickwick, 2016.

Rudolph, David J., and Joel Willitts, eds. *Introduction to Messianic Judaism: Its Ecclesial Context and Biblical Foundations.* Grand Rapids: Zondervan, 2013.

Russell, Mary D. *Children of God: A Novel.* New York: Ballantine, 1999.

———. *The Sparrow.* New York: Ballantine, 2016.

Sales, Francis de. *The Catholic Controversy: St. Francis de Sales' Defense of the Faith.* Translated by Henry Benedict Mackey, OSB. 1886. Reprint, Charlotte, NC: TAN, 1989.

Sanders, Fred. "The Kingdom in Person." *The Scriptorium Daily,* July 28, 2015. http://scriptoriumdaily.com/the-kingdom-in-person/.

———. *The Triune God.* New Studies in Dogmatics. Grand Rapids: Zondervan, 2016.

Sarisky, Darren. *Reading the Bible Theologically.* Current Issues in Theology. New York: Cambridge University Press, 2019.

Schaff, Philip. *The Principle of Protestantism.* Lancaster Series on the Mercersburg Theology, Vol. 2. Translated by John W. Nevin. 1845. Reprint, Eugene, OR: Wipf and Stock, 2004.

Schleiermacher, Friedrich. *The Christian Faith.* Edited by H. R. Mackintosh and J. S. Stewart. 1928. Reprint, Berkeley, CA: Apocryphile, 2011.

Schmemann, Alexander. *Of Water and Spirit: A Liturgical Study of Baptism.* Crestwood, NY: St. Vladimir's Seminary Press, 1974.

Schneiders, Sandra M. *The Revelatory Text: Interpreting the New Testament as Sacred Scripture.* 2nd ed. Collegeville, MN: Liturgical, 1999.

Schreiner, Patrick. *The Ascension of Christ: Recovering a Neglected Doctrine.* Snapshots. Bellingham, WA: Lexham, 2020.

Seitz, Christopher R. *The Character of Christian Scripture: The Significance of a Two-Testament Bible.* Studies in Theological Interpretation. Grand Rapids: Baker Academic, 2011.

———. *The Elder Testament: Canon, Theology, Trinity.* Waco, TX: Baylor University Press, 2018.

———. *Figured Out: Typology and Providence in Christian Scripture.* Louisville, KY: Westminster John Knox, 2001.

Sheehan, Jonathan. *The Enlightenment Bible: Translation, Scholarship, Culture.* Princeton: Princeton University Press, 2007.

Smith, Christian. *The Bible Made Impossible: Why Biblicism Is Not a Truly Evangelical Reading of Scripture.* Grand Rapids: Brazos, 2011.

———. "A Reply to Leithart on Biblicism." *First Things,* August 26, 2011. https://www.firstthings.com/web-exclusives/2011/08/a-reply-to-leithart-on-biblicism.

Smith, James K. A. *Desiring the Kingdom: Worship, Worldview, and Cultural Formation.* Cultural Liturgies, Vol. 1. Grand Rapids: Baker Academic, 2009.

———. *The Fall of Interpretation: Philosophical Foundations for a Creational Hermeneutic.* 2nd ed. Grand Rapids: Baker Academic, 2012.

Smith, Jonathan Z. "Sacred Persistence: Towards a Redescription of Canon." In *Imagining Religion: From Babylon to Jonestown*, 36–52. Chicago Studies in the History of Judaism. Chicago: University of Chicago Press, 1982.

Smith, Wilfred Cantwell. *What Is Scripture? A Comparative Approach*. Minneapolis: Fortress, 2005.

Sokolowski, Robert. *The God of Faith and Reason: Foundations of Christian Theology*. Washington, DC: Catholic University of America Press, 1995.

Sommer, Benjamin D. *Revelation and Authority: Sinai in Jewish Scripture and Tradition*. New Haven, CT: Yale University Press, 2015.

Sonderegger, Katherine. *Systematic Theology, Vol. 1. The Doctrine of God*. Philadelphia: Fortress, 2015.

———. *Systematic Theology, Vol. 2. The Doctrine of the Holy Trinity: Processions and Persons*. Philadelphia: Fortress, 2020.

Soulen, R. Kendall. *The God of Israel and Christian Theology*. Minneapolis: Fortress, 1996.

Stanglin, Keith D. *The Letter and Spirit of Biblical Interpretation: From the Early Church to Modern Practice*. Grand Rapids: Baker Academic, 2018.

Stanley, Andy. *Irresistible: Reclaiming the New that Jesus Unleashed for the World*. Grand Rapids: Zondervan, 2018.

Steinmetz, David C. "Uncovering a Second Narrative: Detective Fiction and the Construction of Historical Method." In *The Art of Reading Scripture*, edited by Ellen F. Davis and Richard B. Hays, 54–65. Grand Rapids: Eerdmans, 2003.

Swain, Scott R. *Trinity, Revelation, and Reading: A Theological Introduction to the Bible and Its Interpretation*. London: T. & T. Clark, 2011.

Tanner, Kathryn. *Christ the Key*. Current Issues in Theology. New York: Cambridge University Press, 2009.

———. *God and Creation in Christian Theology: Tyranny or Empowerment?* 1988. Reprint, Minneapolis: Fortress, 2005.

———. "Theology and the Plain Sense." In *Scriptural Authority and Narrative Interpretation*, edited by Garrett Green, 59–78. Philadelphia: Fortress, 1987.

Tapie, Matthew A. *Aquinas on Israel and the Church: The Question of Supersessionism in the Theology of Thomas Aquinas*. Eugene, OR: Pickwick, 2014.

Taylor, Derek W. *Reading Scripture as the Church: Dietrich Bonhoeffer's Hermeneutic of Discipleship*. Downers Grove, IL: IVP Academic, 2020.

Theodore the Studite. *Writings on Iconoclasm*. Ancient Christian Writers. Translated by Thomas Cattoi. New York: Newman, 2015.

Thérèse of Lisieux. *Story of a Soul: The Autobiography of Saint Thérèse of Lisieux*. 3rd ed. Translated by John Clarke, OCD. Washington, DC: Institute of Carmelite Studies, 1996.

Thiessen, Matthew. *Paul and the Gentile Problem*. New York: Oxford University Press, 2016.

Thirty-Nine Articles of Religion. http://anglicansonline.org/basics/thirty-nine_articles.html.

Thomas Aquinas. *Summa Theologica*. 5 vols. Translated by the Fathers of the English Dominican Province. Notre Dame, IN: Christian Classics, 1948.

———. *Thomas Aquinas's Quodlibetal Questions*. Translated by Turner Nevitt and Brian Davies. New York: Oxford University Press, 2020.

Thomas, R. S. *Collected Poems, 1945–1990*. London: Phoenix Giant, 1996.

Ticciati, Susannah. "Anachronism or Illumination? Genesis 1 and Creation *ex nihilo.*" *Anglican Theological Review* 99.4 (2017) 691–712.

Treier, Daniel J. *Introducing Evangelical Theology.* Grand Rapids: Baker Academic, 2019.

———. *Introducing Theological Interpretation of Scripture: Recovering a Christian Practice.* Grand Rapids: Baker Academic, 2008.

———. *Virtue and the Voice of God: Toward Theology as Wisdom.* Grand Rapids: Eerdmans, 2006.

Turner, Denys. *Eros and Allegory: Medieval Exegesis of the Song of Songs.* Collegeville, MN: Cistercian, 1995.

Turretin, Francis. *Institutes of Elenctic Theology, Vol. 1. First through Tenth Topics.* Translated by George Musgrave Giger. Edited by James T. Dennison Jr. Phillipsburg, NJ: Presbyterian & Reformed, 1992.

van Driel, Edwin Chr. *Incarnation Anyway: Arguments for Supralapsarian Christology.* New York: Oxford University Press, 2008.

Van Inwagen, Peter. "Critical Studies of the New Testament and the User of the New Testament." In *God, Knowledge, and Mystery: Essays in Philosophical Theology,* 163–90. Ithaca, NY: Cornell University Press, 1995.

Vanhoozer, Kevin J. "Ascending the Mountain, Singing the Rock: Biblical Interpretation Earthed, Typed, and Transfigured." *Modern Theology* 28.4 (2012) 781–803.

———. "Augustinian Inerrancy: Literary Meaning, Literal Truth, and Literate Interpretation in the Economy of Biblical Discourse." In *Five Views on Biblical Inerrancy,* edited by James R. A. Merrick and Stephen M. Garrett, 199–235. Grand Rapids: Zondervan, 2013.

———. *Biblical Authority After Babel: Retrieving the Solas in the Spirit of Mere Protestant Christianity.* Grand Rapids: Brazos, 2016.

———. *The Drama of Doctrine: A Canonical-Linguistic Approach to Christian Doctrine.* Louisville, KY: Westminster John Knox, 2005.

———. *Faith Speaking Understanding: Performing the Drama of Doctrine.* Louisville, KY: Westminster John Knox, 2014.

———. *Is There a Meaning in This Text? The Bible, the Reader, and the Morality of Literary Knowledge.* Grand Rapids: Zondervan, 1998.

Vanhoozer, Kevin J. et al., eds. *Dictionary for Theological Interpretation of the Bible.* Grand Rapids: Baker Academic, 2005.

Viola, Frank, and George Barna. *Pagan Christianity? Exploring the Roots of Our Church Practices.* Rev. ed. Carol Stream, IL: Tyndale House, 2012.

Volf, Miroslav. *Captive to the Word of God: Engaging the Scriptures for Contemporary Theological Reflection.* Grand Rapids: Eerdmans, 2010.

Ward, Timothy. *Words of Life: Scripture as the Living and Active Word of God.* Downers Grove, IL: IVP Academic, 2009.

Ware, Timothy (Kallistos). *The Orthodox Church: An Introduction to Eastern Christianity.* 3rd ed. New York: Penguin, 2015.

Warfield, B. B. *The Inspiration and Authority of the Bible.* Edited by Samuel G. Craig. Philadelphia: Presbyterian & Reformed, 1967.

Watson, Francis. "Does Historical Criticism Exist? A Contribution to Debate on the Theological Interpretation of Scripture." In *Theological Theology: Essays in Honor of John B. Webster,* edited by R. David Nelson, Darren Sarisky, and Justin Stratis, 307–18. London: T. & T. Clark, 2015.

Waugh, Evelyn. *Brideshead Revisited: The Sacred and Profane Memories of Captain Charles Ryder*. Boston: Little, Brown, 1945.

Webster, John. *Confessing God: Essays in Christian Dogmatics II*. Cornerstones. London: T. & T. Clark, 2016.

———. *The Culture of Theology*. Edited by Ivor J. Davidson and Alden C. McCray. Grand Rapids: Baker Academic, 2019.

———. *The Domain of the Word: Scripture and Theological Reason*. Edinburgh: T. & T. Clark, 2012.

———. "'Eloquent and Radiant': The Prophetic Office of Christ and the Mission of the Church." In *Barth's Moral Theology: Human Action in Barth's Thought*, 125–50. Grand Rapids: Eerdmans, 1998.

———. *God Without Measure: Working Papers in Christian Theology, Vol. 1. God and the Works of God*. London: T. & T. Clark, 2016.

———. *Holy Scripture: A Dogmatic Sketch*. Cambridge: Cambridge University Press, 2003.

Wells, Samuel. *Improvisation: The Drama of Christian Ethics*. Grand Rapids: Brazos, 2004.

Westminster Confession of Faith and Shorter Catechism. In *Book of Confessions*, Part 1 of *The Constitution of the Presbyterian Church (U.S.A.)*, 117–91. Louisville, KY: Office of the General Assembly, 2007.

Wiarda, Timothy. "Scripture Between the Incarnate Christ and the Illuminating Spirit." *International Journal of Systematic Theology* 21.2 (2019) 120–40.

Wilken, Robert Louis. *The First Thousand Years: A Global History of Christianity*. New Haven, CT: Yale University Press, 2013.

———. "In Defense of Allegory." *Modern Theology* 14.2 (1998) 197–212.

Williams, Rowan. *Arius: Heresy and Tradition*. Rev. ed. Grand Rapids: Eerdmans, 2001.

———. *Christ the Heart of Creation*. London: Bloomsbury, 2018.

———. "Historical Criticism and Sacred Text." In *Reading Texts, Seeking Wisdom: Scripture and Theology*, edited by David Ford and Graham Stanton, 217–28. Grand Rapids: Eerdmans, 2004.

———. *On Christian Theology*. Malden, MA: Blackwell, 2000.

———. *Why Study the Past? The Quest for the Historical Church*. Grand Rapids: Eerdmans, 2005.

Wiman, Christian. *He Held Radical Light: The Art of Faith, the Faith of Art*. New York: Farrar, Straus and Giroux, 2018.

Wittgenstein, Ludwig. *Philosophical Investigations (Philosophische Untersuchungen)*. 4th ed. Translated by G. E. M. Anscombe, P. M. S. Hacker, and Joachim Schulte. Malden, MA: Blackwell, 2009.

Wittman, Tyler. *God and Creation in the Theology of Thomas Aquinas and Karl Barth*. New York: Cambridge University Press, 2018.

Wolfe, Gene. *Shadow and Claw*. The Book of the New Sun, Vol. 1. London: Gollancz, 2011.

Woodbridge, John D. *Biblical Authority: A Critique of the Rogers/McKim Proposal*. Grand Rapids: Zondervan, 1982.

Work, Telford. *Living and Active: Scripture in the Economy of Salvation*. Grand Rapids: Eerdmans, 2002.

Wright, Franz. *Walking to Martha's Vineyard: Poems*. New York: Knopf, 2005.

Wright, N. T. *History and Eschatology: Jesus and the Promise of Natural Theology*. Waco, TX: Baylor University Press, 2019.

———. *The Last Word: Scripture and the Authority of God—Getting beyond the Bible Wars*. San Francisco: HarperSanFrancisco, 2005.

———. *Paul: A Biography*. San Francisco: HarperOne, 2018.

Wyschogrod, Michael. *Abraham's Promise: Judaism and Jewish-Christian Relations*. Edited by R. Kendall Soulen. Grand Rapids: Eerdmans, 2004.

———. *The Body of Faith: God and the People Israel*. Northvale, NJ: Aronson, 1996.

———. "Incarnation." *Pro Ecclesia* 2.2 (1993) 208–15.

Yoder, John Howard. *The Priestly Kingdom: Social Ethics as Gospel*. Notre Dame: University of Notre Dame Press, 1984.

———. *To Hear the Word*. 2nd ed. Eugene, OR: Cascade, 2010.

Young, Frances M. *The Art of Performance: Towards a Theology of Holy Scripture*. London: Darton, Longman and Todd, 1990.

———. *Biblical Exegesis and the Formation of Christian Culture*. 1997. Reprint, Peabody, MA: Hendrickson, 2002.

———. *God's Presence: A Contemporary Recapitulation of Early Christianity*. Current Issues in Theology. Cambridge: Cambridge University Press, 2013.

Young, Frances M., with Andrew Teal. *From Nicaea to Chalcedon: A Guide to the Literature and Its Background*. 2nd ed. Grand Rapids: Baker Academic, 2010.

Subject Index

Author Index

Scripture Index

Revelation (continued)

CPSIA information can be obtained
at www.ICGtesting.com
Printed in the USA
JSHW032107140921
18653JS00005B/193

9 781532 664984